Contents

The
Enchanted
Life

unlocking the magic
of the everyday

Sharon
Blackie

1 3 5 7 9 10 8 6 4 2

First published in 2018 by September Publishing

Illustrations by Leo Nickolls
Typeset by Ed Pickford

Printed in Denmark on paper from responsibly managed,
sustainable sources by Nørhaven

ISBN 978-1-910463-88-8

September Publishing
www.septemberpublishing.org

Why Enchantment, and Why Now?

1. Enchantment matters

The wind at dawn has secrets to whisper
Don't go back to sleep!

Mewlana Jalaluddin Rumi

IMAGINE THAT YOU are entering a small wood on a Sunday morning in late spring; you've come here to walk. You have an immediate sense of wellbeing. How peaceful, you think, as you look around you; how pretty. The trees are lovely and the birdsong is beautiful. There are ferns under the trees, and bluebells. You turn your attention to them briefly and tell yourself how attractive they are. You check your watch as you set off down the gravelled track; you have half an hour for your walk before you have to head back home. You keep to the path; it rained last night and you don't want to get your shoes muddy. Your shove your hands into your pockets; you keep your eyes straight ahead, mostly, but every now and again you look around you and tell yourself how nice it is to be away from the crowds and the traffic fumes.

After you've been walking for a few minutes, you start to think about other things. You can't help yourself; something in your head just takes over. You've been to mindfulness classes but it never seems to stick, and most of the time mindfulness seems a bit boring, to be honest. You hum the same notes of a tune over and over. You replay an argument you had with your husband yesterday and remind yourself how unreasonable he was – just how unreasonable he always is; the muscles in your stomach start to clench as you relive the irritation. You think of all the things you could have said differently, and refine your sentences until they're the deadliest of barbs. Suddenly someone else appears on the path ahead of you, walking towards you; you jump, and realise that you haven't taken in anything around you for the past several minutes. This is ridiculous, you think to yourself; I'm supposed to be walking through a wood, and you try to turn off the voices in your head. You begin to feel a little anxious, because you can't. Your mobile phone buzzes, and though you briefly sigh for the impossibility of ever being truly lost in the world, you're really quite relieved to have the distraction of a text.

It starts to drizzle, and you sigh again and hunch down into your coat. You start to walk faster. So much to do when you get home, and although it's nice to have this break from the vicissitudes of real life, the truth is that you just can't afford the time, really. You start to worry about how you're going to pay for the haircut your teenage daughter wants, at the expensive new salon that just opened down the road. How she seems always to be asking for something you can't afford and how inadequate that makes you feel. How you're going to pay for the summer holiday abroad (and you shudder, remembering the crowds at last year's airports). Whether the interest rates are going to rise, in spite of all the government's promises, and then how will you pay your oversized mortgage . . .

Suddenly a large black bird (is it a crow, you wonder, vaguely? Maybe a raven . . .) flies across your path, right in front of your face. It settles on a low branch, looks you right in the eye and squawks. For a fleeting moment something in your head cracks open a fraction and you glimpse it – a sense of wonder, a sense that the bird is in some way interacting with you – but then you shake your head and tell yourself not to be so silly: it's just a bird, for heaven's sake; you're making things up – and all at once the feeling is gone. The bird flies off. You hurry on along the path, and leave the wood feeling vaguely dissatisfied, looking at your watch and your heart sinking as you realise how little of the weekend is left, and then it'll be Monday and you'll have to face the commuting crowds and five more days doing a job you hate before the weekend comes around again, and you have the chance to relax and take a nice walk in the woods.

Take two. Imagine that you are entering a small wood on a Sunday morning in late spring; you've come here to walk. If you brought a mobile phone with you, it is on mute: there's a time and a place for gadgets, and your attention is on what is actually here, right now in this moment, yourself in this wood. You close your eyes and listen. Rooks chattering high up in the canopy; the warning call of a smaller bird – three sharp notes in succession. A few trees away, another bird replies. News of your arrival is spreading through the wood.

The air is scented with bluebells, and you breathe in deeply. You are breathing in bluebells, you think, and you smile, because that means the bluebells are a part of you now – or are you a part of them? There are nettles under the trees and you have always loved nettles, ever since you heard the story of 'The Wild Swans' as a child, about the girl who had to pick nettles with her bare hands, and spin them into shirts to save her brothers who had been transformed into swans by a wicked stepmother. You bought a ball of nettle yarn which you found by accident in a wool shop you happened upon, a few weeks ago. You're not quite sure what you'll do with it, but you like to finger it, and remember that old story which even now pulls at your heart. It tells you that there's magic in the profoundly mundane. You can't see a nettle now, or a swan, without thinking of the girl in the story, locked into silence for all of the years it took her to complete her task. Love and endurance overcoming malice and injustice, and the wild magic of plants – and the one brother who had the unfinished shirt – the brother with one arm and one white wing, neither wholly man nor entirely bird.

But a nettle is a nettle as well as a set of associations: its growing tips make a fine and nutritious soup, and its fresh or dried leaves make a delicious tea. You don't need to pick them here; there are plenty back in the wild edges of your garden, and in the city park.

You step off the path and into the trees. You'd never get lost; in any place the first thing you do is orient yourself in the world, as if there's some internal compass inside you, just as you imagine migrating birds must have. Your own personal True North. And besides, like Hansel and Gretel, you've laid down a trail of imaginary breadcrumbs. Left a bit at the baby birch, right by the rock that looks like a giant tortoise. You touch everything, gently, as you walk. You are aware that under your feet the trees and plants are communicating and interacting with each other through a vast underground web of fungi which connect them. You once read that resources are shared through this network – carbon, water and nutrients. This isn't just a wood; it's a living, communicating ecosystem, and you are not in it but part of it. There is bluebell inside you. The rocks scattered through the wood are the protruding bones of the earth; the stream over there a vein, carrying its blood.

The stone in that small clearing – a beautiful stone, multiple shades of grey and brown, covered in ivy and moss – looks as if it has a face: head tipped back, two closed eyes and an open mouth, as if it's telling a story. You decide to call it the Story Stone, and next time you pass through the woods you'll remember it, and acknowledge it. You might even sit down and tell it a story yourself, some time. When there's no one else around to think you're crazy. Everything around you is vivid; all of your senses are fully engaged, and you feel at home in this wood. It knows you. You speak to the trees and stones each time you visit; they know your voice, and you watch the trees push out new branches and the lichens creep slowly across the stones, little by little, each year.

It starts to drizzle, and you lift your face to the water that brings this place – and you – life. It feels soft and clean. Suddenly, a crow flies across your path, right in front of your face. She settles on a low branch, looks you right in the eye and squawks. You stop, look right back at the crow and listen. *Crow*, you say, and *Hello*, and a whole other world opens up inside you, layering the richness of its symbols and images on top of the physical world around you. Badb and the Morrígan: all those powerful crow-goddesses in the old myths. Crow represents hidden knowledge, messages from the Otherworld; often it's a Trickster. Clever birds. Crows and humans have always lived together; is it any surprise that there are so many stories about them? You don't know what the crow is saying to you, but you know she is saying something. You know that she is counting you in.

You stand respectfully, drinking in the blue-black beauty of glossy feathers until the crow flies away again and then you walk on. And when you leave the wood to go home sometime later, you carry bluebell in your lungs and crow in your ears.

I suspect that most of us would recognise something of themselves in that first account of a walk through the summer wood. I certainly do. I've been that person; spent a decade or more in that skin. Stressed, fragmented, disconnected. A curiously dissociated play-actor in a life I was never meant to be living. Contemporary life does all that to us – or so we imagine; the unpalatable truth is, we do it to ourselves. We made this world. We're caught up in a great, grinding machine of our own fabrication, and even if we're lucky enough to catch a glimpse of another way of being, to make out in the distance the indistinct shadows of people who seem to be free, all too often we feel that we're powerless to extract ourselves from the mechanism which we imagine keeps us secure. We might not like it, we tell ourselves, but it's what we know. And aren't we mostly safe in the streets (mostly), and warm in our little house-boxes (if we can afford to pay the bills), and fed (yes, of course there are people who aren't, and of course we wish there was more we could do to help), and don't the trains still run (even if overcrowded and rarely on time), and when we're sick we can get treatment (even though, in some countries, only if we're lucky enough to be able to pay), and water comes out of the tap (let's not think about the chemicals), and the great (world-destroying) power stations provide electricity so that we can have our TVs for entertainment and our gadgets to help us manage our lives . . . The disconnection, the constant nagging sense of something critical missing in our lives, is just the price we pay for greater longevity, prosperity and health. It's not so bad, really.

And in one sense, it's true: on average, human beings in Western countries today are safer, healthier and wealthier than in any other civilisation in the history of the world, and life expectancy continues to rise along with these objective markers of 'quality of life'. But there's a catch. The statistics may try to persuade us that, by these objective markers, our 'quality of life' is high – but when it comes to *subjective* markers, our own thoughts and emotions about the matter, a quite different story emerges. 'Life satisfaction' scores in many wealthy countries are surprisingly low, averaging just 5.7 on a scale from 0 to 10 in OECD countries.[1] And in the West, for several decades now there's been a relentless increase in mental health conditions such as depression and anxiety: a 2014 study by the UK Office for National Statistics (ONS), for example, suggested that anxiety and depression affects at least one in five adults. Recently, a pre-existing trend towards alienation has intensified – alienation from ourselves, our fellow humans, and the world we live in. In a 2016 ONS report, around 40 per cent of adults reported that they did not feel a sense of belonging to the places where they lived, and in people under twenty-four the figure rose to a remarkable 50 per cent.[2]

We imagine we're thriving, but we're not. We have allowed ourselves, as the price we pay for so vigorously enrolling in the prevailing Western cult of progress and growth, to become disenchanted with ourselves and each other, and with our lives. But as modern life becomes ever more mechanised, and the social, economic and political systems we once considered to be robust become increasingly fragile, we find ourselves thirsting for something more to hold on to, for new stories to tell about who we are and what our place in the world might be. We're yearning for meaning, for ways to feel at home in the world. We long to see it as we once saw it when we were children: a world that's full of mystery, bursting with possibility; a world that will challenge us to become all that we could ever hope to be. And just like the protagonists in all the finest old stories, even though we know that the journey through this world might not always be easy, we know that it will nevertheless be vital, vivid and rich.

But there's another, critically important, dimension to this problem: whether or not we imagine ourselves to be thriving, it's clear that the planet isn't. And that's because of us. Because our disenchantment with our own lives, with the systems and values on which human civilisation has come to be based, extends to the wider world around us. We've fallen out of love with the world. It's clear from the way we treat it. When you love someone or something, you treasure them, nurture them, take care of them – do all you can to ensure their wellbeing. Many of us might as individuals, but as a species, we don't do that for our planet any more. We might appreciate the continued existence of far-off wild places, and hope we get to visit them some day. We might value a nearby wood we like to walk in (or past), love our cats and dogs, light up when we watch TV documentaries of exotic animals in the jungles and savannahs, sigh over a beautiful sunset – but we long ago ceased to imagine ourselves as real and engaged participants in the wider cycles of life on this planet. Aren't we humans, after all? Aren't we uniquely possessed of reason and intellect – maybe even of souls – and so more valued than any other species on this earth?

Because of this sense of estrangement from the rest of the world around us – a separation that, as we will discover, has its roots in the rationalist classical philosophy on which contemporary Western culture was built – we treat the planet, and the other creatures which inhabit it alongside us, as mere resources to be exploited. And we've taken that exploitation too far. The oceans

To live an enchanted life is to be challenged, to be awakened, to be gripped and shaken to the core by the extraordinary which lies at the heart of the ordinary. Above all, to live an enchanted life is to fall in love with the world all over again.

are polluted and warming, the land is despoiled, the weather is wilder, the atmosphere is richer in greenhouse gases, and animal and plant species are dying out at an unprecedented and alarming rate – but the increasingly dire warnings from scientists and other experts about the consequences of human-induced climate change and environmental damage have little or no meaningful impact on the policies and practices of governments anywhere in the world. And not enough of us are holding them – or ourselves – to account. All of us, together, collectively, are perpetrating these acts of violence against the planet that gives us life. The pursuit of progress is our only religion; unending consumption is our primary motivator. No wonder our psyches are wounded. Our growing modern malaise – anxiety, depression, disease and dis-ease, a multiplicity of dysfunctions – springs in good part from our alienation from the natural order of the world and from our natural selves.

It can't possibly end well. Something has to change – for our own continued existence and wellbeing, and the continued existence and wellbeing of the planet. We have to change. We have to change the way we approach our lives, and to reconstruct our way of being in the world from the bottom up. We have to turn ourselves inside out.

That's what this book is about: learning to shrug off the chains of the old, sterile ways of thinking and being that have been instilled in us ever since we were children, and unburdening ourselves of the sense of alienation and dispossession that so often characterises our lives. It's about the everyday magic of transformation, as the first person in our fictional wood (let's call her Woman A) metamorphoses into the second (Woman B), so coming to feel a sense of wonder, kinship and belonging to the world. Above all, it is a practical guide to *re-enchanting* ourselves, and the world around us.

As a psychologist, I am very much aware that in order to begin thinking about how you might remedy a problem, it's important not only to correctly identify it, but also to understand where it came from. And so, as we make our way along the tangled path to re-enchantment, we will briefly encounter a few of the key thinkers, and brush up against some of the key ideas, that have been responsible for getting us into this mess in the first place. From ancient Greek philosophy to modern cognitive neuroscience, from Jungian psychology to anthropology, we'll craft an understanding of how we came to so profoundly rupture ourselves from the living world around us – and we'll also run into a handful of more recent thinkers who are trying to show us how we might readjust some of our most fundamental perspectives on the way the world is, and our relationship to it. But at the heart of this book is a focus on the practical things we can do, the small and large changes we can make to the way we inhabit and experience the world, which will allow us to grow into a state of enchantment.

I believe that enchantment is an attitude of mind which can be cultivated, a way of approaching the world which anyone can learn to adopt: the enchanted life is possible for everybody. In this book I'll share with you my own experiences, and the experiences of several men and women from around the world, as they demonstrate how we can bring enchantment into every aspect of our daily lives. Because enchantment, by my definition, has nothing to do with fantasy, or escapism, or magical thinking: it is founded on a vivid sense of belongingness to a rich and many-layered world; a profound and whole-hearted participation in the adventure of life. The enchanted life presented here is one which is intuitive, embraces wonder and fully engages the creative imagination – but it is also deeply embodied, ecological, grounded in place and community. It flourishes on work that has heart and meaning; it respects the instinctive knowledge and playfulness of children. It understands the myths we live by; thrives on poetry, song and dance. It loves the folkloric, the handcrafted, the practice of traditional skills. It respects wild things, recognises the wisdom of the crow, seeks out the medicine of plants. It rummages and roots on the wild edges, but comes home to an enchanted home and garden. It is engaged with the small, the local, the ethical; enchanted living is slow living.

Ultimately, to live an enchanted life is to pick up the pieces of our bruised and battered psyches, and to offer them the nourishment they long for. It is to be challenged, to be awakened, to be gripped and shaken to the core by the extraordinary which lies at the heart of the ordinary. Above all, to live an enchanted life is to fall in love with the world all over again. This is an active choice, a leap of faith which is necessary not just for our own sakes, but for the sake of the wide, wild Earth in whose being and becoming we are so profoundly and beautifully entangled.

2. The unendurable everyday

And new philosophy calls all in doubt,
The element of fire is quite put out,
The sun is lost, and th'earth, and no man's wit
Can well direct him where to look for it.

John Donne, from 'An Anatomy of the World'

I REMEMBER MY first experience with what I'd now call disenchantment: the first time I ever actually understood what it was, and all that it implied. It wasn't when, at the age of five, my great-uncle calmly informed me that Santa Claus didn't actually exist (I wasn't entirely sure I'd ever bought into the idea, to be truthful), or when, not so very long afterwards, a schoolteacher told me that there were no such things as fairies (that was just silly. Of course there were. I'd read *Peter Pan*, and I also knew perfectly well that, when she said those words, a fairy died). In fact, I retained a sense of that particular kind of enchantment all through a challenging childhood and well into my teenage years. I knew full well that the world was full of mystery. I discovered it under every leaf and stone in our tiny urban garden, and I fell headlong into it when I read the mythology, fiction and poetry which I loved. If we could imagine worlds filled with such wonders, I reasoned, then at some level they had to be real.

No, my first ever full-on experience of disenchantment came at the age of eighteen. It happened during one of the first lectures I attended after enrolling for a degree in psychology at a university in the north of England. I'd chosen to study psychology rather than literature, as I'd always imagined I would, in good part because I was afraid that that the obsessive textual deconstruction that seemed to characterise the advanced study of literature would take all the enchantment and mystery out of the great books that I loved. And by studying psychology, I believed, I would instead be delving into all the enchantment and mystery of the human mind. I was thrilled by the idea; as the only child from my impoverished working-class family line who had ever made it to university, I so badly wanted to learn, to be inducted into the magical world of academia.

And so it was with a strange sick feeling in my throat that I watched as a sardonic disbeliever-in-everything thoroughly deconstructed the idea of hypnosis. It was a demolition job which involved a fair amount of showmanship, as the lecturer in question gathered a couple of giggling helpers from the admiring audience and demonstrated how to perform the Human-Plank Feat – once declared to be one of the 'proofs' that hypnosis was a unique state of consciousness in which people could be instructed to do things they normally wouldn't dream of – and then proceeded to pick apart all of the ways in which humans indulged in 'magical thinking'. This degree course, he informed us, would knock all of that kind of nonsense out of us, once and for all. It would show us how to think; it would show us how to recognise what was 'real' and what was just a figment of our imaginations.

It's not that I didn't want to learn how to think: I did. It's not that I didn't want to know that what once was held up as a 'proof' of the existence of an irresistibly suggestive hypnotic state wasn't actually a proof of anything at all – anyone with halfway decent abdominal muscle tone could achieve it. I did want to know such things. But what struck me to the core were two fundamental aspects of his approach to the subject: first, his profound and gleeful contempt for people and the way they participated in and thought about the world; and, second, an absolute refusal to entertain any idea that couldn't be empirically verified, and to dismiss it as 'mere imagination', as unreal. What was wrong with imagination? I was bewildered. With the obligatory exceptions of O levels in biology and mathematics, all of my education at school had focused on the arts. Imagination was life – it was everything. It was the best of us. So I wholeheartedly believed (and still do).

With that, the brain-washing began. A year into that degree, and I could hardly say the word 'mind' without shuddering. 'Brain' was fine, because it was a physical entity which we could break into and look at; and 'behaviour' was fine, because we could see it and objectively measure it (even if we couldn't always *trust* it). Internal events, though, were another matter entirely. Thought and emotion? Well, if you couldn't explain them in measurable behavioural or biological terms, you simply shouldn't study them at all. You probably shouldn't even use the words. Best, on the whole, to pretend they didn't exist. People who talked about things like 'mind' and 'consciousness' – well, they were all a bit . . . flaky, to proper scientists like us.

The truth is, it was a fine enough education in its way. It was gloriously broad, as we delved into the relationship between psychology and disciplines as diverse as genetics, neuroscience, social sciences, ethology and linguistics. It was rigorously scientific, and the subjective nature of psychology meant that it was necessary to question everything, always to be aware of and challenge your assumptions. That was good, and I've been grateful, over the years, for that fine education in how to think. We humans need a hefty dose of rationality in our lives; it keeps us honest. I liked the rigour – but I didn't like the fundamentalism which presented science as the only true dogma, and I didn't at all like the ways in which we were actively and determinedly disenchanted, as lecturers wielded copies of B.F. Skinner's profoundly disturbing *Beyond Freedom and Dignity* as if it were their institutional, and very holy, bible.

It took a lot of years for me to recover from that reprogramming; a three-year PhD followed by a stint of postdoctoral research in behavioural neuroscience certainly didn't help. And yet I held on. Throughout it all, I lived a curiously double life: in my spare time I read and studied, just as I had always done, everything I could find about myths and fairy tales, and immersed myself in books and novels imbued with that sense of enchantment which was now sorely lacking in my own working life. I wouldn't, of course, have admitted to it under torture; the persona I presented to the world was always wonderfully . . . rigorous. I was a very successful neuroscientist. It wasn't until I was in my late thirties – all at sea, burned out from several years of corporate disenchantment after I finally left academia, and working my way through what seemed like the last in a whole line of early and mid-life crises – that I found a way to combine psychology with the mythology that I loved, and clawed my way determinedly towards a vision which could bring those two aspects of my own personality back together. Because an enchanted life recognises the need both for rigour and for the free-wheeling imagination. The one doesn't have to exclude the other. The world isn't black and white. A scientific approach is a valuable part of the way we come to understand the world; the problem arises when it presents itself as the only valid way.

But here's the question which consumed me during my university days, and which still nags at me today: how did we ever get to the stage where we thought this might be a good way to educate a human being? Where did we acquire our determined worship of the rational and intellectual, our downgrading of the value of the creative imagination? And how did it so profoundly infiltrate our institutions?

The disenchantment of the world

If to be enchanted is to fully participate in the world, to be open both to its transparency and its mystery, then to be disenchanted is its opposite. To be disenchanted is to be shut down. As we'll see in a later chapter, our way of being in the world is naturally open to wonder and awe when we are children, but then we lose our facility for enchantment as we grow older, and learn to conform to the social and cultural codes which tell us we must actively *dis*enchant ourselves if we want to be thought of as fully adult. My own experience, as a scientist-in-training, might have been extreme in its focus, and in its clearly stated intent to disenchant – but we're all subjected to the process of disenchantment in one way or another. Disenchantment is ingrained in our culture and, as we'll discover, it goes back a long, long way. This way of thinking won't be so easy to uproot.

So what is it, this disenchantment which ultimately replaces the instinctive, enchanted worldview that we possess as children? What does it actually look like, and how does it manifest itself in our lives and in the world around us? How does it happen to us?

It's just a bird, for heaven's sake

At the risk of seeming to over-simplify, to those of us in the English-speaking world, disenchantment arguably begins with 'he', 'she' and 'it'. Because what replaces enchantment is the intensely dualistic – 'us and them' – Western worldview which is instilled into us from the moment, as children, we begin to learn language, and are taught to label things and categorise them. The English language in particular forces us to adopt a position of separation and distance from the rest of the world as soon as we begin to use it. Only humans may properly be given the pronoun 'he' or 'she'. Everything else is an 'it'. An 'it' is usually an inanimate object – something which (even if it is capable of growing, like a plant) isn't alive in the same way that we are

– which lacks characteristics like perception, consciousness and volition. Even though we tend to agree that animals are not inanimate
objects (though not all philosophers have been entirely convinced, as
we'll see in a moment) nevertheless, in proper use of English, we don't
talk about them in the same way we talk about ourselves. Sometimes
it's acceptable to refer to a pet – an animal with which we have a personal relationship – as 'he' or 'she', but a quick online search of 'how
to do grammar properly' resources for writers will confirm their
advice that we should always refer to a wild animal as 'it'.

Already, we are separate. There's us, the humans, and there's
the rest of the world. The one we are told is outside of us – which
we are taught to think of as beginning where our skin ends. A
completely different category: one giant, inanimate *it*.

This perspective – in which we are not participants in the world
but mere observers of it, acting upon inert objects which are *other*
than us – clearly distances us from our surroundings and the (non-
human) beings who we share them with. It not only teaches us
that this strange *it*-ness outside of us is less valuable than we are
(not requiring of us the same linguistic courtesies, for example),
but it profoundly reduces our sense of belonging to the world, for
how can you ever belong to something from which you are so profoundly different, and to which you imagine yourself morally and
intellectually superior?

Our first fictional walker in the woods, Woman A, displays just
this kind of attitude. Everything she encounters is an object, something other than her, something to observe, sometimes admire,
and perhaps classify (if she can). She walks apart on the man-made
path, and engages with nothing that she encounters – a curious
crow is dismissed as 'just a bird'. She is entirely wrapped up in her
own head, in the experience of her own subjectivity. Woman B, on
the other hand, treats everything she comes across as another being
with whom she can have a meaningful exchange – whether it's a
crow, a bluebell or a stone.

In most indigenous societies – and we'll explore this more deeply
in the next chapter – the prevailing view of the world is animistic.
The word 'animism' derives from the Greek *anima*, 'soul', and in
such a worldview everything is alive – not just humans, not just
animals, but rivers and seas, rocks and stones, trees and plants.
Humans are a part of this world, just like all those other living

things. We aren't in charge, and neither are we alienated observers of an inert cosmos: we are all bound up in its unfolding, all of us in it together. A vast meshwork of humans and animals, rivers and seas, rocks and stones, trees and plants.

The corruptions of the flesh

It sounds like a much richer, friendlier way to live, to inhabit a world in which you are enfolded into a vast community of life, constantly surrounded by others with whom you can enter into relationship – but unfortunately this way of being in the world began to erode in the West a long time ago, as philosophers and other intellectuals increasingly began to promote the rational and intellectual above all other types of knowledge, and taught us that we should mistrust the evidence of our physical senses. Our detachment from the rest of the world around us is clearly expressed in the writings of Plato, a wealthy Athenian about whom little is now known, but who, along with his teacher Socrates and his most famous student Aristotle, laid many of the foundations for Western philosophy and intellectual practice as we know it today. Plato argued 2,500 years ago that humans alone possess reason and intellect, and because of this we're not only different from, but superior to, every other living creature that exists.

There we have it: in one fell swoop we are severed from the rest of life on this planet, completely alone in the world.

In contrast to the 'naturalist' philosophers who preceded him, Plato denied the reality of the physical world, arguing that the material world that we perceive with our senses is not the 'real' world at all, but only an image or copy of a real world which can only ever be properly known through the intellect. The physical is profoundly to be mistrusted; only reason can lead us to the truth.

And of course, it's not as silly an idea as it might seem; one of Plato's points was that the way the world is perceived is very subjective. You can argue as much as you like that grass is green, but if the person looking at it has a particular form of colour-blindness, then chances are they'll see it as grey. Which is 'real'? Unfortunately, though, Plato's rejection of the physical and veneration of the transcendental and intellectual passed directly down into later Western thought, and, for example, strongly influenced the doctrines of

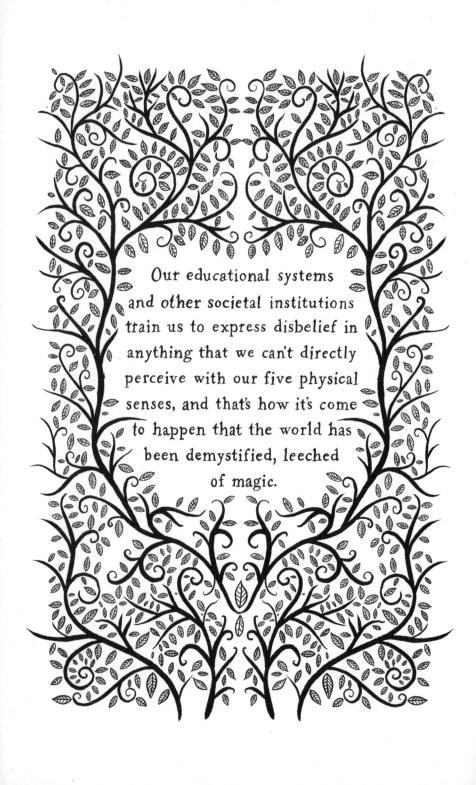

Our educational systems
and other societal institutions
train us to express disbelief in
anything that we can't directly
perceive with our five physical
senses, and that's how it's come
to happen that the world has
been demystified, leeched
of magic.

major religions such as Christianity. The body was scorned as a remnant of our 'animal nature', which we were striving to supersede in our pursuit of reason and intellect, so that we might grow closer to a transcendental, immaterial God. And so phrases such as the 'corruptions of the flesh' abound in medieval religious writings; only by negating the body could you hope to grow closer to God. That's why certain religious communities, especially those of women, were taught to practise 'mortification of the flesh' – in its more extreme forms, a particularly unpleasant form of active self-harm which included flagellation – so that they might free themselves from 'sin'.

Given that we experience the world and live in it as embodied creatures, none of this was ever going to help us feel a sense of belonging to the physical Earth which we inhabit right now. Unfortunately, it was never going to do much for the overall mental health of our species, either: denying what you are is the first step forward on a sure path to madness.

Many of us today are still embarrassed by our physical bodies and their perfectly natural functions. We concoct all kinds of strange words and phrases to gloss over or camouflage the process of eliminating waste from our bodies: in North America, for example, even the word 'toilet' has been exchanged for the bizarrely bashful and utterly inapposite 'restroom'. As a teenager, I could hardly say the word 'menstruation' without blushing, and going into a shop to buy tampons or sanitary pads was positively excruciating. The sexualisation of the female body in particular means that nudity is seen as titillating rather than natural. We cover ourselves up so as not to be a source of 'temptation', and if we don't and we are assaulted or raped, then we are just 'asking for it', because everyone knows that the female body is unbearably arousing and induces men to sin.

Most of us experience a sense of shame because we can't live up to the cultural idea – and men, of course, suffer from body image issues just like women. The presentation of the 'ideal man' – tall, muscular, bronzed – is no more realistic than the presentation of the ideal woman. A 2017 article in *Time* magazine spoke of a 'body image epidemic' in American men – Dr Harrison Pope, director of the Biological Psychiatry Laboratory at McLean Hospital in Massachusetts, said that the increasing equation of masculinity with muscularity has led men not only to feel more and more dissatisfied with their bodies, but for around 4 million of them to use potentially harmful anabolic steroids to increase their muscle mass.[3] The body image issue for lesbian, gay, transgender, bisexual and questioning others is even more complex, with societal stereo-typing adding to the problem, as individuals experience intense feelings of dissonance between who they perceive themselves to be and who they ideally would like to be.

The Chain of Being

Later, Aristotle – a man whose students were nicknamed 'the Peripatetics' because he was known for walking briskly around the school grounds while lecturing them, forcing them to trot along behind – formalised Plato's ideas into a hierarchy of values. Plants were placed at the bottom of his value system, because they pos-sessed only what he called 'nutritive souls', which were related to growth and metabolism. Slightly above plants in his hierarchy were animals, who in addition, he said, possessed 'perceptive souls' of pain, pleasure and desire. And firmly at the top of the ladder were humans – because, he believed, we additionally, and uniquely, pos-sessed the faculty of reason. Later, this notion was expanded by other philosophers into what is now referred to as the 'Great Chain of Being', which proposes the following hierarchy: God at the top, followed by angelic beings – neither of whom occupied the realm of the material and so were infinitely superior to those who did – then humans, then animals, then plants, then minerals. Beings on higher levels of this hierarchy were believed to possess more authority over those in lower positions.

Although it might seem like a rather archaic idea to us now when presented in this fashion, the Chain of Being still informs the way we think about ourselves and our relationship to the rest of the world today. In a recent article in *Psychology Today,* a respected Harvard psychiatrist refers to all things which are not human as 'lower life forms'.[4] The Chain of Being certainly informs our exploi-tation of the environment, and we still often apply Aristotle's value hierarchy in making judgments and choices – for example, when we make choices about what it's okay to eat: humans never, animals sometimes (depending on whether or not you're a vegetarian) and plants always (even if you're the most radical of vegans) because, as a vegan friend declared to me once, 'Even if plants are alive, they don't feel pain in the same way we do.'

Masters and possessors of nature

This sort of thinking pretty much held sway down through the centuries, through the Middle Ages and on into the Renaissance. In the early seventeenth century, it was further advanced by French philosopher René Descartes, who was perhaps best known for his most famous written line, 'Cogito, ergo sum' – 'I think, therefore I am'. Descartes is believed to have been sickly as a boy, and to have suffered a nervous breakdown while studying law at the University of Poitiers. Then, having become disillusioned with the world of books, and in a move that might not seem entirely obvious for someone of such an apparently tender disposition, he decided he would be better served by seeing something of the world – and took himself off to join the Duke of Bavaria's army. So it was, at the age of twenty-three, that he found himself 'shut up in a stove-heated room' while wintering with the army in the German city of Ulm. It was 10 November 1619, the vigil of the Feast of St Martin of Tours – a time of great celebration in the France of the day – and, during the course of the night, Descartes had three 'big dreams' which he later credited with determining the future course of his work. He immediately interpreted them as coming directly from God, and from that moment on, Descartes believed that he had a divine mandate for his ideas. Indeed, he was so convinced of this divine endorsement of his 'mission' that he shortly afterwards made a pilgrimage to the Holy House of Loreto to express his appreciation.

Descartes – clearly by then not a man particularly given to self-doubt – took from those dreams the message that he should set out to reform all human knowledge; he decided to begin with philosophy. Unfortunately for the future trajectory of Western civilisation, Descartes' dream-God seems to have left him with the impression that our job is to make ourselves the 'masters and possessors of nature'. This would be a desirable thing, Descartes wrote, because it would allow us to 'enjoy trouble-free the fruits of the earth and all the goods found there'.[5] But, it hasn't quite turned out that way. As a consequence of our quest for mastery and possession of nature we are, like Mary Shelley's Frankenstein, much more likely to have sown the seeds of our own destruction.

Descartes also extended the Aristotelian view that, as well as being the only creatures who possess reason, humans are unique because they alone possess souls and 'mind'. Animals, he declared, have neither soul nor mind; they have no self-awareness or volition; they're insentient and feel no emotion. Although they might act as if they're conscious, they're really not: they are nothing more than biological machines, programmed to behave in wholly predetermined and highly restrictive ways. The entire non-human world is bereft of animating force, insentient, purposeless and completely lacking in intrinsic value. We can do what we like with it.

Again, chances are that many of us, when presented with such a bald statement as 'We can do what we like with it', would flinch or demur. We don't think like that any more, we might say: we've moved on since then. And yet, many of us don't think twice about killing and concreting over fertile fields and healthy forests to create our cities, or injecting liquid at high pressure into subterranean rocks to force open fissures so we can extract oil or gas, or keeping vast numbers of living animals confined in cages throughout the entire course of their drastically abbreviated lives so we can slaughter them en masse and buy their flesh neatly wrapped up in plastic in our supermarkets and not have to think about where it came from. Aren't we humans, and don't we need more houses and more power and more food for the hungry (human) masses? Don't we have more right than any other being to the space, and the resources of the planet? (And for sure, hardly anyone ever thinks of asking a stone on a beach whether it would be okay to remove it from its natural environment, take it home with us and 'display' it on an indoor windowsill.) Whether we know it or not, the choices we make as individuals, as well as the practices of our civilisation, are still driven by ideas concocted hundreds of years ago by wealthy, educated men such as Plato, Aristotle and Descartes.

Too enlightened for our own good

While Descartes was working towards his vision of mastering and possessing nature, Europe was in the throes of the Scientific Revolution: a term used by historians to describe the emergence of modern science, when developments in fields of study like mathematics, physics, astronomy, biology and chemistry were profoundly transforming our views about the nature of ourselves, and the world. Francis Bacon, one of the early founders of the scientific method, was an influential contributor to the Scientific Revolution in the late sixteenth and early seventeenth centuries. He strongly believed that the only valid approach to science was empirical: in other words, you can only properly test an idea by observing, experimenting and measuring, and if you can't do that, it's not a proper subject for study. Thinking about something and reasoning about it just isn't good enough, and older forms of knowledge such as intuition are completely beyond the pale.

Bacon was originally a statesman who, after becoming Lord Chancellor, was subsequently accused of accepting bribes, and was impeached by Parliament for corruption. With his political career in shreds, he decided to have a go at philosophy. In the *Novum Organum*, published in 1620, he suggested that humans could achieve power over the world by seeking knowledge of it – and so give birth to the 'Empire of Man over creation'.[6] The same fundamental idea: humans better; humans first. Unfortunately for Bacon, in the expression of his own individual Empire it was 'creation' which had the last laugh. In 1626, while performing a series of experiments to test the effects of cold on the preservation and decay of meat, he stuffed a hen with snow and promptly caught a chill. He soon developed bronchitis and, a week later, died.

The theories of Descartes and Bacon, along with others which were developed during the Scientific Revolution, influenced the intellectuals whose ideas, taken together, ushered in the period of history that we now call the Enlightenment – and which is sometimes called the Age of Reason. During this period (the Enlightenment is usually considered to have lasted through the eighteenth century) there were also major challenges to religious beliefs and practices; at the same time, there was a growth in the doctrine of Humanism, which emphasised the primacy and centrality of human beings in the world, instead of God. The old religions were held to be mere superstition; the new, true religion was founded on the application of reason and the acquisition of knowledge – but only if that knowledge could be verified empirically.

This cultural worship of reason and empiricism means that our educational systems and other societal institutions train us to express disbelief in anything that we can't directly perceive with our five physical senses, and that's how it's come to happen that the world has been demystified, leeched of magic. We might, deep down in our hearts, believe that there are more things in heaven and earth than are dreamed of in the empiricists' philosophy, but most of us probably feel we'd be wise not to talk about them in public. I've been a recovering scientist now for thirty years, and I still find myself flinching if ever I should happen to use words like 'holy', 'sacred', 'reverence' or 'spiritual'. I'm not entirely sure I won't someday be burned at the stake if I confess that there's something in me which believes the old gods are alive, still, and walk the land, if only you know where to find them . . .

And yet, 'official' cultural norms aside, many people in the West have their own antidotes to disenchantment. Belief in protective icons and rituals is still strong. Nearly 30 per cent of Americans say they have felt in touch with someone who has already died, almost 20 per cent say they have seen or been in the presence of ghosts, and 15 per cent have consulted a fortune teller or a psychic, according to a 2009 Pew Research Center survey.[7] As many as 72 per cent believe in Heaven, 58 per cent believe in Hell, and 83 per cent are absolutely or fairly certain that God exists.[8]

Dogma and demiurges

And on that note – it's not just scientists and philosophers who laid down the script for our disenchantment: religion was influential too. This might at first seem like an unlikely idea, because ever since the Enlightenment, critics have usually associated religion with exactly the kind of 'irrational' thinking that's sometimes linked with the use of words like 'enchantment'. But many religions, in their dogmatic adherence to one particular way of seeing the world, relieve us of possibility and so fetter our imaginations. Wonder and awe, they tell us, can be turned only in one direction: never onto what is 'worldly', but always in the direction of God.

In many monotheistic religions, to love God automatically requires a rejection of the physical world. Some strains of Christian thought, for example, involve a profound hostility to the physical, the here and now, and value only the transcendental – the unearthly – and the notion of an afterlife far away from the 'corruption' of material things. We find some of the most striking examples of such beliefs in Gnosticism, a religious perspective adopted by some Christians in the first and second centuries AD. The Gnostics believed that the physical world was evil because it was created by the Demiurge: a malevolent 'emanation' of the One God.

The Cathars, recently popularised (and mostly romanticised) in a series of movies and novels such as Kate Mosse's 'Languedoc' trilogy,[9] were members of a Gnostic revivalist sect which flourished in northern Italy and southern France between the twelfth and fourteenth centuries. They're now remembered primarily because of a prolonged period of persecution by the Catholic Church, which didn't recognise their beliefs as properly Christian (especially their belief in two Gods – one good and one evil) and so condemned them as heretics. The Cathars believed that the world was in fact created by Satan, and so this world, this Earth, was inherently tainted with evil. All physical matter was created by this evil God, and because of that, the Cathars also believed that all reproduction – including human reproduction – was a sin.

So there we have it: a millennia-old tradition of Western thought which perceives the physical as bad; the intellectual, rational and transcendental as good; and humans as superior to and masters of the rest of the world – which, by the way, is filled with mindless creatures and objects which have no awareness or agency of their own. And so which have no meaning or purpose at all other than as objects for us to act on, use or consume. Humans, so uniquely clever but so uniquely alone, plonked down by virtue of some evolutionary accident on the hard surface of a largely inanimate planet, completely at odds with the physical bodies which are our only means of perceiving, experiencing and living in the world. Nothing else to have a proper relationship with, nothing to look up to and, as atheism continues to gain ground over religious faith, nothing to consider sacred beyond ourselves.

No wonder we're alienated and depressed.

In the early twentieth century, German intellectual Max Weber, who is now recognised as the founding father of modern sociology, coined a term which he used to describe these multiple historical processes through which a sense of wonder at the world, a sense of all life as not only redolent with meaning, but as sacred, began to

lose ground. 'The fate of our times is characterized by rationalization and intellectualization, and, above all, by the "disenchantment
of the world",' Weber wrote.[10] But of course it is not the world
which is disenchanted: it is ourselves.

Each of us, at some level, in some way, has an instinctive understanding of the many different forms which that disenchantment
can take; there are so many ways in which we have disenchanted
ourselves. But in this book we will explore acts of *re-enchantment*:
antidotes and alternatives to the centuries-old deadening, new
ways to bring ourselves back to life. New ways to come home to
ourselves, and to rediscover our place in the world.

The hymn of the pearl

There is a story contained within a hymn in the Gnostic Acts
of Thomas, one of the apocryphal New Testament gospels
(those which were left out of the modern canon and didn't make
their way into the 'official' Bible). I heard it many years ago, but
never could remember where it came from, and what little of it
I recalled was never enough to identify it to other storytellers I
asked. Recently, I happened across it again, by chance – if you
believe, which I do not, that stories ever come to you by chance.
But we'll come to the hidden lives of stories in another chapter.
For now, I'd like to share this particular story with you; it is called
'The hymn of the pearl'.

Once there was a boy, the son of a king of kings, who lived happily
in a house of great wealth and luxury. But his parents decided to
send him on a journey. Equipping him with gold, silver and precious stones, they removed his clothing – the glittering robe and
purple toga which he loved, and which suited him so well. And
then they made a pact with him, and wrote the pact in his heart, so
that he should never forget it. 'Go west,' they told him, 'and bring
back to us a uniquely beautiful pearl which lies on an island in the
middle of the sea, guarded by a fierce, roaring serpent. This pearl
is yours. If you do this, then when you return to us you may have
your glittering robe again and your favourite purple toga. And you
will inherit our kingdom together with your older brother.'

Enchantment isn't
about magical thinking;
it is about being fully
present in the world.

So the young boy travelled west, accompanied by two guardians – for the way was long and hard, and he was very young to travel it. After passing through many lands and seeing many wonders, he eventually came to the island he had been told about: an island in the middle of the sea where the serpent lived. Once they had arrived safely on that island, his companions left him. And so the boy asked some questions, and discovered where the serpent made his home; and he remained on the island for a while, planning to wait until the serpent fell asleep (which he did rarely) so that he could take the beautiful pearl from him. But while he waited he became lonely and missed his family; and so when a local boy made friends with him, he shared with him the gold and silver and jewels that his parents had given him, and began to dress like him in order to better fit into his surroundings, and not to be treated like a stranger.

Although he had been warned by his parents not to eat the food of these people, most of whom were slaves, he was hungry as well as lonely, and he gratefully took their food when it was offered to him. And so it happened that, clothed in the garments of this strange country, and partaking of its food, he forgot that he was a son of kings, and began to serve the new country's king: the king of these people, who were slaves. And he forgot his pearl, for which his parents had sent him, and it was as if a veil covered his eyes and he fell into a deep sleep. So he remained for many years.

When years passed and still their son did not return home, his parents understood what must have become of him, and they brought together all of the nobles in their kingdom so that together they could make a plan to rescue him. His family wrote a letter, signed by all the nobles of the kingdom, reminding their son that he was a son of kings, and asking him to free himself from the slavery of the country where he now was – and to remember his pearl, for which he had been sent. Remember also your glittering robe, the letter exhorted him, and your purple toga, and come back to your family and your home!

The letter was given to an eagle, and the king of all birds flew west and soon found this boy who was now a man, and landed beside him as he slept. When, startled, he awoke, the eagle spoke to him and dropped the letter at his feet.

And the man read the letter and remembered that he was of noble birth; and he remembered his pearl, for which he had been sent to this strange country. The veil fell away from his eyes. And so he left his room and went at once to the place where the terrible roaring serpent lived, and he sat down at its feet and set about the process of charming it. He sang and he crooned, and eventually he lulled the serpent to sleep. Once it was safely and soundly slumbering, he snatched away the pearl which lay in the centre of the spiral created by its coiling body. He cleaned his filthy clothes and set off across the sea, embarking on the long journey east.

Just as he was approaching the gates of his family home, servants came out to him, bearing the bright robe and the purple toga which once he had worn. He hardly remembered them now, for he had left his home many years ago, when he was a child – but as soon as the clothes were placed back into his hands, all of a sudden they seemed like mirrors of his true self. And so the man put on his old robes – the beautiful, richly coloured, glittering robes he had worn as a child, but which had grown along with him – and returned home, bearing the wondrous gift of the pearl which he had wrested from the terrible, roaring serpent who lived on an island in the middle of the great western sea.

If you're not used to working with stories of this kind, it's easy to become distracted by their literal content rather than seeing them as metaphors whose function is to shed light, as simply and as briefly as possible, on the complexities of the human condition. You could, for example, focus on the wealth and privilege of the prince's upbringing and lose sight of the fact that, in story terms, this is simply a way of indicating that he was a loved and cherished little boy, and that worldly wealth is often a metaphor for spiritual wealth. This story, then, coming out of a Gnostic text, is usually interpreted as metaphorically reflecting a Gnostic perspective on the human condition: that we are (good) spirits lost in a world of (bad) matter, and that we are forgetful of our true origin as inheritors of the kingdom of God.

But here's the thing about stories: they won't be confined and they won't be constrained. The best thing about stories is that they have lives of their own, and sometimes they conspire with you to subvert the 'official' meaning. So this story presents itself to me in another way. We have indeed forgotten who we are. We've travelled a long way from the natural world that is our home, and the sense of enchantment which is reflected in the glittering robes and brightly coloured togas we once wore there, when we were children. We've all felt it: that nagging sense of something missing, something fundamentally wrong at the heart of our lives, a sense of profound disconnection from the wider world around us. We feel it in our burned-out, stressed-out bodies, in our anxiety-ridden thought patterns, in our broken and dysfunctional relationships, in the sense of futility which haunts our days, in the breakdown of communities and the increasingly frightening breakdown of social order, even in countries we've previously believed to be immune. Because we have been scared, hungry and alone, we've adopted the customs of this new country and put on tainted clothing; we've come to worship a new king: a king who is a slave-maker. We've taken it all too literally and forgotten about the metaphor, forgotten that it's supposed to be spiritual wealth we're acquiring, not just more *stuff.* We've fallen asleep. We've forgotten where we came from, and where we truly belong; we've stopped believing that there is anything beyond us, maybe even that there's something greater and worth fighting for. More than this, though, we've forgotten our calling: forgotten that the purpose of the journey we're on is to discover the rare pearl which was always intended to be our unique gift to the world we've left behind.

It's time to remember who we are. In our hearts, we've known for a long time that something is wrong. We've seen the veil shifting, caught glimpses of the finer reality which lies behind it. It's time to finally wake up, read the letter, set off on the long journey home. It's time to change.

🌿 List the ways in which your own life has become disenchanted – the parts of your life in which you have a sense of something out of kilter. Think about:

 ⊙ Your relationships – friends, partners, parents,
   children, colleagues, community.
 ⊙ Your health, both physical and mental.

- ○ Whether or not you feel comfortable in your physical body.
- ○ Your job, and your hopes and expectations for the future.
- ○ The place you live – your accommodation and the wider location in which it sits.
- ○ Your relationship (a sense of belonging or of alienation?) with the world around you, and with the non-human others you share it with.
- ○ Whether or not you have a sense of meaning in your life.

✺ Categorise your disenchantments according to whether these are things you want to change, and whether you believe you have some power to change them, or not.

Change, and the end-of-history illusion

To come right out and call for change begs some important questions. What kind of change, in who (or what), and how? Well, when it comes to change, I have one foundational belief: that for most of us, no matter how badly we feel drawn to do it, changing the world isn't an option. We don't usually have that kind of influence or that kind of power. But changing ourselves is very much an option, and I believe that if enough of us change ourselves in the same ways, then we are going to influence and create changes in the people around us, and so change the world. This kind of fundamental, grassroots change isn't just about critical mass: it's about the strong bonds and connections which can be made among people who share the same values. That's how most of us contribute to the changing of the world. It starts with ourselves.

If we can create a shift in the fundamental ways in which we see and approach the world, so that we come to feel again that sense of wonder, awe and belonging that we felt when we were children, then we will dramatically enhance the quality of our own lives and increase our sense of wellbeing. But more importantly – those internal changes will spark off wider and more enduring changes in our behaviour and our actions, and lead to an entirely new relationship with, and sense of responsibility for, the living world around us.

Changing ourselves, of course, isn't always easy. Sometimes, even if we can see exactly what it is that we need to change in our lives, we can't necessarily see the steps we need to take to achieve it. To return to our fictional example: if you are like Woman A, how exactly do you transform yourself into someone who is more like Woman B? What do you have to do? How do you actually get to be like that? What are the steps you can take which will create that kind of change? Is it even possible?

Sometimes, the extent of the problem, and the extent of the change that seems to be required to address it, can make us feel hopeless. But humans are made to grow; we're made to change. Every one of us is constantly changing. Biologically, we're doing it every day of our lives. We slough off old cells and our body makes new ones; we cut our hair and it grows back again. Our brains are inherently 'plastic' – they continue to develop as we go through life, as we grow and learn from our experiences. Let's just take the example of the prefrontal cortex – the section of our brain which is deeply involved in mediating our thoughts and actions, our plans and decisions, and key aspects of our personalities. This region, and the wider neural networks by which it connects to the rest of the brain, shifts and changes for as long as we are alive. This underpins our shifting sense of identity as we grow older. We are hard-wired to change.

But, as with so much in human behaviour, change is rarely quite that simple. Psychological research carried out at Harvard University, for example, showed that at each stage of our lives we consistently doubt our ability to achieve change. The researchers called this phenomenon the 'end-of-history illusion'.[11] When we look back into the past, their study tells us, we readily acknowledge how different we once were, and how much we have changed in the intervening years. But when we imagine our futures, we just can't believe that we'll carry on changing in such fundamental ways.

The subjects of the Harvard research were 19,000 people aged between eighteen and sixty-eight, and most people, in each of the age groups studied, accepted that they'd changed substantially in the past decade, but rated as extremely low their likelihood of changing much in the decade to come. The researchers drew the following conclusion: 'People, it seems, regard the present as a watershed moment at which they have finally become the person they will be for the rest of their lives.' The Harvard team noted that this has practical consequences for important decisions we make (or perhaps fail to make) about the future. Or, as Daniel Gilbert, one of the study's authors, said to the *New York Times*: 'At every age we think we're having the last laugh, and at every age we're wrong.'[12]

Sometimes, change can seem like a caving in, a betrayal of the person we once thought we were and the beliefs we once held. I remember as a teenager, absolutely convinced that I would be a born-again evangelical Christian for the rest of my life, I was utterly furious at my mother for insisting that I'd soon 'grow out of it'. Change was for dilettantes, for flibbertigibbets, not for serious, thoughtful people like me. At fourteen, brimming over with hormone-inflamed passion, I was absolutely convinced that change was the opposite of, and a deadly threat to, commitment. I would love God forever, just as I would love Bryan Ferry forever. (Whereas, of course, neither love outlived my fifteenth birthday.) Because something, surely, had to last. I was tired of change. My adolescent body was changing by the day; my emotions were changing by the minute – I badly needed something enduring to cling to. God and Bryan Ferry would do.

Just as it was to me as an adolescent, then, change can be threatening or frightening. And so maybe the end-of-history illusion is simply a way of protecting ourselves from the anxiety that anticipated change can generate. Because of that anxiety, so many of us embrace change only when we have to: when we are diagnosed with a life-threatening illness, or with anxiety or depression. When we are divorced or lose a loved one in some other way. But we can also embrace change when we see something we want, badly. When we see a light shining in the distance which encourages us on. When we climb to the top of one mountain range and see another in the distance, and wonder what is beyond.

I believe that the enchanted life is something worth wanting, badly. Something worth the risk of changing for.

Here in the West, so many aspects of our lives are aimed at protecting us from risk and change, and instead establishing a state of what we imagine to be permanence. We manage the minute details of our lives so that we can stay safe – which usually means staying put. We embrace repetition and routine. But when we insist on permanence, when we cling tight to what we know, when we resist change, refuse the journey – we are in a very real sense refusing life. Life is an act of creation, of ongoing transformation. The world changes with every cycle of the seasons. We change with every cycle of our lives, from birth through adolescence to adulthood and, finally, to death. And perhaps, in the end, clinging to permanence is a way of protecting ourselves against death – an impossible feat, but one which we blindly pursue, anyway.

Change is possible, and change is life.

Confronting our fear of change

It's important to understand that there's nothing intrinsically wrong with fear; fear is a natural part of life. None of us are fearless. The problem comes when you believe that the presence of fear means that what you're contemplating is dangerous. It isn't, always. We don't begin the process of re-enchantment by freeing ourselves of fear; that's not possible. We do it by accepting that change can be frightening, and resolving to change anyway.

Here are some of the reasons why people might be afraid to change, to begin to reverse the process of disenchantment and to live a more enchanted life. Which of them do you recognise in your own life? Are there others, not listed here?

- Fear of the unknown.
- Fear of being different from other people.
- Fear of ridicule or rejection from friends and family.
- Fear of not being taken seriously, of being thought to be foolish.
- Fear that you lack imagination.

> ❧ Fear that you have too much imagination, and are
>   deluded!
> ❧ Fear of change, because sometimes it's painful.
> ❧ Fear that we'll have to give up something valuable.
> ❧ Fear that we won't be as safe or secure.
> ❧ Fear that our lives up until now might have been meaningless.
> ❧ Fear of giving up control, represented by the status quo.
> ❧ Fear of losing one's boundaries.
> ❧ Fear of failure – of feeling that you're not capable of
>   change after all, and that you'll never be able to live a
>   more enchanted life.

What is enchantment, anyway?

In this chapter, we've explored the nature and onset of our disenchantment, and it's certainly a concept which has been studied and analysed in many different ways, over the years. Economists, philosophers and cultural commentators have picked it to pieces using the theories that are beloved of their own disciplines, often taking Max Weber's ideas as their starting points; theologists concerned about the secularising of the world have put their own more religious spin on the term. But although there's been a good deal of focus on *dis*enchantment, there has been relatively little analysis of the state of enchantment itself. What does it actually mean, to be enchanted? How do you do it? What are the components of an enchanted frame of mind? What is actually going on inside us when we're enchanted – what is the lived experience of it for us as individuals? As a psychologist, these questions interest me much more. And as a human being planted in a world which is in various and varying states of growing crisis, they seem to me to be infinitely more essential.

When we turn to the usual sources of definitions for clues about what enchantment is, they offer us very little help. The Oxford Dictionary[13] provides two possible meanings, which are echoed in other major dictionaries in the English-speaking world:

1. A feeling of great pleasure; delight
2. The state of being under a spell; magic

In other words, the word as it is commonly used today is associated either with the practice of magic, or with a feeling of pleasure at something which is charming. But if we return to Weber's idea of disenchantment as characterised by 'rationalization and intellectualization', as a stripping away of everything that we once held sacred in the world, then we approach much more interesting territory when we begin to think about what the opposite of that state might be.

I believe that the state of enchantment has four major components:

1. It is founded upon a sense of fully *participating* in a living world – a feeling of belonging rather than separation.

2. It incorporates feelings of *wonder*, and curiosity. To be enchanted is to be comfortable with the fact that not everything can be explained; to tolerate, even welcome, the presence of mystery.

3. Enchantment is not all in the head, it is very much a function of our lived, *embodied* experience in the world.

4. Enchantment is an emanation of the *mythic imagination*, and is founded on an acknowledgement of myth and story as living principles in the world.

In the next part of this book we'll examine these ideas, and meet some people who are putting them into practice in their daily lives and their work. And then we'll explore the changes, great and small, which each of us can make – whoever we are, wherever we live – to bring a sense of enchantment to the way we approach the world, every single day of our lives.

What Is Enchantment?

3. To inhabit the living world

Man feels himself isolated in the cosmos. He is no longer involved in nature and has lost his emotional participation in natural events, which hitherto had a symbolic meaning for him. Thunder is no longer the voice of a god, nor is lightning his avenging missile. No river contains a spirit, no tree means a man's life, no snake is the embodiment of wisdom and no mountain still harbours a great demon. Neither do things speak to him nor can he speak to things, like stones, springs, plants and animals.

C.G. Jung[14]

'IT'S LIKE A dance,' he tells me. 'And your dance-partner in the sky is a thermal.' The man who is speaking is David Knowles, a former pilot in the Royal Air Force. But he's not talking here about flying fast jets; he is talking about hang-gliding, which he practised for almost twenty years. Hang-gliding, for those of you who don't know much about it, requires you to clip yourself on to an aluminium frame which is braced with steel wires and covered in a 'skin' of fabric. The harness you wear is a bit like a sleeping bag – after you've used your legs for take-off you lie forwards and tuck them up into the back of the harness and close it with a zip. Then you are lying flat, belly down, with your arms ahead of you, flying a bit like Superman – except that you are holding on to a thin aluminium bar which allows you to control the glider: to bank left or right, and to raise or lower its nose to control speed.

'I was on leave in the middle of pilot training when I started hang-gliding. Which maybe sounds like more of the same. But flying was something I had always dreamed of – vivid dreams with physical sensations. Flying the nimble, sleek training aircraft in which we learned our craft in the RAF fulfilled many aspects of those dreams. Except . . . well, except that in the dreams I had felt the air flowing over my face, my skin. And my whole body had somehow been involved in the flight, arching and flexing as I manoeuvred. To get those kinds of sensations while flying you really need to fly a hang-glider. Which I went on to do for a thousand or so hours all told, all over the world, sometimes in competitions but more often just for the joy of exploring a landscape like a bird.'

Once upon a time in the American Midwest, when I was thirty-eight years old, I learned to fly a small plane to overcome a fear of flying, and to begin wrestling with a crisis which led me to seriously question the trajectory my life was taking. It largely worked (on both fronts) but I liked the illusion that the flimsy tin can which surrounded me gave me some protection from . . . well, I don't really know what, because it was flimsy enough, for sure. But, no matter how foolish, that illusion made me feel safe. The last thing I wanted was to feel the air on my own fragile body. And I flew in constant fear of an engine failure, so I can't begin to imagine what it must be like to fly in a contraption which has no engine at all.

'Well,' says David (who also happens to be my husband), 'what it means is that inevitably, you'll naturally drift downwards as you fly. You have wings: it's usually a gentle enough drift, but it's no fun; your flight will last no more than a couple of minutes and then you'll have to pack up the equipment and trudge it all the way back up the hill you originally took off from if you want to fly some more. But what you really want is to fly for hours at a time, to explore the world of the birds, the mountains, the clouds. For that you need nature's help. You need a thermal.'

All of this is so second nature to him that he laughs when I tell him that I'm not entirely sure what a thermal is, and how it works. I know that birds coast along on them – I *think* that birds coast along on them – but beyond that, all I know is that it has something to do with warm air. Where that warm air comes from, or how you find it (or does it just happen to you?) I have no idea.

'When the sun warms the land,' he explains, 'it doesn't do it equally. Rocks or hollows which are protected from the wind get warmer than their surroundings and heat the air above them. And that warm air rises. So if somehow you manage to fly inside this rush of rising air, you rise up with it. On the right sort of day, the warm air forms into a column that towers upwards for thousands of feet, until it finally cools. Then the water vapour it contains condenses to form one of those pearly white cumulus clouds we associate with the best of summer days. Of course, these natural elevators are invisible. But as a bird you know, and as a pilot you learn to intuit, where they might be in that vast, seemingly feature-less open sky.'

French philosopher Maurice Merleau-Ponty (who we will meet again soon) used the example of a 'blind man's cane' to explain the ways in which objects which otherwise would be perceived as being outside of us actually become extensions of the self: a means through which we experience the environment. When David talks about hang-gliding, it is clear that the glider serves a similar kind of function. It gives you wings. And, he says, 'when you approach the thermal, at speed, your wings tremble. But it's not out of emotion, or fear: they tremble in the way that a dog trembles in anticipation of being let off the leash to follow a scent.

'The problem with thermals, though, is the downdraughts which surround them. They're tricky things, and always worse than you anticipate. If you picture pushing the flat of your hand through water you'll have an idea of what a downdraught is like – some water is pushed down along with your hand but the rest spins back chaotically to fill the hole you have left. Downdraughts take you by the scruff of the neck and dunk you. You're nearly weightless under the force of it. You're flying along and, all of a sudden, your flightline slews and yaws without warning or hope of negotiation. That's how you know that the thermal must be close and it will be wild and headstrong. But on you fall, and still the turbulence pummels you. And just as you're beginning to be afraid, there comes the upward surge, like a punch in the guts. Under your left wing, say, which bucks skywards while your right staggers and tries to get a hold. Any hesitation now and the thermal will push you out, turn you away back into the waiting arms of the downflow. If that happens you'll lose hundreds if not thousands of feet in the blink of an eye. And when you finally manage to regain control and turn back to find the thermal again, it may have pulled up its skirts and have disappeared way above you. A thermal only lasts for a short time. You might be lucky enough to find another nearby, but you might equally well be headed for the ground and looking for somewhere, anywhere, safe to land. In a hurry.'

The experienced hang-glider's response to a downdraught is clearly instinctive. 'It is,' he confirms. 'You lean left with all your heart. The shape of your shoulders, the curve of your body as you lie horizontally in the harness, cry "Turn!", and the great mantle of sailcloth that sprouts from your back follows the lead, reining in the left, urging the right. Now you need to commit. Your arms extend to raise the nose of this man-wing to face the challenge. Full on, and nothing in reserve. Either you carve up and left into the heart of the lift and dance with this frenzied partner, gripping it around the waist – or you're thrown out, too slow. You've staked your speed on entering the dance, defenceless against the chaotic turbulence you'll face if you fail, falling like a leaf in a storm. 'And yes, that is the moment you remember in your dreams. Aerodynamics is a wonderful science, and it can explain to you all of the ways the air flows around a wing, the way it breaks and fails at the moment of maximum output, when a wing stalls. But the *feeling* of a wing, your wing, giving everything it possibly can, tightening up to the edge of stalling but not falling over that edge – well, that's a thing alive. And here's a strangeness: we talk about the five senses easily enough, but when you go on to talk about a sixth, people imagine that you are talking about something spooky or supernatural. Not so. There is actually a very powerful, physical sixth sense. Imagine that you board a ferry – one of those big roll-on-roll-off ones. Say that it is pitch black or that you have a blindfold on and are standing inside a cabin while the ship is still alongside. Do you fall over? No. But how do you know which way is up? Well, your whole body knows fine well which way is up. Fancy apparatus in the ear has a lot to do with it. But also every muscle and tendon in your body tells you continuously what is going on. Now the ship gently sets sail. Do you feel it? Sure. Do you fall over now? No. Your whole body is looking after you, making the necessary adjustments, telling you that the voyage has begun.

'The same thing happens when you take up hang-gliding. When you first attach yourself to a hang-glider, a non-rigid wing, the sensations are strange and separate. But if you work at it and are open to it, eventually the lines of communication open up. The hang-glider feels you and your movements, and you feel what the wing is feeling. After long enough the gap closes. You're a creature with wings now; you just fly.

'You fly, and you dance. Why not? You dance with the air, and you long to dance most of all with the crazy, hip-grinding beauty of a strong summer thermal. So yes, it's worth the battering of the turbulence, the gamble of airspeed and safety, to enter into the music.'

I'm keen to know what this dance feels like; he thinks for a while. It's a sensation he has never thought to put into words. 'Once you're established in a thermal a quietness comes on you both. On you and the thermal, I mean. The rushing noise of speed and the brute force needed to control your flight during the transition are done. Now there's only the two of you in this dance, way up there, so high that nobody on the ground notices you – or if they do they might take you for a bird and go on with their day. The dance goes around and you feel each subtle movement of the thermal, the way it surges and syncopates.

'But it isn't enough just to feel these things, of course. You're not in the audience; you're in the dance. You have to respond. Gentle movements now – tightening or loosening the circle, slowing luxuriously into the embrace or sweeping wide to give space to your partner.'

And does the thermal respond to you, I ask him?

'Hmmm . . .'

A rather precocious student of philosophy before he launched himself out of the safe predictability of Oxford University and into the RAF (after first dying his spiky green hair brown again, and removing the earring from his right ear), he is always careful with his words, and especially cautious when we encroach on the subject of metaphysics.

'I can only say that it feels like it does. Of course the thermal is way, way bigger than I am and has a strange boundless identity. And there may be birds there with me, and the thermal is dancing with them at the same time – I've flown close with many species of birds: with buzzards and vultures, swifts and crows. Those are no doubt the thermal's favoured partners. But still. If I dance, if I fly with courtesy and with openness to the patterns and creations in the air around me, then yes, I am dancing with a summer thermal and the thermal is dancing with me. That's how it feels. And if you dance clumsily or without courtesy the thermal will throw you out in a second – back out into the turbulence and the downdraughts. That's how it should be. I'm the junior partner here.

'You see, the thermal has never thought itself separate from the rest of the world; the boundaries between masses of air are not like the skins that cover us and give us that sense of being shut inside, closed off. Energy and substance flow in and out of it at every moment. But that doesn't change the fact that the thermal is very much itself, too: it expresses its own specific creativity, makes its own unique interpretations of the music as it rises. For a time I also flow into it and am a part of it. I'm attentive to its movements and I respond to them with my own. How could it not be the case that it also flows into me, and becomes a part of me that persists in the shape and flow of my life, long after we've parted?'

Participating in a unified reality

In 1975, the Scottish poet Kathleen Raine wrote about an experience which her eighty-year-old mother once confided to her: an experience she had had as a girl. '"I have never told anyone before," she said, "but I think you will understand." It was simply that, one day, sitting among the heather near Kielder, "I saw that the moor was alive."'[15]

Raine went on to describe a similar experience which she herself had, as she sat at her writing table one evening in front of the fire, looking at a hyacinth.

All was stilled. I was looking at the hyacinth, and as I gazed at the form of its petals and the strength of their curve as they open and curl back to reveal the mysterious flower-centres with their anthers and eye-like hearts, abruptly I found that I was no longer looking at it, but was it; a distinct, indescribable, but in no way vague, still less emotional, shift of consciousness into the plant itself. Or rather the plant and I were indistinguishable; as if the plant were a part of my consciousness. I dared scarcely to breathe, held in a kind of fine attention in which I could sense the very flow of life in the cells. I was not perceiving the flower but living it.

What Raine was describing is what David is describing, when he speaks about hang-gliding: a sense of kinship with the world; a feeling of oneness, in the sense that we and the world and other creatures and objects in it are not really separate and fundamentally different from each other, but are merged in the same living system. Such moments of deep relationship have been described by mystics throughout the ages, but in 1964 the American psychologist Abraham Maslow secularised them and gave them a new name: he called them 'peak experiences', and described them as 'rare, exciting, oceanic, deeply moving, exhilarating, elevating experiences that generate an advanced form of perceiving reality, and are even mystic and magical in their effect'.[16] According to Maslow's early studies, peak experiences can be triggered by exposure to art, time spent in nature, sex, creative work, and listening to music.

Today, we see these experiences as remarkable and unique, because they occur rarely during each of our lifetimes; indeed, some people report never having had them at all. But when they happen they are always transformative, jolting us out of the every-day, leading us to see the world, and our place in it, in a very different way. Kathleen Raine wrote that when she returned to 'ordinary reality' after her experience with the hyacinth, it was 'as if I were experiencing at last things as they are, was where I belonged, where, in some sense, I had always been and would always be. That almost continuous sense of exile and incomplete-ness of experience which is, I suppose, the average human state, was gone like a film from sight.'

They might be rare, transient experiences for us, but anthro-pologists have suggested that this way of perceiving the world once would have been the norm rather than the exception for all human beings, and that it still is the norm for many indigenous peoples around the world. It arises out of a belief not only that the world and objects in it are alive, just as we are – but more than that, they are capable of interacting with us. In contrast, in her remark-able novel *Ceremony*, Laguna Pueblo writer Leslie Marmon Silko describes the way Westerners see the world:[17]

They see no life.
When they look
they see only objects.
The world is a dead thing for them
the trees and the rivers are not alive
the mountains and stones are not alive.
The deer and bear are objects.
They see no life.
They fear.
They fear the world.
They destroy what they fear.
They fear themselves.

At the beginning of the twentieth century, French philosopher Lucien Lévy-Bruhl used the term *'participation mystique'* – 'mystical participation' – to describe the worldview of what he called 'primitive peoples', in contrast to the more logical, rational worldview of 'civilised man'. Participation, he wrote, is a belief that 'mystical forces' which can't be perceived by our physical senses are present in the world, and can somehow affect the world. Objects can of course simply be themselves – a stone is very much a stone, and a stone is something we can act upon – we can pick it up, move it, use it to build a wall – but objects can also be something more. A stone could represent, for example, or in some sense be inhabited by, other powers and influences which are able to make themselves felt beyond the stone. And so the stone, or those powers and influences which the stone represents, can affect us, or act on us, just as we can act on the stone. In other words, the relationship isn't just one way: it's reciprocal.

Even here in the 'modern' West, I think that many of us – whether we are aware of it or not, or would admit it publicly or not – still retain a residue of this aspect of *participation mystique*. I certainly do. I invest all kinds of objects with a significance which goes well beyond their natural physical forms. One of my most treasured possessions is the bright blue empty shell of the egg of a grey heron. My husband retrieved it from the floor of a heronry in the woods behind an old riverside cottage we once lived in, in Donegal. To me, this delicate and fragile shell is two things. First, it is at some level, quite simply, an exquisite sky-coloured egg: a rich reminder of the beauty that can so readily be found in the natural world. But second, it carries in it all the mythical power of the heron in my native Irish mythology. Heron is an edge-dweller, a stalker of riverbanks and lochsides, a walker-between-worlds who passes easily from water to land to air; she guards the entrance to the Otherworld. As we'll see in a later chapter, heron haunted my early morning walks along the river, and in many ways personified for me that magical green river valley where we spent three years of our lives. The shell, then, is essence-of-heron, essence-of-Otherworldly-guardian, essence-of-liminality, essence-of-the-cycle-of-birth-and-rebirth . . . it's a magical object, something which, when I hold it (very carefully!) in my hand, conjures up a remarkably rich panoply of archetypal and mythical images which are overlaid onto the beauty of its natural form.

Is the eggshell, then, in my head, inhabited by 'other powers and influences' which are able to make themselves felt beyond it? Yes, indeed.

Am I a 'primitive' at heart? Perhaps I am. But my life is richer for it.

What is interesting here is that, in my understanding, indigenous people who subscribe to such a worldview don't differentiate between the supernatural and the natural, the material and the spiritual, the self and the non-self. It's all the same thing. To see the world in a participatory fashion is to refuse such dualisms, to refuse to be separate from the world, to insist on always participating in it and with it, and with the other objects and forces which are present in it. It is also, at its heart, about seeing *meaning* in a stone, or in the discarded shell of a heron's egg.

Some scholars have argued that this state of participation is indeed primitive, because it's nothing more than anthropomorphism – in other words, people who live like this are really just projecting human qualities onto other objects and processes in the world, mostly because they are naive, or lacking in proper understanding. According to this perspective, you can't look at a participatory approach to the world as a form of consciousness which happens to be different from ours, but which is equally legitimate – instead, you should see it as a misguided and unsophisticated worldview that most of us in the West have, happily and rather cleverly, now outgrown.

But other writers and thinkers have suggested that *participation mystique* might be rather more sophisticated than that: people in such indigenous societies might really see other objects and processes as genuine, autonomous presences which are part of the same life-world we inhabit, and which are capable of interacting with us. Maybe they see something we don't. Maybe stones, rivers and storms are alive, just as people are alive, and maybe all things in the world can have relationships with other things. For example, when asked how they have come so perfectly to understand the medicinal uses of plants without the benefits either of randomised or double-blind clinical trials, or chemical analyses in the laboratory, most indigenous people will patiently try to explain themselves to Westerners using some version of the words, 'The plants told us'. Why then shouldn't a woman drift for a while into the consciousness of a hyacinth, or a man accept the invitation to dance with a thermal?

> ❧ Have you had an experience which might fall into the
>   category of a 'peak experience'? What was the nature of the
>   experience, and what words would you use to describe it?
> ❧ Are there other times when you feel or have felt especially
>   at one with the world?
> ❧ What examples of *participation mystique* do you see in
>   your own life? Are there objects or places which hold
>   significance for you beyond their physical form? How did
>   they come to acquire that significance?

The web of life

Lévy-Bruhl's notion of *participation mystique* has been taken up
and refined by a diverse range of scholars over the years; one of
its most enthusiastic interpreters was the psychologist Carl Gustav
Jung. To Jung, 'participating consciousness' could be problematic,
sometimes: it might be a sign of childishness, of being trapped in
a state of infancy; or it might be a sign that a person couldn't adequately differentiate himself from other members of the community
and so become a 'proper' individual. But Jung also recognised that
it might be a sign of a kind of psychological wholeness which had
long since been lost to us, in the West. Later Jungians took a more
positive view, linking *participation mystique* with experiences of
mystical union with the world or objects in it which, far from being
infantile or primitive urges which badly need to be outgrown, are
profound and unforgettable, and often life-changing.

One of Jung's leading and most favoured disciples, Erich
Neumann, believed that participatory experiences are examples
of something which he called 'unitary reality'. Neumann argued
that our notions of 'inner' and 'outer', when it comes to the way
we think of ourselves and the position we occupy in the world –
the idea, that is, that the world is outside of the head that we are
inside – are nothing more than categories which are forced on us
by our culture. Such dualistic ways of thinking are simply illusions

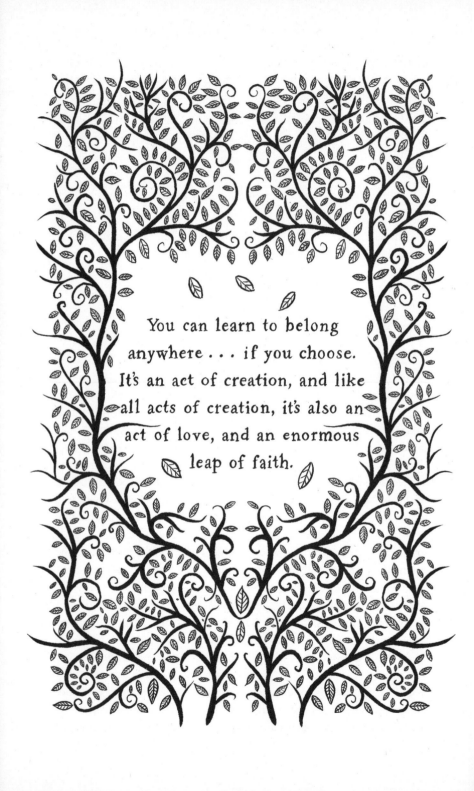

You can learn to belong
anywhere . . . if you choose.
It's an act of creation, and like
all acts of creation, it's also an
act of love, and an enormous
leap of faith.

of the human mind. They have little to do with true reality, he said, which has an underlying unity. Neumann thought that human experiences of this unitary reality are related to a special type of knowledge which he called 'knowledge of the field': the field being a web of reciprocal interactions between human beings, animals, objects and their environment. In this field of unitary reality – the true reality – Neumann suggested, the mental and physical are not opposites, and the boundaries of form which seem to define (and so confine) a person or object in their physical bodies are blurred.[18]

Jung believed that synchronicities – the 'meaningful coincidences' which he wrote about at some length – were examples of unitary reality, or what Neumann called the field, in action. According to this idea, events which occur together aren't always connected by cause and effect: sometimes they're part of a larger pattern which is connected by *meaning*. I'm sure most of us can remember examples of such seeming synchronicities in our lives: the right guide or teacher who appears in our lives at exactly the time we need them; the perfect house which has unexpectedly popped onto the market again just at the time we are looking. These are the events which make us want to exclaim, 'What a remarkable coincidence!' And indeed, synchronicities are coincidences which are so remarkable that we can't begin to imagine how it came to pass that on one specific day, at one specific time, all the stars aligned and all the right people were at all the right places at exactly the right times to do exactly the right things. Coincidences which are so statistically improbable that the chances of those specific circumstances coming together at the same time is way off the scale. We're often Doubting Thomases, inclined to pass them over as the result of mere chance – but what if these apparent coincidences are in fact expressions of our profound entanglement in the web of unitary reality – an underlying reality in which our ideas of isolated objects, space and time, and cause and effect, are largely meaningless?

It might perhaps be more easily recognised among indigenous peoples, but a sense of participation is actually an innate, spontaneous human tendency which we all possess. It is the state which naturally exists before, as children of Western civilisations, we are taught to see ourselves as separate, or as other, and so become blind to this underlying unity in the world and begin to feel that we don't really belong to it. Alienation is the almost-inevitable consequence.

Can we, as 'modern' Western adults, ever hope to achieve such a sense of underlying unity in our daily lives? Interestingly, Lévy-Bruhl suggested that there were intermediate stages between the 'primitive' (mystical) and 'civilised' (logical) ways of looking at the world. In these intermediate stages, you might not be able to perceive a sense of participation directly, but certain aspects of it make sense to you. The mystical mentality, he said, is never completely supplanted by the undisputed reign of logic. In every human mind, there is always some rational thought and some mystical thought – and regardless of what we've been taught to believe, that's really not such a bad thing at all.

But what would it be like to see the world in a more participatory way, almost at will? What might it actually look like? And how might you learn to do it?

Speaking to stones

Woman B displays some of the characteristics we might associate with a sense of *participation mystique*. Her encounter with the stone in the wood, for example, suggests that she certainly sees it as a stone – she notes its colours, and the moss and ivy growing over it – but she also sees it as something more. It represents something else to her; it represents the power of story, and perhaps specifically the power of story which is hidden in the land (we'll come to this in chapter 8). This example is based on an experience of my own, because I am a lover of rocks and stones; something in me is drawn to them. Perhaps it's because I've spent some of the richest and most transformative years of my life in the boulder-strewn, rocky landscapes of the Outer Hebrides and the west of Ireland. I'm fascinated by the life stories of rock. The rock of Connemara, where I live now, began to form around 850 million years ago; it has lived through so many of the ages of the world. Volcanic rock, formed from the slow crystallisation of magma below the earth's surface; metamorphic rock, constantly transforming itself when subjected to high heat or pressure. How could you not believe that rock is alive? In the ancient Chinese tradition, stones are believed to have spirit or life-force (chi) and stories of their own. Sioux philosopher Vine Deloria said that, for his people, 'stones were the most perfect beings because they were self-contained entities that had resolved their social relationships and possessed great knowledge about how every other entity should live.'[19] In the perspectives of indigenous peoples around the world, then, of course rock is alive; of course it's developed the most remarkable wisdom over the long ages of its existence.

In 2010, when I moved back to Ireland after several years in a remote croft on the Isle of Lewis in the Outer Hebrides, I felt as if I'd been cast adrift. There was no question in my mind that I wanted to return to Ireland, a country which I'd grown up thinking of as home, and where I'd lived in the 1990s – but I had been so deeply attached to the bleak, rocky landscape that I had inhabited on Lewis that I didn't know how I'd ever come to feel that kind of belonging again. But as a result of that profound attachment to the land, I had learned something about the art of belonging (for it is an art, which can be learned) and I knew that the process of learning to belong to any new place is in part a process of internal mapping. Not just physical mapping – I know where this track leads; I know what is over that hill – but emotional mapping, as the landscape begins to reveal its mysteries to you, to hint at its stories, and you begin to form a bond with it. Like any new relationship, it is about building attachments to particular locations and features which, over time, become familiar and loved. You can learn to belong anywhere, in this way, if you choose. It's an act of creation, and like all acts of creation, it's also an act of love, and an enormous leap of faith.

And so I found somewhere to attach myself to, in those early days. I thought of it as an anchor – literally, something which anchored me to that place, the first specific location which I began to love beyond our own small patch of land and the fast-flowing river which ran alongside it. Somewhere to head for on my early morning and afternoon walks with the dogs, a place I looked forward to arriving at, and to sit in for a while as the dogs collapsed panting in the heather. It was the best kind of anchor of all, because it was a rock: a huge rock, twice as tall as me, and wide.

It sat on a high point in the bog, and from there I could look out at the Seven Sisters mountains, and down onto our cottage in the fertile green valley below.

It was host to woody vines which crept over its surface, and to heather which grew in its cracks. It was covered in lichens, of all textures and colours. It sheltered a beautiful little rowan seedling which, characteristic of its kind, had placed itself in an unlikely but protected hollow, sheltered from south, west and northerly winds. This rock had everything: a flat sloping side with a dry, soft, strawy place to sit, so that you could lean back against it and face south to the magical, conical Mount Errigal.

I loved that rock. It was more than a rock; it was an ecosystem. I sat there every day in all weathers, watching the creepers and lichens and the wildflowers around it grow and change as the weeks passed by, worrying about whether the rowan seedling would survive the seasonal incursion of sheep onto the moor; listening to the crows who sat on top of the rock sometimes, and who shouted their insults into the dawn sky. And then one morning, approaching the rock from a different direction, I noticed something which transformed my relationship with it. I saw that it had a face. A face which looked as if it belonged to a head which was thrown to one side, eyes closed, and mouth open in a big oval 'O', as if it was telling a story.

There is a word for people like me: apparently we are 'pareidoliacs', possessed of a tendency to see patterns and faces 'where none exist'. But whether or not the face I saw 'existed' was beside the point. The point was that my rock now had a name: the Story Stone. I am a storyteller, and that pleased me immensely. And so, from time to time when the weather was fine and the dogs happy to sit panting at my feet for a while, I would sit and tell a story to the Story Stone.

Did the rock hear me? Whether you believe it did or not, what mattered was that now I felt myself to be in relationship with it. I was communicating with it, in the primary way that humans like to communicate with each other. I was speaking to it. I felt as if I was having a conversation. And for the first time, I felt that I was actually participating in that landscape. I wasn't just walking through it, a stranger; I was a part of it, someone who might now be recognised by it. I was beginning to belong.

A few months later, I offered up an exercise, right at the beginning of a creative retreat for women that I was leading in the far south-west of Ireland. Go out alone, I said to the women, and find a place. Any place. Sit in it for a while, and talk to it. Talk to the place or an object in it. Tell it a story, tell it something that happened to you, read it a poem – anything. Do that, and then come back tonight and tell me what happened.

The first woman I asked to speak in our fireside circle that night had never done anything like this before; she hadn't been entirely sure, she said wryly, that it was entirely sane. She lived in Amsterdam, and had certainly never thought of having a conversation with her native city, or any non-human inhabitant of it. But she had done as she was asked: she had gone out and sat by the sea. On the sand, at the water's edge, she had spoken to the sea of a childhood memory: a story, I think I remember, about the loss of a dog. 'What did that feel like?' I asked her, and she shook her head. 'It felt strange at first,' she said, 'and a little bit silly. But then it was easy. And I spoke much more than I had intended to. And at the end – well, it wasn't so much that I felt that the sea was listening to me. But for the first time, I felt that we were not different, after all. I felt that we were not apart.'

The Sit Spot

My experience of sitting with my rock up on the high bog is similar to an exercise which is often practised in nature-based retreats and courses. It's called the 'Sit Spot'.

A Sit Spot is a place that you should visit regularly (as close to every day as you can manage) and sit in for a while, tuning in to what is happening in the world around you. Ideally, it should be close to where you live; it should be a place where you can observe nature; and it should be a place where you feel safe and can remain alone and undisturbed for a while. It could be your garden, a city park, a wood, a field, a beach – it doesn't matter. What matters is that you cultivate the practice of visiting it regularly, and sitting in the same spot.

The aim is simply to notice. To settle down, focus your thoughts on the present moment and notice the flow of life around you. It's about using all your senses, too: not just sight, but smell, hearing, touch. Taste, even, if you safely can. Go there in all kinds of weather – yes, sit there in rain, hail and gales! The world is different in such weather, which has its own magic. Notice the animals – birds, insects. Watch how the plant life changes through the seasons. Stare up into the sky. Tune in to the rhythms and cycles of the season – see how the light changes throughout the year.

And sometimes, if you are happy that you will not be overheard (or if you are comfortable to be overheard) let your Sit Spot hear you speak. Talk to it. To a tree, a flower, a river, the wider place. Tell it anything. Sing to it. Recite a poem. In this way, you become more than just an observer of this place: you become a participant in it.

The world is alive

My first encounter with the ideas of Australian philosopher Val Plumwood came when I read an article she wrote after almost being eaten by a crocodile in Australia's Kakadu National Park. Perhaps not surprisingly, her near-death experience led her to reflect deeply on the relationship humans have with animals and the rest of the natural world. In her article 'Being Prey',[20] she described the crocodile's attack and its aftermath; it was, she wrote, a 'humbling and cautionary tale about our relationship with the earth, about the need to acknowledge our own animality and ecological vulnerability'. Plumwood argued that the idea of humans as prey threatens the old vision of human mastery, in which we humans manipulate nature from outside, only ever as predators. She described her own paradigm shift in the following way: '. . . I glimpsed a shockingly indifferent world in which I had no more significance than any other edible being. The thought, *This can't be happening to me, I'm a human being. I am more than just food!* was one component of my terminal incredulity. It was a shocking reduction, from a complex human being to a mere piece of meat.'

I then discovered that much of Plumwood's work (unlike, frankly, that of many contemporary philosophers I'd attempted to read following my husband's persistent but ultimately unconvincing attempts to persuade me that philosophy held the keys which would unlock all the secrets of the universe) was not only rather more accessible than most, but also addressed many of the issues I was grappling with in my own life at the time. Val Plumwood spent her academic life arguing against the hyperseparation of humans from the rest of nature, and what she called 'the standpoint of mastery': the old Western philosophical perspectives we've been thinking about here, in which not only the natural world and its non-human inhabitants, but women and indigenous people too, are seen as inferior to anything associated with reason and the intellect. But the thing that interested me most about Plumwood's work was her adoption of a 'panpsychist' approach to the universe.

What would it be like, to believe that the entire world around us is alive and capable of interacting with us? Trees, rocks, winds, clouds – maybe even bricks and roads – everything pursuing its own purpose in the world, just as we are? There's a term which is often used to describe such a perspective: 'animism'. In his wide-ranging study of animistic worldviews throughout history and across the world, Australian scholar Graham Harvey[21] defines animists as people who 'recognise that the world is full of persons, only some of whom are human, and that life is always lived in relationship with others'. Panpsychism, a term preferred by Plumwood and many of her fellow philosophers, is related to animism. 'Pan' means 'everything', and 'psyche' means soul, or mind. Panpsychism, then, holds that there is some kind of mental dimension to everything; that all objects in the universe possess an interior, subjective reality, even those objects which we usually think of as inanimate, like rocks and rivers.

A panpsychist perspective is threaded through the writings of Western philosophers and scholars like Thales, Plato, Spinoza,

Leibniz and William James – though after the Enlightenment it very much went against the materialist/empiricist framework which prevailed in the intellectual circles of the day. But in the late twentieth century, panpsychist ideas began to undergo something of a mainstream revival. Unlikely as it might appear, that revival seems to have originated in good part in the academic field of environmental ethics. If you were to see the human and natural realms as 'unified and kin', writers in this field suggested – if you should believe that all features of the environment possess consciousness, reason and volition, just like human beings – then this must inevitably have consequences not only for the ways you make value judgments about the natural world, but for the way you treat it.

As evidence began to mount up about climate change, the mass extinction of species and other ecological disasters caused by human activity, environmental philosophers took up these ideas and made them the intellectual foundation stones for environmental activism. Val Plumwood was among the most influential of them, and she wrote extensively about 'intentional panpsychism': a belief that everything in the world possesses some qualities that we usually think of as reflecting 'mind', including qualities that look like choice, goal-directedness and purpose. She wrote:

> *Mountains, for example, present themselves as the products of a lengthy unfolding natural process, having a certain sort of history and direction . . . Trees appear as self-directing beings with an overall 'good' or interest and a capacity for individual choice in response to their conditions of life. Forest ecosystems can be seen as wholes whose inter-relationship of parts can only be understood in terms of stabilising and organising principles . . .*[22]

Throughout the rest of her life, Plumwood argued that we should all return to a panpsychist worldview which respects the needs, goals and purposes of other objects, creatures and ecosystems within the natural world. This was the only way, she believed, that we could bring ourselves back into balance with the needs of the planet which gives us life; the only way forward that might hold out any hope of stopping – maybe even reversing – the damage that humans were inflicting on the Earth.

Val Plumwood died in 2008, but her friend and colleague Freya Mathews, a philosopher based at La Trobe University in Australia, has written a number of books about panpsychism and the consequences of adopting such a worldview for the way we live our lives.[23] For Freya, the cosmos itself is the place where mind originates. All material objects and entities participate in that primal cosmic mind, she suggests, though only some of them – living things – also have minds of their own.

Freya grew up, she told me, in the rural outskirts of Melbourne in the long period of peace and prosperity that followed the Second World War. 'I look back in wonder on that time, because there was no sense of environmental threat whatsoever: nature seemed permanent, the touchstone of all meaning.' She described her childhood as 'very blessed', and especially credits her forays into the country on her ponies with showing her that other beings – not just humans – could be potentially communicative and companionable. 'They opened me to their own alternative ways of seeing things, and they carried me into dimensions of landscape that I couldn't have discovered in any other way. So my early experience was unquestionably one of total belonging to the world – it was a seamless blend of everyday materiality and equally taken-for-granted enchantment. There was always a shimmer, a kind of transparency to the landscape, that gave the sense that there was something on the other side.'

This sense of inner affinity with the natural world that she experienced growing up was the starting point for Freya's journey towards panpsychism. 'I never felt wholly inside the bubble of modern civilisation,' she said. 'I had one foot in it, of course, but one foot outside of it as well. In my teenage years this enchantment with the intricate living but also "dreaming" fabric of the world was expressed in drawings and poetry, and I stumbled into philosophy accidentally, with no intention of making it my career. But discovering metaphysics, through the philosophy of Spinoza and Leibniz, made philosophy an interesting field of exploration for me.

'But even before then, I was strongly drawn to indigenous cultures. This happened very early, really before I knew anything about them. So at eighteen I found myself, incongruously, in "swinging London", enrolled in a philosophy degree, but voraciously reading old anthropology books instead. It was in those old books, particularly Lévy-Bruhl and a swathe of out-of-date ethnographies of Australian Aborigines, that I found hints of what I was looking for: the notion of *participation mystique*, for instance, and views of the world as suffused with a Dreaming dimension.'

Speaking of Dreaming, it seems to me that the influence of indigenous Aboriginal thought runs very deeply through Australian culture; Freya agreed. 'The word "country", for example, as it's used in Aboriginal English, has now entered Australian English. "Country" is used for land that has a spiritual as well as a geographical dimension. Country is land which belongs to a people and to which a people belongs. Country sees, hears, smells, feels, speaks – it is sentient and responsive to its people. To accept this is to accept that such a thing as land-psyche or land-soul exists, in addition to the psyche or soul of humans and animals. Country is a communicative player in human affairs, rather than a mere backdrop to the human drama.' And that last, of course, is precisely how many of us in the West view the landscapes we inhabit: as inert, two-dimensional stages across which we, the players, stroll.

Underlying Freya's work is a belief that it is important to rise above the materialism which prevails in modern culture, and to see our world in more-than-materialist terms if we are truly to care about it and feel implicated in it. Because panpsychism isn't just an interesting theory; it's a way of life, and something that can help put us back on the right track. 'If you think of ecosystems as purely physical systems, devoid of inner qualities such as self-mattering and self-meaning, then how can you really expect people, whose values and deepest motivations are shaped by those qualities, to become emotionally engaged with the land, and with ecosystems, which are said to be "blind" to them?

'If humans are ever to truly reinhabit the world, to truly want what we need to want if the world is to flourish, then first we'll need to start thinking of life-systems as meaning systems – imbued with psychoactivity as well as physicality, and as subjects and not just objects. So environmentalism needs to be underpinned by panpsychism, I think. But I also think that such an attitude to reality – an intimate and even erotic relationship with reality – is key to our own humanity, to the meaning of our own existence.

I am standing in the midst
of an aliveness, and that
aliveness deserves my
attention, my respect, my
care . . . The insects and
birds and animals are singing
themselves into being; this
autumn land is dreaming and
I am a part of that dreaming.

When you step into indigenous communities in which an intimate and erotic relationship with reality has survived, you can hardly fail to notice the contrast: you find a much greater depth of warm humanity there.'

I asked Freya to explain what it might feel like, to inhabit a panpsychist universe rather than a materialist one – how does it change the way you actually perceive the world? 'Okay; to appreciate the contrast,' she suggested, 'let's perform a little thought experiment. Let's imagine stepping out into the garden late one evening. It's a clear night. The moon is not quite full. There are gum trees. We can hear the electric click of a few bats flitting about overhead. There is a strong perfume in the air – some night flower is shedding its scent. There are lots of stars. We look around us quietly, taking it all in.

'What kind of world is it we imagine we are seeing? For most of us who belong to modern Western societies it will be the familiar universe of space and time and celestial bodies such as stars, moons and planets. We may feel that there are presences around us in the garden – the bats, for instance; perhaps even the trees and shrubs. But when we lift our eyes, we are gazing into a vast loneliness, an emptiness of indefinite space, a predominantly unpopulated expanse of galaxies. The way we imagine it may be more or less sophisticated – we may imagine it in simple Newtonian terms as a vast arrangement of particles in a void, or we may imagine it in sophisticated Einsteinian terms as an elastic field of dynamic deformations. But either way, we generally see it as empty, devoid of any informing presence. Some may think of it as the work of a Creator God who stands outside of it, and who perhaps keeps it in existence. They might even think of that God as somehow "available" to his Creation. But still, the Creation itself remains empty, possessing no animating principle of its own.

'Now, let's repeat the experiment after adopting a panpsychist perspective. We step out into the night garden again. The moon has climbed higher in the sky. Bats continue to flit about and the stillness is even deeper than before. We look up at the stars. What do we see this time? We are no longer gazing out into a vast chasm of emptiness and loneliness. The stars no longer shine down with cold indifference. All this now has something of the aspect of the inside of someone's mind. It has qualities of awareness, and it all feels nearer somehow – as if, at a certain level, distances have collapsed. The stars and bats and other figures in the field have a new poetic status, as potential elements of meaning in a communicative exchange between ourselves and this larger subject. This universe is alive and breathing. It is a spirit-thing. We are not alone. We have stepped into a different night.'

This is close to the way that our Woman B approaches her foray into the woods: she sees every creature, plant or object not just as something to observe, but as something with which she can be in relationship, and which has a presence, a being, of its own. Her walk in the woods is an example of precisely this kind of 'communicative exchange'. But what happens when she leaves the woods? What does her life look like, and how does she approach it? 'How do you think it changes you, if you begin to see the world in this way, then?' I asked Freya. 'And, perhaps more interestingly, how does it affect the choices you make about how to live?'

'I believe that the shift from a materialist world to a panpsychist one is so profound that it transforms our most basic way of being in the world,' she said. 'And I suspect that the average modern Westerner drawn to a sense of the spirit of land or place doesn't necessarily anticipate the depth of transformation that such a spirituality will require. It's not a matter of just closing the office door, hopping into the four-wheel drive and running off to some charged or ancient site and then going home again to carry on exactly as you were before. To truly engage with the "spirit" of land or place must surely be to have your inner perspective rearranged to such a degree that it simply isn't possible just to scuttle back to town and resume your place among the cogs and wheels of a civilisation that rests on an incompatible metaphysical premise – that the land is inanimate. It's no coincidence, after all, that traditional indigenous people who exhibit a reverential attitude to land also behave, personally and socially, in every department of life, in ways profoundly different to the ways of most modern societies.

'To begin with, I think that the most appropriate response to a world which you recognise as having a subjectivity of its own is to seek to *encounter* it. To approach it as if it were possible to have a relationship with it, and so to expect a response from it. Every action we take, every posture we assume, now becomes an interaction with a responsive world. And when the world is regarded as a "spirit-thing", with ends and meanings of its own, then we also need to be able to let it be – to stop feeling that we should take charge of it, and to allow it instead to unfold in its own way. Because we are part of it, our own self-realisation depends on its self-realisation. In letting the world realise itself then, we also further our own richest self-realisation: we come into being, most fully and richly, in a world which is itself most fully and richly coming into being.'

I asked Freya to clarify what she means by 'letting the world be', because it seems to me that, for humans used to intensely managing their surroundings, this might be the trickiest thing of all. 'Letting things be means just that,' she insisted. 'Not interfering unduly with the unfolding of the things around us, allowing natural cycles to take their course, letting rivers run, mountains mount and beings be. At the ideal limit, letting-be might involve gathering our food from the wild, and making our shelters and garments from materials at hand, so that these activities of ours feed back into and nourish the natural cycles that produce our livelihood, as the subsistence activities of all other species do.'

This makes sense to me, but we live now in modern societies, and often in cities, and for most of us that kind of hunting-and-gathering practice (beyond foraging for a few nettle tips for soup, for example, or some blackberries from the hedges or mushrooms from the woods) is no longer remotely practical. So what does it really mean to 'let be' today?

'It's true that in modern societies we can't just pluck food from the forests, and can't always grow it in ways that contribute to the self-realisation of the land,' Freya agreed. 'We're going to have to be more proactive if we're to meet our needs. But that needn't take the form of recutting the cloth of our world to suit ourselves. It needn't mean manipulating and controlling that world, imposing our own designs on it. Rather, we can learn to identify the patterns of energic flow already at play and try to hitch a ride with them.

'So – to take a light-hearted example – when people look for adventure they'll often do so by choosing some exotic tour package, like horse-riding along the old Silk Road of China or picking wild apples with Kazakhstan nomads or having themselves lowered in a cage into the ocean to meet white sharks nose-to-nose. But we might equally well scrutinise our own immediate neighbourhood for the unknown, the offbeat, for the numinous and unpredictable elements that the neighbourhood might contain. We might take a pilgrimage to the source of our local creek or river, for instance, or explore the half-forgotten labyrinth of the city's underground storm water system; or we might simply shoulder our pack and set off down the road, without a premeditated plan. It's about adjusting our goals to what's in front of us, and this requires flexibility, detachment from fixed ideas, and an eye for opportunities if and as they present. It might not get you to where you thought you wanted to be, but it will get you to a place that will be appropriate when you get there.'

When I think about panpsychism, and about the idea of the world having mind, or soul, my thoughts naturally turn to wild places – to forests, mountains, rivers . . . but so many of us today live in urban environments that have been built by humans. 'And so what about those places?' I asked Freya. 'What happens to panpsychism in the city?'

'A spirituality which focuses its devotion on the world doesn't make sharp divides between the living and the non-living, "nature" and non-nature,' she answered. 'Reality carries rocks, apartment blocks and factories as well as forests and arid shrublands into the patterns of its unfolding. We act in harmony with such a world not by insisting on ecology after the event – erasing suburbs to restore lost woodlands, or felling mature exotics to plant indigenous seedlings – but rather by taking the pulse of the world-as-it-is, then finding within that pulse the trajectory of the world's unfolding. To tear down and rearrange things according to our own designs – even our ecological designs – is just to perpetuate the cycle of domination-and-control.

'And ultimately,' she told me, 'although we can't en masse replicate today the hunter-gatherer practices that were associated with panpsychist consciousness in our ancestors, we can all participate in activities such as engaging attentively with specific communities of life through hands-on restoration or conservation practices. And in doing so, we may find ourselves rediscovering panpsychist consciousness as a consequence. Because when the landscape "opens" to us in this way, we can experience not only organisms and eco-systems, but reality itself, as alive.'

It's not just philosophers who are increasingly buying into the notion of panpsychism again; it's alive and well in the world of physics too. Gregory Matloff, a long-time physicist at New York City College of Technology, recently published a paper arguing that a 'proto-consciousness field' might extend through all of space. Stars, he suggests, may be 'minded' entities which purposefully control their paths through space, and indeed, the entire universe may be self-aware.[24]

Matloff isn't the first physicist to propose such ideas: the possible relevance of quantum physics to panpsychism began to be considered in the early twentieth century, when thinkers such as philosopher Alfred North Whitehead started to draw on the concepts of indeterminacy and uncertainty, which are fundamental to quantum physics, to defend panpsychist ideas. American physicist John Wheeler, perhaps best known for having coined the term 'black hole', has speculated that perhaps the universe as a whole exists in a state of uncertainty, and only achieves actual *being* when it's observed by a conscious entity. 'We are participators in bringing into being not only the near and here, but the far away and long ago,' Wheeler said in 2006, describing what he referred to as the 'participatory anthropic principle'.[25] If he is correct, then the universe is conscious; but it is only through the active participation of other conscious minds – such as our own – that it comes into existence at all.

All of this, of course, is highly speculative as well as being very theoretical; does it actually make the slightest bit of difference to the way we live today?

For me it changes everything, and profoundly. If the world is alive, if nature has consciousness, then I am not just some singu-lar, solitary being plonked on a lump of inert matter surrounded by inert space in an inert universe. Everything around me is alive – there is no such thing as 'inert'. I am standing in the midst of an aliveness, and that aliveness deserves my attention, my respect, my care. It deserves my awe and my reverence. The stars are no longer cold, unknowable objects, scattered shining but ultimately life-less across the vast empty distances of black space: they are active participants in their own journeys of becoming. The insects and birds and animals are singing themselves into being; this autumn land is dreaming and I am a part of that dreaming. That beautiful emerald-bodied dragonfly over there by the beehive is no longer a soulless creature, capable only of mechanically carrying out the simplest of genetically preprogrammed tasks. It has its own purpose and path. It is a participant in the unfolding of the world, just as I am; a unique expression of the prodigious, indiscriminately varied life of the cosmos, no more and no less than I am. I see a dragonfly; what does it 'see' when it sees me? There are patterns and webs and weavings – lines of becoming all around me that I cannot ever begin to imagine I understand. The world is *alive*, and in the infinite extravagance of its multi-faceted aliveness it is full of mystery again.

What could be more enchanted than that?

4. The wonderment

If I had influence with the good fairy who is supposed to preside over the christening of all children I should ask that her gift to each child in the world be a sense of wonder so indestructible that it would last throughout life, as an unfailing antidote against the boredom and disenchantments of later years, the sterile preoccupations with things that are artificial, the alienation from the sources of our strength.

Rachel Carson, from *The Sense of Wonder*[26]

AS A SMALL child, I inhabited a world filled with possibility. There were so many things to wonder at that I hardly knew where to begin. Like most children, my curiosity about the world was intense, and I asked questions all the time. Life was a beautiful mystery, and that mystery was there, wherever you looked. It lived inside our heads, and was all bound up with the things we could imagine. It hid between the pages of books, and revealed itself in the soft dusty pigment of a butterfly's wing.

I couldn't understand how it was that adults didn't seem to see it. Why did they always look so tired when you pointed out to them marvel after marvel, right there in the world around them? Why didn't they share your curiosity? How could they so easily dismiss it all, and turn back to the strange, mundane things that filled up their days but never seemed to make them happy? 'Too busy,' they said. And, 'Yes, dear, I know' – but I could see that they didn't know anything at all. Did they never know it, or had they just forgotten? Is that what growing older was all about – learning less, rather than more? In that case, I was with Peter Pan. I'd remain a child forever, thank you very much, if this was the only alternative.

My childhood world was filled with wonder not because I grew up in an easy place: on the contrary, I spent my days, while my single mother was out at work, with an elderly and notoriously crotchety great-aunt on the fringes of a council estate in a north-eastern English steel town. But, grim and grimy as it might have seemed on the surface, I always felt that I was surrounded by mystery, and my mind brimmed over with vivid imaginings. The pitchfork-shaped, steam-spewing industrial structures across the River Tees were devils; moths were night-angels, fallen to earth. Living stories marched across the industrial landscape to the south and sailed in on the tides to the east. Nothing in this world was fixed. Everything was fluid, transforming; everything was in a constant process of becoming. What would I become, in such a world? Anything was possible; anything I could imagine could be real.

Until, gradually, it wasn't. Until I learned that there were rules, and that good girls should always obey them. Until I learned that imagination was nothing more than just 'making things up', and that certain things were allowed to be real while other things weren't. Until I was thrown into an education system in which I excelled, but which nevertheless seemed designed to imprison my awakening mind, rather than freeing it. Freedom could be dangerous, it seemed, and so I learned to knuckle down and follow those rules which had been so thoughtfully fashioned for me by rich white men. I took the degree that might lead to a 'proper career'; I married the wrong man; took out a crippling mortgage so I could live in a tiny house in a city I didn't want to be in; applied for a 'better' (corporate) job so I could pay that mortgage, and as a consequence worked such long hours that I was hardly ever in the house I didn't actually want but was now selling my soul for. I spent three hours each day commuting among frazzled and frantic London crowds, served the soulless corporations, bought the right suits to keep my bosses happy, regularly mowed my suburban lawn to keep the neighbours happy, and smiled brightly through it all to keep my mother happy. I didn't do all that for very long, but I did it for long enough to break.

Finally, when I was older still, I picked up the pieces of my fragmented self and learned how to flout all those rules – and the world of mystery peeked out of the dark closet where I'd locked it away for safekeeping and revealed itself to me again.* On a Welsh hilltop at night watching the stars; in the soul-searing light on a stormy west-of-Ireland beach; listening to a fox yapping in an autumn wood. I relearned wonder and awe. I remembered that the world of the imagination is just as real as any other, that it is part of the fabric of reality. I reclaimed what indigenous peoples around the world know, what (as the old literature clearly shows) my Celtic ancestors once knew, and what I – a working-class girl brought up in the industrial edgelands of a deprived and dingy

---

* This journey is described in my book *If Women Rose Rooted* (September Publishing: 2016).

town – had known perfectly well when I was a child. The understanding that everything, *everything* is alive. Everything is vivid. Everything has its own path, and the intersection of our paths is life's greatest blessing.

And in that process of re-enchantment, I came clearly to understand one thing: that this way of being in the world is a natural part of the human psyche, regardless of our culture. We know it when we are children – but then we are required to unlearn. We are forced into our cultural corsets and social straitjackets, and all that we once knew is squeezed out of us, along with much of what gives our lives meaning. Because this is what, as we contort ourselves into new and unnatural shapes to better conform to what 'civilisation' requires of us, we strip away from the natural world: not just magic, but *meaning*.

What was missing in my life for so many years, and what is missing still from the lives of so many of us, is an ongoing sense of meaningful participation in a world which we believe matters. Which we maybe even hold to be sacred. Most of us experience moments that are rich with meaning in our lives; but how many of us feel that the very fabric of our lives is woven from such moments? How many of us occupy a ground of being in which reverence and respect for an animate world around us overwhelms the cultural programming which tells us that our individual human lives are the only things that matter? Where wonder, not knowledge, is the foundation of possibility, and mystery is something to sit with, not to solve?

Wonder, curiosity, mystery, imagination – all are key constituents of enchantment. Cultivating them is essential to living an enchanted life.

Wonder is different from awe, which is usually defined as the sense of having an encounter with some presence larger than ourselves, something more powerful, and a little bit frightening. In a state of awe, we feel humbled. In a state of wonder, we feel *possible*.

Many different kinds of experience can induce wonder. Some people find it in art, or music; some people find it in mathematics and science; some find it in the practice of their religion or spirituality. I find it almost exclusively in the natural world, in situations which offer me a new sense of our deep connectedness. In the last chapter I wrote about my Story Stone in the high bog, which looked out onto the Seven Sisters mountains of Donegal. Each of those seven mountains, of course, has a name in Irish, and in my early days there, two of the names interested me more than the others. An Eachla Bheag, translated locally as 'The Little Horse', and An Eachla Mhór, 'The Big Horse': two mountains next to each other which seemed to tower over our little stone cottage by the river. I walked through the labyrinth of boreens* in the bog for many months, finding myself strangely drawn to their feet, gazing up at them, examining them, wondering what it was about those two particular mountains that had caused them to be named for horses – for no naming is casually performed in this old country. Names hold power, and memory; names tell the stories of people and their relationships with the land.

I drove past the two horses from time to time; I viewed them from all directions; I sat and stared at them in all weathers. And then, one day, when the morning sun was especially bright behind An Eachla Mhór, when detail vanished and contrast increased so that only its contours could be clearly perceived, I saw it. Shadow resolved into shape, and there it was, so very clear that I couldn't imagine how I had missed it all these months: the outline of a large horse, lying down in the bog, head turned and long nose curved around to rest against its back. Next to it, a smaller version, nestled against the Big Horse's rump, lying down in the same fashion but facing in the opposite direction.

It was as if I had been taken up by a great ocean swell, sweeping me off the ground. I came to a complete halt, and exclaimed; I stopped breathing for a moment and then I exhaled, laughed, madly, exhilarated, my heart racing with excitement. It was as if this place had finally chosen to reveal itself to me, as if I'd passed some kind of test, stayed the course, never stopped asking the question – and at last I'd been granted the answer. What I felt in that moment was profoundly emotional, as pure a sense of wonder as I've ever known. The mountain was alive. The mountain was a great, potent animal. It was a *horse*, and I could walk on its back. I was stirred, engaged, joyful; the world had communicated itself to me, and I radically belonged to it. It was a homecoming, a sense of

* From the Irish word *bóithrín*, little road.

In a state of awe
we feel humbled.
In a state of wonder
we feel possible.

returning to something that so many of us have lost. The boundaries between myself and the mountain were blurred; I was somehow continuous with it. I was like it, and it was like me. Somehow, we were the same.

Such experiences break us open, and invite us to open ourselves up to the possibility that there might be an order of reality which lies beyond that which we can experience through our physical senses. Is it a 'mystical' experience? Maybe. Maybe this is another example of the kind of mysticism that Lévy-Bruhl was talking about when he spoke of *participation mystique*. To me, An Eachla Mhór and An Eachla Bheag were, above all, mountains – there was no question in my mind about that. I knew their geology, their structure, the way they drew certain kinds of weather to themselves . . . But they were also something more. They represented some force, some power of the land which transcended all logic, which couldn't be perceived with the rational mind, and which even now I have difficulty explaining with words. Whether you choose to consider such an experience mystical or not, it is nevertheless a kind of revelation: the sweeping aside of a veil, an expansion of the potential that we see in the world. Wonder allows us to break through the constraints, to reach beyond the restrictive cognitive frameworks we've been tethered to, so that we can entertain the possible rather than simply observing the actual. When we are filled with wonder it is as if we've encountered the world, in all its beauty and mystery, for the very first time. If we are to re-enchant the world, re-animate our thought processes, then wonder is a habit we need to cultivate.

William James, brother of American novelist Henry James, a philosopher and the founding father of modern psychology, wrote extensively about wonder; he believed that it was a key to human potential. He suggested that our sense of wonder is founded on a greater perception of reality: one which usually escapes us amidst the busyness of our everyday lives. (James also had a particular fascination with mystical experiences, which led him to experiment with substances such as chloral hydrate, amyl nitrite, nitrous oxide and peyote in an effort to break out of ordinary reality. I have enormous sympathy with the fact that he apparently claimed that it was only when he was under the influence of nitrous oxide that he was able to understand the rather challenging nineteenth-century German philosopher Georg Wilhelm Friedrich Hegel.)

Later, Abraham Maslow suggested that the experience of wonder was a key feature of peak experiences.[27] He urged educators and others to promote experiences of wonderment in order to produce more creative individuals in the arts and sciences,[28] arguing that wonder enhances creativity because it is all tied up with our ability to imagine new possibilities.

  List the things which have made you gasp with wonder or awe. How can you introduce more experiences like that into your life?

The Wonderment

If wonder, then, is a perfectly natural state for children, is there anything that we disenchanted adults might be able to learn from them? Thirty-five-year-old Amy Spittler Shaffer thinks so; she is the creative director and co-creator of a project called The Wonderment,[29] which is based in her home town of Salt Lake City. Its official mission statement is 'to connect kids to develop a new sense of humanity together'.

'The starting point of our work with kids,' she told me, 'is the recognition that they don't think like adults do.' Amy believes that children have a natural free-flowing creativity which helps them conceive of novel solutions to problems – solutions that adults somehow don't seem able to imagine. The Wonderment, then, is all about capturing that creativity before it's lost.

And it is being lost. Ongoing American research conducted since the 1990s has shown that children's creativity scores have consistently decreased over the past couple of decades.[30] In the words of one researcher, the data indicates that 'children have become less emotionally expressive, less energetic, less talkative and verbally expressive, less humorous, less imaginative, less unconventional, less lively and passionate, less perceptive, less apt to connect seemingly irrelevant things, less synthesizing, and less likely to see things from a different angle.' This, added to the well-known fact that children also begin to lose their sense of wonder at the world as they grow older, doesn't offer much hope for the psychological wellbeing of future generations. Many different complex, interwoven factors contribute to this loss. An over-reliance on passive technology for entertainment rather than active play; an enormous and ongoing reduction in hours spent outside or exposed to the natural world; and an education system which teaches us how to categorise, label, control and define, but which – in spite of the best efforts of many inspired and dedicated teachers – has no time for nourishing youthful imaginations which are still longing to take flight. So it vanishes, and far too early, that fervid curiosity, that utter rapturous delight in the unfolding mysteries of the world. And by the time we turn into adults, we're primarily looking for safety and predictability. We tether ourselves tightly to the mundane, the routine, the humdrum, and tell ourselves that's a life.

'I think that loss of wonder and imagination has a lot to do with the way the relationship between our inner and outer worlds is shaped at a very young age,' Amy told me. 'At about the age of six, for the very first time, we start to think about the idea that there is a world beyond ourselves. This recognition kicks off a period of intense synthesising, as we begin building cognitive systems to try to reconcile the rich fluidity of the reality that we've spent the early years of our lives immersed in, with the concrete world around us that we are for the first time seeing as something "other".

'This first experience of "otherness" also collides with a crucial window for a neurological process called "synaptic pruning". To offer a very basic spin on it: you are born with nearly all the neurons you will ever have, and then you spend the first few years of your life developing synapses at a furious rate to connect these neurons into the useable infrastructure of your brain. By the time you reach middle childhood, you've developed approximately 130 per cent of the synapses that you'll have as an adult. So some shedding is going to happen. And synaptic pruning works in exactly the way it sounds – your brain assesses which routes are used most, and how essential a function they seem to perform, and then takes out the straggler synapses to give greater strength and emphasis to the main thoroughfares.

'The most important period of synaptic pruning in life, then, happens just when kids are grappling for the first time with the nature of their place in the world, and with how to connect their native inner reality with an exterior world that suddenly feels very foreign to them. So they're looking for a blueprint of how the world is, and of course they look to adults to provide that. What kind of blueprint do you think the vast majority of kids think that we adults are building from, when they look at the world around them? It's certainly not a blueprint which values an ecological or imaginative approach to the world – which puts it at odds with the flow of their imagination-driven development to that point.'

Clearly, the way we educate our children – both at school and at home, and especially in their early years – has a major effect on those blueprints which children develop of how the world is. Writer and filmmaker Carol Black[31] notes that, at the turn of the twentieth century, educational theorists were quite open about the fact that they were designing schools for the specific purpose of adapting children to the new industrial order. Children must shed their 'savage' wildness, and develop 'civilised' habits like punctuality, obedience, orderliness and efficiency, she says. The purpose of school, said William Torrey Harris, US Commissioner of Education from 1889 to 1906, was to 'elevate' children out of their 'totally depraved' natural state and train them to take their place in man's grand project of 'subordinating the material world to his use.' She quotes Ellwood P. Cubberley, dean of the Stanford University School of Education, as saying, in 1898, 'Our schools are, in a sense, factories, in which the raw materials – children – are to be shaped and fashioned into products . . . The specifications for manufacturing come from the demands of 20th century civilization, and it is the business of the school to build its pupils according to the specifications laid down.'

These original purposes, Black suggests, were so effectively built into the structure of modern schooling – with its underlying systems of confinement, control, standardisation, measurement and enforcement – that today they are accomplished even without our conscious knowledge or assent. And so little has changed. In the UK, a recent article in the *London Review of Books* discussed the pride that some secondary schools apparently take in focusing predominantly on the acquisition of facts, and refusing to teach children higher-order skills such as learning to use their knowledge in unusual or unfamiliar situations.[32] In the most-viewed of all TED talks around the world, arts education expert Sir Ken Robinson claims that creativity is as important in education as literacy – and yet instead, schools educate children out of their innate creativity. Every education system on Earth has the same hierarchy of subjects, he suggests. At the top are mathematics and languages, then the humanities, and at the bottom are the arts. Schools, he proposes, should seriously think about teaching dance. But instead, 'as children grow up, we start to educate them progressively from the waist up. And then we focus on their heads. And slightly to one side.'[33]

One of the many beauties of children is that they have no objection at all to the improbable. All things are possible, but then we adults stifle those possibilities with probabilities – with facts and statistics – and subject children to an educational system which punishes them (and their teachers) for daring to explore different paths. Their innate creativity is nurtured by freedom to explore, but it is crippled by the continuous evaluation, adult supervision and direction, and pressure to conform which define children's lives today.

That precious but endangered imagination, Amy told me, is precisely what The Wonderment is looking not just to maintain, but to harness. And not just for the sake of the children themselves, but also for the future world we might build. 'I believe kids dance on the quantum froth, and we call it "play" because we don't have a good word for it, or an understanding infinite enough to reflect what is really occurring. We say things to kids, like "it's just in your imagination", because we've completely lost any sense of how real and powerful that can be. It is a dance, to be sure, one that weaves an interface between the imaginal and physical worlds. A wonderment. I think it's the state that we as humans were created to experience – it's both our place and our purpose in the cosmic ecology. The more we relinquish it for the role we believe we must play in an economy, the less we feel like we intrinsically belong. Eventually we forget the feeling of belonging – and we forget how to see and value the things that might remind us.

'The Wonderment, then, is a platform where kids can share their creativity with each other around the world, and use it to make the world a better place. One of the things we like to say around The Wonderment is that we're not creating a better world for our kids, we're creating it with them. I know that might sound like a glib tagline, but it's true – I've seen kids do incredible things in this world when they're supported by understanding adults. In fact, I think we adults may be their greatest work! It takes honest listening, radical willingness to show up like that with kids (and trust me, they know when you do), but then they can show you paths to a whole other world – quite different from the one we adults have resigned ourselves to. And they do this simply by being themselves – alongside us.'

I asked Amy to tell me about The Wonderment's projects: what exactly do they do to harness this imaginative capacity of children for building a better world? 'Well, so far, kids from over fifty countries have contributed over 12,000 ideas and creations on our online app-based Wonderment platform to help make child-initiated projects happen in Guatemala, Peru, Costa Rica, Utah and Kenya. The most powerful example I have seen of this process in action centres around one of my favourite people in the world: Adriana, a seventeen-year-old girl in Chimaltenango, Guatemala. She has more ideas in a day than she or anyone around her has any idea what to do with – and, luckily, she has a dad who throughout her life has encouraged her to follow, question and build on them.

'One of Adriana's ideas brought her together with her friends to propose a project to us: to build a mobile library out of an old school bus which could serve kids in rural areas around their city who didn't have access to books or learning resources. The project was incredible, but what really impressed me was watching Adriana in the months after the bus was delivered.

'She and a group of other students at her school started going out with the bus to meet and work with the kids and, particularly, to teach them to read. Literacy is an ongoing challenge in Guatemala and doesn't get a lot of emphasis – something that Adriana (who loves to read more than anything) could never understand.

'As she started this process, she realised that simply going out and delivering standard reading curriculum wasn't going to work with these kids; she had to find a way to capture their attention and imagination. So she and her friends started asking them questions: about their lives, about their homes, about their fears, about the things they thought were funny. They started asking them to tell

'I believe kids dance on the quantum froth, and we call it "play" because we don't have a good word for it, or an understanding infinite enough to reflect what is really occurring.'
Amy Spittler Shaffer,
The Wonderment

stories. They even gave them surveys asking them how they liked to learn, and what was working well.

'Then, every week, this group of young teacher-students would meet to discuss what they'd heard from the kids, and to build a framework for how they could structure a range of activities ranging from physical games to national history to local folk stories to art – and then tie it all back to reading.

'So these high school students began to figure out and implement in real time a responsive, integrated learning experience for a diverse group of kids with different needs and challenges – and it worked! They had kids begging to know when they would be coming back with the library bus. They are starting to see results that you could spend millions of dollars in research and "official" programs to achieve – and still you wouldn't find the right approach, because this had to be done peer-to-peer, with a totally open beginner's mind – and these kids who cared were able to step into it so beautifully just by wondering how.

'This year, Adriana and the bus will be continuing to develop their efforts and, as they do, we will be facilitating them to share their experiences throughout the Wonderment community. Their idea has also already inspired other projects around the world – their mobile library bus in Guatemala sparked an idea for a group of kids to create a mobile creative community centre for refugees in Salt Lake City. We think there are children who have ideas, solutions and stories like these all over the world; if we adults could discover, facilitate and support them, there is an incredible web and ecology of growth that reflects their power. A whole new perspective could emerge. And it all orbits around the radical, everyday acts of noticing, following your curiosity and sharing together. That's a wonderment, for certain.'

It sounded to me as if this kind of project required a radically different way of approaching children, given that as adults we're infinitely more inclined to tell them how to think rather than respect their ideas or ask them for help. Amy nodded. 'Just to show up and be willing to lay aside the assumption that you have the answers because you're the adult goes against almost every current of our society. But when you really feel the coherence that starts to emerge when you do, you start to see the possibilities, and a whole new blueprint lights up.'

How to raise a creative, innovative, connected child

Projects like The Wonderment are a marvel, but what can parents do every day, at home, if they would like to reinforce the natural curiosity, imagination and sense of wonder that their children have?

Amy had plenty of suggestions to offer. 'First,' she said, 'you have to recognise what's going on in your interactions with your kids. One of the best opportunities to witness our adult programming in action is the moment when we believe something is threatening our children, or that they're not doing well. Our first instinctual response tends to be immediate and visceral: "How do I fix this?" or "How do I protect them?" When we anxiously look around us to the adult world for answers, those answers are predictable: get them into the best/most competitive programmes, put all of their (and your) time and energy into making them successful in said programmes, and then measure the hell out of them to make sure it's working.

'But if we could make ourselves pause before launching ourselves into a sequence of predictable actions, and instead think of considering a few different possibilities, that would be a moment with huge power.

Possibility 1: That the answer for how to raise a creative, innovative, connected child doesn't exist in simply taking establishment processes, values and products and applying them with escalating determination until your child eventually smooths out his or her "edges" in order to do better. And that, even by doing that, you can never guarantee that it will make them happy, or safe, or fulfil any of the desires for them which you may originally have had.

Possibility 2: That no one else has the answer – but your kid does. And you are the key to help him or her unlock it, and use it. Supporting your child to recognise their place in the world and thrive in it is a very personal process: although the world, with all of its opportunities and challenges, is one we all share, what we each bring to it is as individual as each child is.

Possibility 3: That kids' perspectives have as much to offer you as you have to offer them. What would happen if a generation of parents, teachers and leaders genuinely listened? Perhaps we'd rediscover a world which would reflect back to us the wonder of discovery – and which would help us to remember the power of listening, whether it's to the earth, ourselves or each other.'

In her many years of working imaginatively with children, Amy has learned a few simple tricks which have, she said, helped her to stay in a state of authentic possibility and exchange with kids and teachers around the world, as well as with her own son:

1. NOTICING

This is one of the awesome (and exasperating) abilities of young kids – their entire energetic bandwidth seems to be devoted to noticing everything around them. What if you mimicked that approach when looking at them? Being seen is crucial to helping kids recognise things within themselves which they can then connect to their interactions with the outer world – and you can be their bridge.

2. CULTIVATING YOUR OWN CURIOSITY

How can we support kids to be curious if we ourselves don't remember what that feels like any more? Nurturing and trusting our own inquisitiveness gives both permission and example to our kids; it tells them that what might sometimes look scary or messy or unknown is actually part of a process that you nevertheless value enough to participate in. And it creates a sense of equality in our engagements with kids: a wise teacher once said that one of the things she found worked best in building a strong connection within her classes was to make sure that she asked them questions that she didn't already know the answer to. Kids know when you're asking because you genuinely want to know or discover something – and they trust you (and themselves) more because of it.

3. SHARING

Trusting this approach of open exchange with your kids can feel a little weird at first. It can seem too simple to be of real value, or too open-ended to offer up any tangible impact. It can also feel a little lonely, as it's not the authority-driven message or system you'll find reinforced in most schools or communities. And it's not, in and of itself, a result or answer – it's a way of being and thinking which cultivates the capacities within our kids that are unique to them, and which models ways they can use those capacities in the world. As you spend more time in this way of being yourself, you'll start to find and recognise other people and programmes that are also creating new ways of doing things. Hug these people and build with them! Sharing your experiences, work and ideas with like-minded individuals and groups is crucial – then we can build communities that will stretch across the seemingly untenable divides that politics and committees can't cross to do the right thing for our kids. THIS is what our kids really need – and seeing how to create it alongside you is the most priceless resource you could offer them in this dynamic, chaotic era of change.

Into the mystic

It is the dim haze of mystery that adds enchantment to pursuit.

Attributed to Antoine de Rivarol

The world is strange, and it is stranger still to be in it. That rich, velvety mystery which embraced me as a child has never gone away. For years, when I was a teenager and in my early twenties, I had a quote from Sean O'Casey's play *Juno and the Paycock* pinned to my wall:

An', as it blowed an' blowed, I often looked up at the sky an' assed meself the question – what is the stars, what is the stars?

What is the stars, indeed, and what is this planet? Those were the mysteries that occupied me then, and still do now. What was it like before us, because we're new in it: long geological ages of this planet unfolded before the Earth ever dreamed of us. Were the myths real, did the old gods ever walk the land? Will new gods walk it again after us, for this continued existence of this planet does not depend on our small lives?

The mystery is inside us as well as outside us. What are we, really? Like Ted Hughes's 'Wodwo', constantly wondering 'What am I? Nosing here, turning leaves over . . .' We inhabit such strange worlds of our own, and the mystery is in other people too. What do they think, what do they know? What different worlds live inside them, and how can we ever approach them? Why are we alive, and what happens when we die?

Is the world really as we see it, or are we poorly equipped with senses to understand the fullness of what is there? In *The Republic*, Plato's Socrates speaks of an underground cave in which people have been chained to chairs since birth, facing the rear wall of the cave. Behind the prisoners is a fire, and between the fire and the prisoners is a raised path with a low wall, behind which people walk carrying objects or puppets 'of men and other living things'. The wall ensures that only the shadows of the objects can be seen, not the people who are carrying them. The prisoners cannot see anything that's happening behind them; they can only see the shadows cast upon the cave wall in front of them. The sounds of the people talking behind them echo off the walls, and so the prisoners believe these sounds come from the shadows. 'To them,' Socrates said, '. . . the truth would be literally nothing but the shadows of the images.' Plato used this example to argue that there is a whole realm of 'forms' or 'ideas' beyond the perceptual world. The truth, like the sunlit world above the cave, is much larger, more intense and overwhelmingly brilliant than the world of shadows. But when you are in the shadows, the worlds beyond you are in the mystery.

To be enchanted is to experience wonder, and to experience wonder is, more often than not, to experience mystery. Mystery is unknowable to the rational mind. It has nothing but laughter to offer empiricists who insist that mysteries should be capable of being explained, and who don't much value those which can't. As philosopher Soren Kierkegaard maintained: 'Life is a mystery to be lived, not a problem to be solved.' It's the difference between an *apparent* mystery, merely waiting for a magician to reveal

There is something in us which is always seeking a new frontier, which requires an enigma that can't be easily penetrated.

his sleight-of-hand, and living in the presence of the numinous: what early-twentieth-century theologian Rudolf Otto called the *'mysterium tremendum et fascinans'* – the 'fearful and fascinating mystery' – which underlies all life. And here's another innate human quality: there is something in us which is always seeking a new frontier, which requires an enigma that can't be easily penetrated, which needs a myth that can't so easily be debunked.

To live an enchanted life, then, is to be comfortable in the company of mystery: to be willing to penetrate beyond the shadows; to take a walk in the dark. When we walk in the dark, our senses are heightened, our instincts are sharper – we feel not only more alert, but more alive. Bump up against people, knock a few things over – it's all part of the journey. Sooner or later, we'll emerge from the shadows to sit by the fire.

Mystery relieves us of the fiction that we know where we're going. It keeps us on our toes; it keeps our lives alive. The world, once again, declares itself to be a place of potentialities. More than that – if we can fully dwell in its mystery, then the world is transformed into something to be revered: something sacred, maybe even holy. Abraham Maslow had something to say about that, too – he called it resacralisation: restoring a sense of the sacred to the everyday world.[34] And this is the most interesting aspect of mystery for me: as we'll see in the next chapter, we don't have to look for it in transcendental experiences; rather, the mystery lies in fully inhabiting our own sensory responses – our embodied responses – to the physical and imaginal everyday world we inhabit.

Cultivating a sense of wonder and mystery

- Watch young children exploring a new place or participating in a new activity. How can you bring some of that childlike curiosity and wonder into your own daily routine?
- Explore your own creativity. You don't have to be a writer, singer, dancer or painter to be creative. Anyone can take

up photography, for example: focus on photographing the familiar in different ways, through different lenses and filters, from different angles.

- Learn something new. Read, or take a class – preferably in a field of study you don't already know much about, but of which you are curious or find strange.

- Go to an art gallery or museum. Choose one object, display or room and spend time with/in it. What does it make you feel, imagine, wonder?

- Stop in your tracks from time to time, and look at the familiar world around you as if you've never seen it before. How might it look from someone else's perspective? What would a visitor think of your town, your house?

- Slow down. Cultivate the art of *flânerie:* a French word which means 'idle behaviour'. This is the word from which the word 'flaneur' is derived – meaning someone who strolls, apparently without purpose, but nevertheless taking in the rich variety of the streets or landscape around him, participating fully through observation, stumbling across new and surprising places.

- Go somewhere new, whenever you can. Even if it's just walking a different way to work or to the shops. If you want to develop a sense of wonder, it's critically important to break out of the habits and routines which have come to define your everyday life.

- Start to cultivate your intuition and your instincts. Whenever you make a decision, for example, examine it from all angles: your emotions and your 'gut feel', as well as what your head tells you. If you get an uncomfortable physical feeling when you're trying to make a decision, pay attention. Pay attention to your dreams, too; are there repetitive themes that have relevance to the things you're grappling with? Slow down and stop listening to the chatter in your head; that'll make it easier to focus on

these other ways of knowing. Do they offer up different
answers to the issues you face?

❧ Above all, no matter how foreign it has become to you, and
no matter how challenging an idea it might be, learn to play
again. We find so many things to occupy our days that have
purpose, but unstructured play has no purpose other than
pleasure. Practise it with a child, a dog, a cat, your lover,
a friend. Or practise it alone: just learn to mess about, to
fiddle with things, to splash in puddles, make sandcastles
or snowmen, paddle in the shallows, like a child.

5. At home in our skin

Ah, Not To Be Cut Off

Ah, not to be cut off,
not through the slightest partition
shut out from the law of the stars
The inner – what is it?
if not intensified sky,
hurled through with birds and deep
with the winds of homecoming.

Rainer Maria Rilke[35]

MY MOST PROFOUND experience of feeling utterly at home in my body, and as a consequence utterly at home in the world, happened in water. I guess it's not so very surprising; I've always been a bit of a water baby, ever since I was taught to swim in the frigid waters of England's North Sea as a very small child. But this particular experience happened in a very much warmer southern Missouri, in the remote depths of the beautiful Ozark forest. I was there for a collection of unlikely reasons; with a weekend to while away between business trips, I had planned to drive from New Orleans to Arkansas, and was looking for something restful to do.

All of this took place fifteen or so years ago, at the end of a period of several years spent working for a major multinational corporation. I'd been living in America because, six years earlier, I'd had to flee my suffocating first marriage. In the process, I'd been forced to leave behind in Connemara not only the beautiful, tiny old stone cottage of my dreams, but my first attempt to escape what I've elsewhere referred to as the Wasteland that is modern civilisation. Now, I was back where I'd started several years earlier, driven once again to escape the disenchantment of corporate life and of contemporary Western culture. As I described in chapter 3, I'd been learning to fly to overcome my fear of flying, to try to regain some sense of control over my life. As a result, I'd made a few scary but positive decisions. The most significant of them was that I was going home again: I had just bought a seven-acre croft – a unique form of tenanted smallholding – in the far north-west of Scotland. But, control or no control, I was forty-two years old, all burned out and all worn out, and I wasn't entirely sure who I was any more. I certainly had no idea who I might be going to become.

By some strange serendipity (or synchronicity?) I had happened across, while browsing online, a small retreat centre which didn't require too great a diversion from my path; it was called Aquaest, and it seemed to be just what I was looking for. Sara Firman, along with her then-husband, had just launched this unique venture, which they described as combining elements of retreat and spa with ideals of right-livelihood and environmental consciousness – especially around water. I was to be one of their first guests. The retreat was located on twenty secluded and wooded acres, beside a healthy creek which had been classified as an 'Outstanding State Resource Water'. It aimed to use the resources of the land (water, wood, wild food and herbs) whenever possible, and always with care and respect.

My own plans to return to Scotland and work the land had arisen out of a growing ecological awareness, and a strong drive to live an alternative and simpler lifestyle. But after so many years locked into the great, grinding corporate 'machine', I wasn't entirely sure how to do it. I'd also been reading, for the first time in my life, a number of books about contemporary 'green' spirituality. There was so much there which resonated with me but, still very much a product of that profoundly empiricist and rationalistic higher education system in which I'd participated for so many years, I found myself frequently worried about whether a lot of this might not actually be a little bit 'woo-woo'.* What would people who lived alternative, greener lifestyles be like, I wondered? Were any of them remotely like me? Could I ever possibly fit in? Most of the people I'd come across who inhabited that milieu had an easy grace, a carefree informality which I had never had, even as a young child. How could I shake off the stiffness, the awkwardness, the sense of being shut in, locked inside my own head, which had haunted me for so much of my life? I felt sure that at Aquaest I'd find some of the answers to those questions – but I nevertheless embarked on my journey with some trepidation, not entirely sure what I was going to find.

'The people who came to stay at Aquaest cared about the environment and enjoyed nature,' Sara says, 'and they wanted to learn more about themselves – and in particular, to access their own

---

* A wonderful new word which, according to the Merriam-Webster Dictionary online, was first coined around 1992, and which means 'dubiously or outlandishly mystical, supernatural, or unscientific'.

creativity.' Which, along with an inexplicable but compelling sense of needing to be healed of something I didn't fully understand at the time, is a fair description of my own situation when I arrived at Sara's door one Friday afternoon in late summer, with all the clothes and contraptions associated with my fading corporate life hastily shoved into the boot of my rental car.

Shortly after I'd arrived, a sudden storm caused us to eat a dinner which had been cooked on a camping stove, by candle-light. In the intensity of this situation – which was more intimate than usual, even for Aquaest – and of the conversation which followed, my first concerns were answered very soon: these people were not the slightest bit woo-woo. Something about Sara, a tall, quiet, composed Englishwoman with long blonde hair tied elegantly back – the most unlikely person I'd ever imagined finding here in the American backwoods – made me feel calm, and curiously safe. But more than that: in spite of a week-end-long conversation which ranged across a number of esoteric subjects that I'd never spoken about before to anyone – from the philosophy of yoga to the theory and practice of tarot – there was a grounded, down-to-earth rootedness in the land on which she lived which underpinned not just her work, but the way she presented herself in the world. This woman didn't just live in her head, and she was no New Age mystic: she lived firmly in her body too. Yes, I found myself thinking. I could be like that, and be proud of it.

Although other movement meditations were also offered to guests, Aquaest was originally inspired by a form of aquatic bodywork which was their signature offering, and which was based on the practice of 'Watsu' (a word which derives from 'water shiatsu'). Watsu is a form of aquatic bodywork in which a practitioner holds you close to them and then gently cradles, moves and stretches you in chest-deep warm water. For me to allow anyone, especially a stranger, to impinge on my personal space in that way required both a letting go of tightly held bound-aries and opening up to a capacity for trust which was not my natural way of being in the world at the time. But Sara's air of perfectly matter-of-fact self-containment reassured me, and so I willingly followed as she led me into the main spa building, a pic-turesque log cabin which held a sparkling round pool contained within a wooden frame. It felt like a sanctuary. Sara lit candles around the edges of the pool, and smudged the air in the cabin with a white sage stick. An underwater speaker transmitted a gentle, soothing music into the pool water. 'These rituals,' Sara explains, 'were all carefully designed to put guests at ease, and also to offer a sense of the magic and mystery inherent in water.'

We slipped into the pool in our swimsuits, I took a deep breath, and the journey began. 'When I float someone in the water,' Sara says, 'they often drift into a child-like state of trust, or sometimes even sleep. My feet on the floor of this round pool filled with chest-deep warm water keep us connected to the earth. I hold them in my arms, lightly but securely. Then gently, slowly, I move them until the pool becomes an ocean or seems as endless as the cosmos. The experience can not only bring comfort, but also a deep sense of being boundless, supported and connected.'

And the primary sensation I felt as Sara led me in this most beautiful of water-dances was indeed that of boundlessness. I transcended the boundaries of my own body and merged with the water so that I no longer knew where I ended and it began. I wasn't *in* the water, I was *of* it, and it was of me. I was aware only of lights, sounds, scents. My mind drifted; I thought of nothing. I remember feeling safe, held, supported, connected. The world made sense, and me in it. There was no sensation of time passing; I could have been there for minutes or hours.

'There is a physical freedom in water,' Sara suggests, 'even for those who say they're stiff on land. Bottled-up emotions may rise to the surface and float away. Some people enter a kind of trance state which, if they can stay aware, brings insights that go beyond their usual reality. In my experience, people find in it what they need. This aquatic healing art meets you right where you are, taking you no further than you are ready and willing to go. But it always expands and softens you.'

I found in it what I needed: the elimination of a sense of separation from the physical world, of a feeling of 'otherness' that had haunted me all my life. Because the boundlessness which I experienced was profoundly sensory in nature. There was nothing transcendental about it at all: I was more present in the world than I had ever been in my life. That was the healing I hadn't understood I was looking for, and it was a healing that was deep and surprisingly complete. There was a sense of profound grieving, then, when an hour and a half later Sara propped me up gently against the side of the pool, arms crossed over my chest and let me slowly return to myself. There was a grieving at the thought of returning to the old ways that we humans have of defining ourselves by and confining ourselves inside our skin. But what I took away with me, and it is something that I have never lost – more: something that I've been able to build upon – was the knowledge that I truly was part of this world, belonging entirely to it and it to me. In that pool, all sense of separation vanished. This knowledge was all the more transformative because it wasn't rational or intellectual – the kind of knowledge which was well within my comfort zone in those days. Rather, it was founded on a deeply felt physical and sensory experience, the memory of which I still carry with me in my body today. Not in my head – in my body. My body remembers what it was to become water; my body remembers what it was to dissolve into the world and feel entirely at one with it.

Why is it then, I ask Sara, that this practice can help people feel so profoundly connected to the world in this way?

'It's true that the sensory experience of being in a body can be exquisitely fine-tuned when you're immersed in warm water,' she agrees. 'Perhaps because we're largely made up of water, and so it's a medium we closely resonate with. Most of us feel at home in water. There is an evolutionary theory that we were once liminal creatures, aquatic apes living in the warm shallows. But whatever we might once have been, for most human beings today, watching the play of light over water or listening to the sound of falling water is profoundly soothing. And we are naturally streamlined and buoyant in water. Which is why I often think that people who fear water (often for reasons they don't understand) may also fear life itself.

'And so my belief is that, perhaps, if someone can have the experience of being at home and safe in water, they'll begin to feel more at home in the entire natural world around them. And floating, just like we once did as a foetus in our mother's womb, helps to recover our sensitivity and our innate vitality. I've seen this happening – even in big men, who could never possibly be held or moved in that way on land. I've seen it in people who are

I love autumn and winter
more. Something opens
up in me then — something
soft and deep and glowing —
which is far too shy to expose
itself to the inexhaustible
light of summer.

fragile through illness and injury; in those who fear that aging is relentlessly depriving them of their freedom, and in people who are simply lost or stuck in a myriad of different ways. I like to think that the water contains and connects together the truths of everyone who has floated there.'

Sadly, Aquaest ceased to exist several years ago, and Sara (who describes herself as a 'wanderer who stays a while') has now returned home to England. In between, she spent three years working at a private spa in India. 'My pool looked out into forest trees, visited by macaques and all kinds of birds. Though the people I was floating would soon close their eyes, they were always aware of the sunlight filtered through the leaves, shifting and changing as we journeyed around the pool. The creatures in the forest were curious onlookers, and sometimes big spiders would come to the poolside to perform their bowing dance, as if they were joining in ours. And so my guests had a profoundly heightened awareness of being a part of the world around us which they may not have experienced in their everyday lives.'

The dangers of disembodiment

> *Do you have a body? Don't sit on the porch!*
> *Go out and walk in the rain!*
> *. . . Wake up, wake up!*
> *You've slept for millions and millions of years.*
> *Why don't you wake up this morning?*
>
> Kabir

To live an enchanted life means that we have begun to fully belong to the physical world around us. To do that, we must pass beyond a simple intellectual understanding of what those words might mean, and truly feel it in our bodies – feel it with all of our senses. And that's something which we don't always know how to do. How can we feel as if we belong to the wider world when so many of us don't even feel a true sense of belonging to our own physical form?

The idea that we might respect, let alone revere, the physical body has long been out of fashion in the West. We have been taught for so long to see ourselves as superior to animals, but the body and its various and often messy functions are, to many people, a rather embarrassing reminder that this is precisely what we are. We have also developed an unfortunate tendency to objectify the body rather than fully inhabit it: our bodies have become tools for 'self-improvement', as we are urged to exercise and surgically sculpt ourselves into whatever form contemporary culture deems to be physical perfection. Our bodies are tools which permit us to compete with others in the realms of sex and beauty, which might be used as bargaining chips, or even as commodities to be bought and sold.

Our culture's distrust of the sensory and disavowal of the physical makes us feel as if we're detached from the world around us, and fosters the illusion that we ourselves are not a part of the world that we observe. Caught up in a mass of abstractions, chained to and dependent on increasingly complex and pervasive technologies, we have a tendency to forget that we experience the world primarily through our physical senses. All too often, we live almost entirely in our heads, and this is encouraged by a culture which operates on the assumption that reason and intellect are 'higher' faculties than sensory and physical perception, a culture in which the product of the intellect is usually valued and rewarded much more than physical work. It's not surprising, then, that Hermann Hesse, in his novel *The Glass Bead Game*, imagined a distant, post-apocalyptic future in which a community of celibate men dedicate themselves to the pursuit of intellectual truth, and remain oblivious to the world outside their country Castalia, which is reserved for those devoted to the life of the mind. But as Hesse's main character Joseph Knecht ultimately discovers, the intellect can only be wise and true when it is firmly in contact with the physical world.

We have developed a tendency to think of the body primarily as a housing for the mind – for our 'consciousness', or our 'self' – and an inconvenient one, because it can't always be relied upon to know what is 'true', and it has an irritating tendency to break. We wall our body off from our conscious experience, ignoring it and often neglecting it – until the time comes when we are uncomfortable, or begin to actively hurt. It's true that physical existence is a precarious thing, fleeting, and often filled with pain. It's not surprising that we should want to shield ourselves from its vulnerabilities. But belonging begins with the body, and if we cannot be enchanted with the miracle of our own physical existence, how can we ever hope to become enchanted with the wider world, and our place in it? If we shut ourselves off from the vicissitudes of bodied existence, and hold the world at a safe distance, we seal ourselves away from its joy and wonder. From the pleasure of contact with human and animal, the softness of mist on early morning skin. From the cold shock of a briny sea, and the scent of bluebell slipping in through our nose and on down into our lungs.

In all of these dysfunctional beliefs and attitudes we've once again been heavily influenced by the ideas of Plato and his philosopher-descendants. In the second chapter of this book we encountered René Descartes, and his judgement that only humans were possessed of 'mind'. Descartes also declared that our understanding of the fundamental truths about the world – how reality really *is* – can only ever be determined by the intellect, free from any 'worldly' influence. The evidence of our senses, he said, is at best irrelevant – an idea with which I'm confident that those who live with chronic illness or chronic pain would certainly take issue. And so, in his 1641 volume *Meditations on First Philosophy*, Descartes wrote that, in order to truly perceive the nature of reality, we must actively 'withdraw the mind from the senses'. His is a curious and profoundly dualistic worldview, in which a disembodied human consciousness which has no material existence acts as a kind of 'receiver' for the external world, but bears no essential relationship to it.

When you put it like that, it sounds rather silly, but the truth is that these beliefs still pervade our Western worldview, and so define the way we approach our lives. In the field of cognitive sciences – the interdisciplinary study of mind and intelligence which embraces philosophy, psychology, artificial intelligence, neuroscience, linguistics and anthropology – the model of the human mind which still predominates conceives of it as a kind of computer-like black box (in other words, something that you can't see inside of, and don't entirely understand) which lives somewhere inside our heads. Information comes into this black box from the outside, is processed inside it (ideas derived from computer science have been influential here) and then an output (a behaviour) is generated in response. According to this perspective, perception is a one-way process in which data from the environment is gathered into the mind and organised; our physical body, our senses, are simply passive receivers of this information.*

We value this individual, separate, disembodied human mind above all else, and it's no coincidence, impregnated as it is by such ideas, that Western society has been on a long trajectory to individualism; it's one of the defining features of our civilisation. As a doctrine it places the worth and wellbeing of the individual over the worth and wellbeing of the community (or arguably the planet). And although as a psychologist I have some sympathy with its aims and achievements, the modern therapy culture which has emerged over the last century has nevertheless accelerated this pre-existing tendency to believe that the maintenance and advancement of our own individual consciousness is worth more than anything else in the world. We are encouraged to endlessly focus on and analyse our own thoughts, beliefs and emotions, and so we become exhaustingly self-referential, learning to value and evaluate everything around us primarily in terms of what it might mean for our own cognitive or emotional 'process'. The body doesn't get a look-in.

Many of the popular practices which bridge the therapeutic and the spiritual also have a tendency to focus people on the inside of their heads to the exclusion of all else, and some mainstream forms of meditation are among the prime culprits. I experienced this for myself several years ago, when I signed up to attend a five-day silent meditation retreat. I did it because, for more than three decades, I'd

---

* However, a new theory has begun to emerge in the cognitive sciences: it is called 'embodied cognition', and its advocates are now studying the role that the body, and the wider environment, play in shaping the mind. According to their perspective on the world, mind is to be understood not in the traditional sense of a mechanism which is contained within the head, but as a wider pattern of interaction between the whole body and the environment which it finds itself in. The mind, again, is not located in any one place at all, but distributed among the brain, the body and the world. As two researchers in the field recently suggested, the difference between the old approach and the new can be captured by the slogan, 'Ask not what is inside your head; ask what your head is inside of'.[36]

been worried about the fact that I couldn't meditate 'properly'. My interest in meditation had begun around the age of sixteen, when I first heard about 'transcendental meditation', and imagined that it might help me very literally transcend the challenges of the difficult world around me. At the time, I was all for escapism. I was also fascinated by the idea of enlightenment (whatever that was), and enlightenment, from all that I had read, was always going to be found on 'another plane'. The physical plane – this world – was just too hard and cruel.

But the trouble was, at that time and through all the long years that followed, whatever form of meditation practice I tried, I just couldn't ever make myself want to do it. In fact, mostly, I really hated it. So I never could form a meditation habit, and I'd always felt that was a failing. I imagined that this was partly because of lack of discipline (and it's true – for this particular activity I had none), but partly also because I was probably 'doing it wrong'.

And so I set off from the late-spring, storm-strewn bleakness of the Isle of Lewis in the Outer Hebrides, where I was living at the time, and headed across the sea and down-country to the remarkable lushness of Herefordshire in May. I hadn't seen trees for months, and I'd forgotten how green the rest of the world could be. Here, it was warm and sunny; I'd come from a land of rain and gales. I found myself in a lovely, slightly dilapidated old mansion in the middle of nowhere, with wild-fringed gardens overburdened with bird-song. It was heaven. All I wanted to do was sit outside and bask in it, let it all melt into me. Instead, it quickly became apparent that 'outside' wasn't on the programme. And so, while the sun shone and the birds sang and the trees danced; while the owners' dogs lay on their backs in the grass with their legs in the air and the sun on their bellies – I was going to have to sit for three full days in a dark, dank room with other people, all of us crammed into a tight circle, sitting still, closing our eyes, and meditating on various ideas and images that the facilitator would present to us for approximately eight hours each day. And into the bargain, this was a silent retreat. I wasn't allowed to talk; I wasn't even supposed to vocalise at all. Laughter was off the menu, for sure.

I lasted till the coffee break on the first morning before I began to feel panicky, as if I'd been incarcerated. I was used to spending long hours outside walking the dogs or working on our croft; I didn't know how to do this intense *insideness* any more. Another hour, and I began to feel weepy. My back ached and my backside was numb from trying to sit still, and I was longing for light and air. A group of magpies were having a very loud conversation in the trees outside and I badly wanted to go and join in. But all of these things were the 'distractions' I was supposed to overcome in order to sit in this dark, crowded room and focus on the content of my own head while everyone around me focused in on the content of theirs. All of this, as a useful side-effect, was supposed to make us love each other (and the divinity which apparently lived within us) all the more. By lunchtime, I hated everyone in that room.

Soon enough, my emotional pendulum swung again and hilarity (or possibly hysteria) set in, and by mid-afternoon I realised that I was going to have to flee. And so I did. I ran for what seemed like my life. Took off in the car like an escaped convict, heading north. I spent the night in another green valley in Wales, and sat on a hillside enjoying the warmth of the evening sun on my shoulders and the light breeze on my skin. I thought of nothing; I just let my body relax and merge into the sounds of the land and its many, mostly avian, non-human inhabitants. All of my senses were singing. And by the time I arrived back on Lewis late the next day, I discovered that I had cured myself forever of the odd notion that what I needed to find in order to attain 'enlightenment' was ever going to emerge out of the confines of my own skull, locked away from the vibrant, living world around me.

American Buddhist teacher Reginald Ray has written about what he calls the 'modern crisis of disembodiment', suggesting that one of the major issues which the rapidly growing tradition of Western Buddhism faces is the fact that most of its many practitioners believe that enlightenment can only be achieved in a disembodied state, and so try to dissociate themselves from the physical. This misses the original point, he suggests, which is that in its most ancient form, Buddhist meditation (including the increasingly popular practice of 'mindfulness') is a technique for letting go of the objectifying tendency of thought, and instead encourages us to enter more fully and deeply into our embodied experience.[37] Ray is a strong advocate for a return to such practices here in the

West, and indeed, we badly need to break out of the prisons of our own heads – to crash through the barriers that cut us off from the sources of our own life. But for many of us, determinedly disembodied creatures that we are, it isn't until we receive the proverbial 'wake-up call' of illness that we are called back to our physical selves, when the diagnosis of a chronic disease or the threat of physical disability can shock us into valuing and properly nurturing our bodies for the first time.

Sometimes, if we learn to listen, physical symptoms can make us aware of things which have eluded the conscious mind. In my thirties, locked into a corporate job which I hated, trapped in a life which made no sense to me and living in an urban environment which was stifling, I began to develop symptoms of chronic hyperventilation, or over-breathing: a constant gasping for breath. It took me long enough to figure out what my body was saying: literally, *You can't breathe here.* A little later, after I'd carried on plodding along, utterly failing to address the problems which were causing those symptoms, I began to have the sensation of a lump in my throat, and then a spasming, as if a pair of hands were around my neck, squeezing and letting go, then squeezing again and letting go. *Hello!* my body was saying. *Anybody home? Are you listening yet? You really can't swallow this!* There was no underlying physical cause in either case, and the symptoms vanished as soon as I made a series of meaningful changes in my life.

According to neurologist Suzanne O'Sullivan, estimates suggest that up to 30 per cent of general practitioner encounters in the UK every day are with patients who have a form of psychosomatic illness: the experience of physical symptoms brought on by psychological states, and in particular by emotional distress.[38] A 2005 study suggested, she says, that the annual cost to the American health system of psychosomatic illness was $256 billion – at the time, double that of diabetes.[39] It sounds like a surprisingly high figure, but I think most of us would accept that we can have physical responses to stress: for example, headaches and indigestion are particularly common. More often than not, our response is to medicate the symptoms: to take an aspirin or an antacid and hope it will all go away. But if the symptoms are caused by chronic muscle tension because of stress or trauma, then the only thing that's going to help in the long term is a major shift in the way you live or the way you approach your life, so that you can come back into balance. Sometimes, our body has an important story to tell, and if a physical symptom persists in spite of there being no clear organic cause for it, then it's probably time to look a little deeper into what that story might be.

How, then, can we learn to fully inhabit our bodies, and to listen to the wisdom which our bodies carry? How do we cultivate the practice of what I would much rather call 'bodyfulness' than 'mindfulness'?

Cultivating 'bodyfulness'

Tuning into the wisdom of the body

If you are a meditator, you might be interested in a practice from the Tibetan yoga tradition which Reginald Ray offers in his classic article 'Touching Enlightenment': it's an exercise aimed at developing what he calls 'somatic awareness'. This tradition recognises the existence of two kinds of breath: the 'outer' breath – our normal, everyday respiration – and the 'inner' breath, or *prana*, which is thought of as a universal life-force which also resides within us. Prana follows, or is held by, the outer breath, and according to Tibetan teaching, it's possible to bring prana to a certain location in your body by visualising that you're 'breathing into' that location. Breathe in, he says, and then imagine that you are directing that breath, and the prana which it carries along with it, into specific areas of your body – your feet, abdomen, throat . . . As you do this, you'll begin to become aware of any discomforts, blockages or tensions.

But Ray's more fundamental point is that, although you might initially feel as if you (as a subject) are bringing your awareness to different parts of your body (as an object), as time goes on you begin to sense that what is really happening is that those places are already aware, and what you are actually doing is tuning into the awareness that already exists throughout your body. Through this practice, he suggests, there comes a shift in emphasis, as the subject-object distinction begins to break down and you begin to understand that your body is a living force, a source of intelligence, wisdom, maybe even intention. You begin to shift from feeling that your body is an object you control with your mind, to realising that mind, or intelligence, is located throughout your body.

I strongly recommend that you try this exercise outside. Whatever form you might imagine it to take, we can probably be fairly certain that the life-force which you are trying to harness is infinitely more plentiful there.

Respecting the body's rhythms

I love the long, dark half of the year. After summer solstice – the longest day of the year – something inside me shifts and settles as the hours of darkness begin gradually to grow. It's not that I don't appreciate summer: I do. I love it deeply, from the first rich flush of hawthorn blossoms to the last fading mauves of August heather. I love the green and the growing, the treasures of the hedgerows, and the always astonishing abundance of the land which surrounds me. It's just that I love autumn and winter more. Something opens up in me then – something soft and deep and glowing – which is far too shy to expose itself to the inexhaustible light of summer.

Unlike many of my friends, I welcome the season of the long dark – and not just because I happen to thrive on it, but because it is a real and necessary part of the year, and there is no sense in fighting it. The texture of our days alters with the seasons: our bodies are made that way. In winter, the slightest sense of hibernation presses down on us, and if we allow ourselves to, we can enjoy a deeper, more velvety sleep. There is a slowing down, a taking stock. A stasis, a moratorium on new projects, a long brewing in the dark cauldron of transformation, out of which who knows what will emerge in spring?

But one of the major problems so many of us face today is our inability to live according to the natural rhythms of the seasons, and to the different things our bodies need at different times. For those of us who go out to work, or who care for children who go to school, for example, our days are tightly defined by schedules which are imposed on us by others, and which permit us little or no flexibility. We struggle to get up on time in winter without the daylight, and we go to bed long after it's dark; we work long days indoors under artificial lighting and heating or cooling, and spend little time outdoors, even in the lush light of summer when everything else around us is blooming and thriving.

For women this inability to respond to the body's natural rhythms can be especially difficult, because our energy, moods and sleep patterns are strongly affected by our menstrual cycles. During menstruation, most of us have a natural inclination to want to be quieter, to be alone and to turn inwards – but our lives rarely permit us this luxury.

For many of us, making radical changes to the shape of our lives to allow us to live more naturally is not an option – but there are always things that can be done. Try to find some regular times – even if it is just at weekends, during vacations or during 'retreat' time away from your family, carved out for yourself – when you can sleep and eat when your body needs to, instead of according to the rules or requirements of others. During the days when you are menstruating, try to be still and quiet. Avoid filling up your calendar with social engagements and other commitments. Allow yourself time to sink down into that archetypal dark, blood-red cave. There are many richnesses to be found there, in the beautiful, nourishing stillness.

Remember to move

We have become sedentary creatures: social and technological changes over the past sixty years or so have significantly reduced our physical activity levels, and we spend more and more time sitting down. According to a recent study, the average American adult spends more than half of his or her average waking day sitting, but higher levels of overall sedentary time are correlated with increased mortality from all causes, including heart disease and cancer.[40] Another study in postmenopausal women found women who were sedentary for at least ten hours a day to be biologically older: their cells aged faster than those of women who were less sedentary.[41] And the problems begin early: a study in adolescents suggested that the more time you spend sitting at a screen, the more likely you are to suffer from depression, suicidal thoughts, anxiety, low self-esteem or other psychological distress.[42]

We need, quite simply, to move more. It's not just about setting aside more time for organised exercise – about going to the gym or swimming. It's important that we don't make movement an optional extra – something separate, that we can decide not to do on the days when we feel too busy. It's about weaving movement into every aspect of our lives.

I think better when I'm moving. I don't just mean going out for a walk to problem-solve: the process of writing itself, for me, is a curious blend of time spent sitting at a computer tapping out words, and an equal amount of time getting up from the computer and moving, stretching, dancing around the blissfully large, open room which is now my workspace. I run my hands over the spines of books that I love, and which have travelled with me halfway round the world and back, as I've moved from place to place. I throw my head back and my arms out, and whirl around as I stare up into the vaulted ceiling which reminds me of the inside of a church. I open the sliding doors and stick my head out into the wind or rain. I try to make all my movements flowing and fluid. By the time I've circled the room a few times, when I come to sit down again, my imagination is reinvigorated. All of these things transform me into something which most people find rather unexpected: a writer who, far from loftily imagining that she is putting down words which she alone has formed inside the confined spaces of her head, instead draws them from a deeply embodied reciprocal engagement with the world around her. It's an act of co-creation.

When I am cooking or cleaning, I'll do the same thing. (Preferably when no one is watching!) Rather than a series of automated, mindless actions, those chores become a strangely creative engagement with pots and pans or ovens and sinks. These objects are familiar to me; they've become part of my story. And so I move around them with delicacy, respect and affection, taking care in the placing of a vessel that holds the warm food which will nourish us. Its weight and balance as I move it from counter to the table teach my fingers and my arms how to be steady in the world. Even cooking is a dance, a form of gesture-as-ceremony, as utensils come into the orbit of bowls, and pans fall under the sway of the ancient iron Rayburn-monster which dominates the kitchen. Yes: there is enchantment in everything, if you choose to believe it, and to feel.

A world of embodiment

If we can successfully erase the ages-old distinction between the body and the mind which we've come to think of as normal, another question immediately arises: where, then, do we imagine that the individual mind-body complex stops and the rest of the world begins? Where is the self, and what are its boundaries? Does it stop at the skin? Over a century ago, psychologist William James suggested that our notion of 'self' incorporates whatever we happen to identify ourselves with – and his list includes our body, clothes, family and even our home. But can we go even further than this, and somehow learn to extend our sense of self so that we also identify ourselves with animals, trees, with the wider world itself?

We've spent quite a bit of time already considering the ways in which Western philosophy locked us into worldviews which have subsequently turned out to be distinctly dysfunctional and determinedly disenchanted. Happily, during the twentieth century, several philosophers emerged who began to challenge the old perspectives. One of them was a Moravian philosopher named Edmund Husserl (who was known to be so zealous that, when he wanted to sharpen his knife as a young boy, he sharpened it again and again until there was nothing left). Around the turn of the century, Husserl established a school of philosophy which he called 'phenomenology' to address exactly this kind of question about our ideas of what is 'inside' and 'outside' of us. Unlike much of philosophy, the aim of Husserl's methodology is not to try to explain how the world really *is*, but to look at the way the world (whatever it is) makes itself known to us – in other words, to think about the way we actually experience it. Husserl's investigations led him to believe that the lived body (not the mind) is the centre of experience. The fact that it moves freely and experiences a wide range of sensations, he said, means that it plays a key role in how we encounter and make sense of the world.

Maurice Merleau-Ponty, a French philosopher who, like his friend Jean-Paul Sartre, was a member of the Resistance during the Second World War, further developed Husserl's ideas. In direct opposition to his fellow countryman Descartes' declaration, 'I think, therefore I am', in the preface to his 1962 book *Phenomenology of Perception*

How do we cultivate
the practice of 'bodyfulness'
rather than 'mindfulness'?

Merleau-Ponty announced: 'The world is not what I think, but what I live.' Firmly rejecting several hundred years of Western philosophical thought, he declared that, as Husserl had suggested, we can't possibly understand the world from the perspective of a disembodied mind which is somehow separate from our physical being – the body is our primary vehicle for knowing the world.

But Merleau-Ponty went further than Husserl. More than this, he said: we experience and perceive the world precisely *because we live in that world and are intertwined within it.* We are part of it, and it is part of us. And so we can only find a sense of meaning in life by establishing connections with the various physical phenomena with which, and through which, we live: plants and animals; landscapes, and the other objects and processes (like weather) which are a part of them. Mind, in his perspective, is firmly rooted not just in the body, but in the body's interaction with the wider world; distinctions between mind, body, and world are really rather arbitrary.

We are, Merleau-Ponty said, constantly drawing from and adapting to the world around us. Our sensing and perceiving bodies exist in a web of other sensing and perceiving bodies, influencing them and being influenced by them in turn. And so to be human is to be thoroughly embroiled in a web of life; our mind/body cannot possibly be imagined as separate from that of the world's. He used the example of touch to explain this perspective: my hand, he wrote, is able to touch something precisely because my hand is touched by that something at the same time. I experience that 'something' that I'm touching as independent of me – but it is not. My body and this 'something' that I'm touching – my body and the world – are merging into one another, because this touching that I imagine *I* am doing in fact is a mutual process which is being done *to me* at the same time. Touching wouldn't be possible without that which is being touched – without the world. It's a two-way, entirely reciprocal, process. And so our perception of the world is at the same time the world's perception of itself, through us. We are the world; the world is us. My embodiment is part of the world's embodiment. There is no real separation.

To see this idea in practice, let's return to our fictional Woman B in the wood: 'The air is scented with bluebells, and you breathe in deeply. You are breathing in bluebells, you think, and you smile, because that means the bluebells are a part of you now – or are you a part of them?' By breathing in the scent of bluebells – a chemical emanation of the plant which has passed into the air and travels towards her – she is literally taking bluebell into her body. And so, Merleau-Ponty might ask, where then would we say the bluebell stopped and the woman began? As Michael Ondaatje's 'English patient' Almasy writes: 'We die containing a richness of lovers and tribes, tastes we have swallowed, bodies we have plunged into and swum up as if rivers of wisdom, characters we have climbed into as if trees, fears we have hidden in as if caves . . . I believe in such cartography – to be marked by nature . . .'[43]

Some scholars have suggested that our sense of separation from the world around us arises in part because our culture places such great emphasis on sight as the most important of all our senses, and because vision is by its nature objectifying, and distancing. In the case of the bluebell, for example, our eyes see a specific (bluebell-like) shape, and perceive that there is a clearly defined boundary associated with that shape. If we didn't confine ourselves to the primarily visual, and instead, like other animals, relied more on our sense of smell, perhaps it might be easier to see how the boundaries between ourselves and the world around us might blur.

But in fact, exactly the same principle applies to vision, as perceptual psychologist Laura Sewall writes in her ground-breaking book *Sight and Sensibility*: billions of photons of light bounce off surfaces and stream into us during every open-eyed moment. Light constantly vibrates into us, as waves.[44] From that perspective, just as in the case of the bluebell scent, the distinction between in-here and out-there quickly blurs, and the extent to which we are fully embedded in the world around us becomes clear. We become bluebell not only because its scent passes inside us through our noses, but because bluebell also passes into our bodies through our eyes in the form of light. And each of these examples teaches us that we're in relationship with the world whether we understand ourselves to be, or not. The idea of non-belonging is an illusion; it's a rejection of what is.

Weathering

To persons standing alone on a hill during a clear mid-night such as this, the roll of the world eastward is almost a

palpable movement . . . to enjoy the epic form of that gratifi-
cation it is necessary to stand on a hill at a small hour of the
night, and, having first expanded with a sense of difference
from the mass of civilized mankind, who are dreamwrapt
and disregardful of all such proceedings at this time, long
and quietly watch your stately progress through the stars.

Thomas Hardy, *Far from the Madding Crowd*

A few years after my profoundly embodied experience in Sara's
Ozark pool, after I had returned to Scotland where I subsequently
met my husband David, we sold the croft I'd lived in when I first
came home from America. We moved to the Isle of Lewis, an island
in the Outer Hebrides, some distance from the north-western shore
of Scotland. Our old stone cottage squatted on the edges of a tiny,
thinly populated townland, at the end of a narrow, winding road
which has been described as 'the longest cul-de-sac in Europe'. This
was the farthest, remotest south-western coast of the island, where
not only the road but Lewis itself gives out into the ancient gneiss
mountains of the Isle of Harris to which Lewis is attached, and
which borders it to the south. It was the croft at the end of the
world, and the extremity of its location was perfectly matched by the
extremity of its weather. Prevailing gales from both the south and
the west regularly battered a house which boasted no shelter from
them, and the vast, open skies seemed perpetually to leak water.

Wind was a constant. Tenacious, sodden westerlies sweeping
in from the sea; fractious, dry easterlies sweeping down from the
mountains. Warm southerlies, icy northerlies. We had it all. When I
moved to the island, I was no great fan of wind; after a few months
of living there, I was tearing out my hair. I had read about the
fierce and dogged Mistral wind of Provence, and now understood
completely why local lore suggested that it would drive humans
and horses mad. But the nature of my life on Lewis permitted no
escape from the wind. We occupied a croft which was populated
by sheep, cows, pigs, geese, ducks and hens – all of whom needed
to be cared for, whether the weather was clement or not. We had
three active dogs who needed regular long walks to keep them out
of mischief – and I was an active human who also needed regular
long walks to keep me sane.

Day after day, then, I'd go out into the wind. Since there was no escape from it, I simply gritted my teeth and learned to live with it. And then, curiously, after a while, I found myself enjoying it. But the process by which I became truly attuned to the wind began in earnest at the moment when I realised that the weather and the land could not be extricated from each other, any more than, living in this land, the weather and I could be extricated from each other. We were all bundled up together. It sounds rather obvious as I write about it here, but it was a major perceptual shift for me at the time. I had been muttering to myself, returning cold and saturated from another walk, hunched down into my not-so-very-waterproof jacket and scowling, that this would be such a lovely place if only there were a little less wind and a little more sun – when suddenly the foolishness of what I was thinking struck me and made me laugh out loud.

I remember the moment very clearly. All at once I realised that these uniquely wild islands were the way they were precisely because of the wildness of the weather. The wind and rain that I was railing against are the forces which had shaped its physical attributes over the millennia, and determined the nature of the land which I loved so fiercely – the water-logged moors and bogs, the hundreds of tiny lochs scattered like fragments of broken mirror across the peatlands to the north, the vastness of a vista that stretched for miles, and across which your gaze could travel uninterrupted by trees or shrubs. (They are unable to tolerate the salt winds. I remember a conversation with an elderly native of the island, who had recently visited the mainland for the first time in her life. 'And what did you think of it, then?' she was asked. 'Well,' she replied, 'it was fine enough in its way, but I couldn't see the point of all those trees. It's a terrible thing, how they get in the way of the view.')

You couldn't extricate the land from the weather – and it hit me then that I didn't live in a landscape – I lived in a sort of weatherscape. And I wasn't walking on the surface of the land, while weather happened above it and apart from it: I lived *inside* a coalescing world of sea, land and sky, all tangled up together, in which the weather was dynamic, always changing, always engrossed in its own process of becoming. The wind was not *happening to* me, the wind was *in relationship with* me. And so, from that moment onwards, my attitude towards the wind changed. I participated in it; I courted it. I danced along with its currents; I let it hold me up, facing into a westerly so strong that when I threw my arms out to the side and tilted forward, the immutable force of it prevented me from falling. We became playmates of sorts, the wind and I – and every kind of wind offered a different way to engage with it. The strong, buffeting westerlies were the wildest and the most relentless; these were winds to test yourself against. The easterlies were dry, fractious and irritable; they tested your psychological, rather than your physical, mettle. The northerlies were sly and cold; they taught you about endurance. The southerlies were harlot winds – warm, wet and unstable; here one minute and gone the next.

I understood now that I inhabited this living biosphere – that I was a living being, living inside the body of another living being, immersed in the land and the air and the weather, just as fish are immersed in a warm or a cool, and a calm or a choppy, sea. The way that I imagined the world, and my place in it, underwent a radical shift of perspective, and it was as if some curious hole which I'd carried inside me all my life suddenly filled up with meaning. This sensation of hollowness is akin to what the novelist John Fowles referred to as the 'nemo': 'a man's sense of his own futility and ephemerality . . . of his virtual nothingness.'[45] At the moment when you become truly grounded, enmeshed in the world you inhabit, the nemo vanishes in a puff of smoke.

What does it mean, to live in a way which acknowledges our embeddedness in the world, and our relationship with everything which participates in it along with us? It begins with remembering that, when you are in a relationship with someone or something, communication goes in both directions. Try approaching the world like this: don't just identify that bird as a robin, and listen to his complex and beautiful song – talk to the robin in return. Let him listen to and come to know your song, just as he would come to know the caw of a crow or the husky night bark of a fox. Don't just see that this is an ash tree, and listen to the sound that is made when the wind passes through its leaves. Let the tree listen to the sound that is made when air passes over your vocal cords. Open your mouth and let the sound out. Let the tree hear your voice. Read it a poem – maybe a beautiful poem in praise of trees. Why not praise the tree? Maybe this is what that song thrush is doing, singing way up there in its heights.

If you are a dancer – or even (or especially) if you are not – dance with the tree. If the wind is shifting its branches, dance as if the wind is also moving your limbs. *Let* the wind move your limbs. Don't just look at the tree and admire it, in a detached kind of way – interact with it. Act as if you are a part of the world around you, not just a spectator of it, and that is what you will become. My friend Ruth follows what she calls a 'land-based dance practice'. What she is trying to do, she tells me, is to shape her own movements to the shifting movements of the natural world around her. How quickly she moves, whether she is active or passive, her position in the landscape and the angle at which she holds her body – all are determined by what's happening in the environment she occupies at the time. 'It's a direct response to the land,' she tells me. 'If I'm moving on a beach it's very different from moving in a forest. It's not just that the land constrains you in certain ways: it's that the response it evokes in you might be different. On a beach there's a sense of sky and of openness, and so my movements might be more sweeping, reaching up and outwards. I might move in time with the ebb and flow, chase a wave or allow myself to be chased by it. In a forest, my movements might be smaller, tighter, more focused on what's under my feet and in line of sight, rather than what's overhead.'

There is a courtesy involved in interacting with the land in this way. Just as we acknowledge our fellow humans when we meet, why shouldn't we acknowledge the land and the other beings which inhabit it? Speaking of the Australian Aboriginal relationship to place, or 'country' – what Freya Mathews earlier described as land that has a spiritual, as well as a physical dimension; land which is a communicative player in human affairs – ethnographer Deborah Bird Rose writes: 'People call out to country, and if they did not do so it would be a sign that they were sneaking around. The country . . . would know and respond, just as it is held to know and respond when the proper people address it in the proper way.'[46] I try not to sneak around; as we saw in chapter 3, one of the ways that I weave myself into a place, and try to build relationships with the non-human creatures which inhabit it along with me, is to tell them stories.

It seems quite natural to me: I'm a storyteller. My stories are the stories of a silent land; there are few voices in the Irish hills and bogs. Except for the sounds of distant farm animals and domestic pets, or the buzzing of a fly or a wild bee, most of the voices you'll find here belong to birds. The harsh cry of a heron or a crow; the haunting song of a diver; the rising alarm call of a wren. In this sparsely populated place, another voice – my voice – inevitably stands out.

A jungle, on the other hand, is home to a tumult of voices, a positive cacophony, and it's to this ferment of vocal forms that restoration ecologist Suprabha Seshan contributes her own. Suprabha sings to the jungle. 'It's what I do,' she says. She sings to elephants, langurs, treefrogs and crows. She sings to whatever is there. Suprabha, who lives and works in the mountains of southern India, told me why.

'Partly because they sing so sweetly to me all the time!' she said. 'It's their generosity that I aspire to match. But singing is also my direct announcement to others in the forest: I am here. I walk alone. I come in peace, I am happy, I am sad. I'm looking for jamuns, bombax flowers, the crinkled seeds of todayan, otterspoor . . . I know these creatures are aware of me whether I sing or not, but I sing, in part, because I believe that singing transmits much more than mere presence. It carries, through tone, beat, volume, phrase and melody, some information about the state of my body, the state of my emotion, and my intention. They can of course choose to stay or to leave, but usually they are not alarmed, and they know it's me, it's the singing woman from that hill. They know me from my voice, from my body's resonances and reverberations, from the particular notes and melodies I emit. They know me from my habits, the way I walk, where and when I walk, perhaps even why.'

This notion of singing as a way to weave yourself into a world filled with the song of others brings me back to the etymology of the word 'enchantment':

> *c. 1300, 'act of magic or witchcraft; use of magic; magic power,' from Old French* encantement *'magical spell; song, concert, chorus,' from* enchanter *'bewitch, charm,' from Latin* incantare *'enchant, cast a (magic) spell upon,'*

from in- 'upon, into' (from PIE root *en 'in') + cantare 'to sing' (from PIE root *kan- 'to sing'). Figurative sense of 'allurement' is from 1670s. Compare Old English galdor 'song,' also 'spell, enchantment,' from galan 'to sing,' which also is the source of the second element in nightingale.[47]

To enchant, then, is literally to *sing into*, and it seemed to me that this was precisely what Suprabha was describing. I asked her how her singing habit began, and she started by telling me about her home and workplace in the Gurukula Botanical Sanctuary, which lies at the edge of a rich and beautiful forest, filled with thousands of species: orchids, tall trees and mosses; elephants, snakes, small mammals, frogs, 220 or more species of birds, and many, many insects.

'It all began after about fifteen years of living here,' Suprabha said, 'when one day I struck out and began to stray farther from home. I started to swim in a forest pool, and then to walk a trail in the bottom of the valley where only wild creatures live. I started to inhabit certain places there, in reed thickets, rock outcrops, the buttressed base of specific trees. I did this at different times of the day and night, over a couple of years. Mostly I went alone; sometimes with one or more dogs. It was in going to the wildest places on the land by twilight, and many times in the night, often by moonlight, when my eyes fell quiet, that my ears opened out, and I felt as if I'd shot through some kind of sonic barrier.

'Now,' she said, 'I sing to the jungle all the time. And it's only after many years of walking, participating, unfolding into the musical present, repeating, practising, responding, syncopating, or swelling out with my own song, and noticing all the time how they respond, that I have this hunch that different non-humans not only recognise me, they also listen to me just as I'm listening to them.

'Today, for example, I joined the crow pheasants. In the half-hour session of listening and imitating, I noticed these things: the calm regular sounding, the steady announcement and response, one here, one there and one further away. The slight differences between their *hoooohoooo*. One whose beat was faster, with an earlier accent on the first notes and then the fall. One who steadily and slowly descended, at a lower pitch than the first. The third one who came in was louder, with a force in the voice – I would say aggression, not the calm sweet steady vocals of the first two. Then he settled down, and then there were three. When I mimic their calls I know I don't get the exact intonation, or even the correct number of hoots. But it gets closer all the time. There will come a day when my voice will be mistaken for one of theirs. My heart's desire is to perch in a quiet place and start hooting, and a crow pheasant will appear.

'I sing in a full-bodied way,' she told me. 'I stand up, bend my knees, sway a little, relax my belly and shoulders. I also use a lot of open vowel sounds, as well as lip rolls and trills. When movement is married to a specific expression or set of expressions, when your singing becomes *action* singing – in other words, a dance – you experience the give and bounce of life. This kind of music – sound movement combined with body movement, performed to an audience in a setting that is unique to every moment – is a form of improvisation, of jungle jazz.

'I think that to live for long years in a place works the body, the vocal cords and the mind in a specific and exact way. We are shaped by our environment, by everything and everyone we touch and are touched by, as well as all the stories and messages passing through. The land, the forest, this community are all abuzz with vibrations: little sonic ripples and dances of molecules. The art of listening is to be open to these, to become aware and conscious of the effect of them on your body.'

The world is multi-layered, multi-faceted; how much more alive would we feel if we travelled on in awareness of those many and varied facets? Awareness of the lifeworld of rock, of animals and plants, of stones, soil and weather . . . of the wind, which dances over the land, interacting with it, interacting with us as it goes. In a world like this, there is no possibility of true disconnection – there is only our own blindness and forgetting. But what we have forgotten, we can surely remember again; and we only need to be reminded how to look in order to begin to see. And above all, in this wholly embodied, radically present conception of what it is to be fully alive, we begin to remember not only what the world is to us, but what we are to the world.

Enhancing our identification with the world

- Don't just be a spectator of the world. Engage with it, with all of your senses. We are not tourists in this world, driving from place to place in search of the picturesque, insulated from it, getting out of the car only for a moment to take a photograph of a beautiful 'view'.
- Like Suprabha, go outside and mimic the birds who live around you. Call back to them when they call. Try doing this with a raven or a crow. You might be surprised to find that an entire conversation ensues!
- Go outside into the world and dance with it. Choose a tree, or dance in front of a crow sitting on a telegraph pole. Begin by mirroring, mimicking whatever your dance partner is doing. Open your arms out like wings, sway with a tree. Bend with a flower; turn your face to the sky or the ground in the way it does. Get down onto its level.
- Reawaken your senses! Ecopsychologist Laura Sewall argues that this is an integral step in renewing our bond with the Earth. Focusing specifically on vision, she offers the following perceptual practices in order to help us, literally, to come to our senses:[48]

    1. *Learning to attend.* Psychological research suggests that where we place our attention determines our subjective reality. We should, then, be more mindful of where we place our attention – and make active choices about what we allow to influence us.

    2. *Perceiving the relations.* We are trained to perceive *things*, rather than the relations between them or the context in which things operate. But if we practise a relational view, Sewall suggests, we will be acting in response to a world that is revealed to be vibrant, dynamic and alive. One way to make the shift from

perception of objects to perception of relations, she offers, is to observe the interface between water and land. As water flows over rocks or sand, reflects, flows over and around and under it, we begin to see that this process is all about relationship: erosion meeting resistance, hard meeting soft. We might then, dipping our hands into the water, perceive ourselves as part of this process of relationship and exchange.

3. *Perceptual flexibility.* This is a fluidity of mind in which the magic of the visible world is revealed by letting go of your expectations and nurturing a freshness of vision. Some of the finest photographers of landscape elements excel at perceptual fluidity, and it seems to come naturally to those of us who are predisposed to see faces in rock. Sewall suggests that exploring optical illusions is a good way to train your perceptual flexibility.

4. *Perceiving depth.* We are not, Sewall reminds us, simply standing on the surface of the planet: we are occupying a place within the biosphere. We tend to focus on horizontality, and our position on the ground; we should teach ourselves to focus more on verticality too, becoming more aware of the sky above us (and the weather which is a part of it) and the earth beneath our feet – all the way down to the hot core of the planet. It's a change from a two-dimensional way of looking at the world to a recognition of depth.

6. The mythic imagination

I will tell you something about stories,
[he said]
They aren't just entertainment.
Don't be fooled.
They are all we have, you see,
all we have to fight off
illness and death.
You don't have anything
if you don't have the stories.

Leslie Marmon Silko, from *Ceremony*[49]

A FEW MONTHS ago, I was invited to open a series of events on 'The Feminine and Social Change' at St Ethelburga's Centre for Reconciliation and Peace, in London. The evening began with a conversation between myself and the organiser, during which she asked me a number of questions about my work and writing. Her last question came as something of a surprise to me; after we had talked for a little while about the extent of the ecological and social challenges facing the planet, she asked simply and finally, 'What gives you hope?'

For a moment, I didn't know what to say. It's such a big question, and, as is the way with answers to big questions, it would be so easy to sound glib or anodyne in reply. So I answered it in the only way I could think of – the only way I can ever seem to think of, when questions are aimed right at the heart of my way of approaching and being in the world: I answered it with a story.

When Things Fall Apart

There is an island to the far north-west of these lands, close to the end of the world; you'll maybe have seen it in your dreams. Long white beaches, rocky coves, stormy seas. If you stand on the cliff-tops on its westernmost shores, they say you might sometimes catch a glimpse of Tír na mBan, the Isle of Women, way out on the horizon. When the sky is blue and the air is still – which happens rarely enough in those parts. Here, the wind blows hard and long through the dark days of winter, and summer is precious and fleeting. Somewhere along the stormiest section of that westernmost coast is a high, inaccessible cave where they say the Old Woman of the World lives still – but no one I've met has ever found that cave, though many have searched, and many have drowned in the process.

No one knows how long she's been in that cave, the Old Woman of the World; she's not even sure herself. She only knows that she doesn't remember ever having been anywhere else. Are you wondering what she does there? She weaves. You might catch her at it, if you should be lucky enough to happen across that cave – right at the back there, creating an enormous tapestry which she plans will be the most beautiful weaving in the world. Oh, the complexity of it! – and the rainbow colours of the threads, some thick and some thin, some soft and some shiny. Right now, she's getting ready to make a fringe for the weaving, and she wants the fringe to be as intricate and unique as the body of the tapestry. So she's making the fringe from sea urchin spines. Because it seems right, somehow, to the Old Woman of the World, that such a beautiful piece of craftsmanship should be finished off by sharp and thorny spines which can sting you if you don't take care. After all – she's weaving the world, and this is the way the world is. She has to flatten the spines to work with them, and so she bites them; and because she has flattened so many of them during the long history of the world, her teeth are little more than stubs.

Over on the other side of the cave is a big fire. They say that the fire has been burning in the cave forever; certainly, the Old Woman can't remember a time when she hasn't tended it. Over that fire hangs an enormous black cauldron, and in that cauldron is a soup which contains all of the seeds and all of the herbs and the essence of all of the growing and living things in the world. As well as weaving, it's the Old Woman's job to tend to that soup. But sometimes she gets so caught up in her weaving that she forgets about the soup, and it starts to stick to the bottom of the cauldron and it splutters and splashes – and then she jumps up and crosses to the other side of the cave to stir the pot.

But there's another inhabitant of that cave, and he's biding his time, waiting for the Old Woman to leave her weaving for a moment. He's been watching her, you see – watching all the beautiful shiny threads going back and forth – watching, and waiting. He's a big black crow, and his name is Trickster. I wouldn't say that he was a companion to the Old Woman, but wherever she goes he seems to be there too, as if they're bound together somehow, like the weaving and the soup. So when the Old Woman leaves her loom to tend to the soup, Trickster Crow

flies down from his rocky perch at the back of the cave and stands
in front of the tapestry.

And then he begins to peck at it. Thread by thread, he begins to
unravel it. Faster and faster, picking and pecking, until by the time
the Old Woman turns away from the soup and makes her way back
to the loom, all that is left is a tangled mess of threads on the floor.

What does the Old Woman do now? Does she weep and wail,
sit down by the tangled chaos of her work and grieve because she'll
never create anything so beautiful again?

She doesn't. Because as she stands there, eyes moist, staring at
the mess in front of her, a beautiful rich green thread catches her
eye. Who knows why it's that particular thread? But she happens to
glance at it, and before she can even begin to think about it, her hands
are reaching out and she's picking up that thread and she's weaving
it back into the fragments of warp which remains on her loom – and
before she really understands what's happening, a new pattern is
already beginning to emerge and a new tapestry is taking form. And
Trickster Crow cackles and caws, and flies back to his perch.

The Old Woman isn't thinking about the beautiful work that
was lost, or wasting her time getting angry at Trickster Crow.
Because the Old Woman is a weaver, and weaving is what she
does. Weaving is what she is for. So, on she goes, warp and weft,
thread after beautiful thread, weaving a new pattern, until the
next time that the soup needs stirring, and Trickster Crow flies
down again from his perch. Because Trickster Crow understands
this: that if the weaving is ever finished, in all its beautiful perfection, the world will come to an end. And so Trickster keeps
on disrupting, and the Old Woman keeps on weaving, through
all the ages of the world, so that new patterns are always in the
process of becoming, and the end of the world is held at bay for
a few ages more.

And that, I told the audience, is why I have hope: because there's
always a thread to be salvaged from the rubble of our dreams, or
the world's; there's always a beautiful new tapestry waiting for eyes
to notice and fingers to reach out for that single bright thread with
which a new weaving begins.

I could, of course, simply have exactly said that in response to
the question I was asked; it would only have taken a moment or

two, and time was beginning to run short. But such a reply would have lacked the many-layered images, the mythic resonances and the fragments of hope, yearning and dreams which accompany the ideas this story conjures up in my imagination. And that is the essential power of story: it breathes life into our thoughts and dreams; it illuminates who we are, and shows us how we might possibly play our own unique part in the ongoing becoming of the world.

The storytelling animal

> The first true storyteller is, and will continue to be, the teller of fairy tales. Whenever good counsel was at a premium, the fairy tale had it, and where the need was greatest, its aid was nearest ... The wisest thing – so the fairy tale taught mankind in olden times, and teaches children to this day – is to meet the forces of the mythical world with cunning and with high spirits.
>
> Walter Benjamin, from 'The Storyteller'[50]

We don't always appreciate the extent to which stories dominate our lives, and the many ways in which we've been shaped by them. After all, what is story? Little more than a set of oral or written conventions which somebody made up sometime, long ago, and which we choose to follow in order, primarily, to entertain ourselves?

Nothing could be further from the truth. The fact is, we can't extricate ourselves from story – we are storytelling animals, hardwired for story. It's so obvious in children; they're born with a remarkably imaginative and seemingly innate storytelling capacity. In their pretend play, toddlers as young as two and three years old create their own uniquely plotted dramas, populating them with people and animals, pitching their voices differently for different characters, and ascribing clear personality traits to them. Their play-acting covers a wide range of human experience, too – it's not all about polite chit-chat at dolls' tea parties. Sometimes it's positively existential, portraying a world which is changeable and dangerous – just like the fairy tales they almost always love to be told.

Contemporary neuroscience offers up some interesting evidence which may help explain why stories are so important to us. It seems that when we listen to stories, watch movies or read books, the parts of our brain which are activated are exactly the same areas which would be implicated if we ourselves were indulging in the activities that are being described in the story. As far as our brains are concerned, it's as if we are literally living the story we're engrossed in, and Keith Oatley, an emeritus professor of cognitive psychology at the University of Toronto (who also happens to be a novelist), has suggested that reading stories produces a simulation of reality which can be so vivid that we feel as if we are right there, inside it.

It's not just about our own individual imaginings, though: the beauty of stories is that they can bind people together, bring us to see the world in common ways. Other studies carried out by Oatley and his colleagues show that people who read a lot of fiction seem to be better able to understand other people, empathise with them, and imagine the world from their perspective. This idea is extended by the work of Uri Hasson, a neuroscientist based at Princeton University, who conducted a series of studies based on functional magnetic resonance imaging (fMRI) in the brain. These studies indicated that the brains of different people begin to show similar activity when they hear the same story. In one study, for example, five people listened to the same story, told aloud. Before the recording began, everyone's brain activity was quite different; but once the story started, their brain activity began to become 'aligned', to use Hasson's phrase. In a related experiment, Russian speakers and English speakers listened to the same story told in their own languages, and the brain activity of the two groups still became aligned; this alignment occurred even when the story was conveyed to each of them in differently worded paraphrases. All of this implies that the brain activity alignment is taking place at the level of the story itself, and is not just a function of linguistics.[51]

Stories can bring us together, then – or they can tear us apart. Stories can change minds, hearts, even the course of history. 'So you're the little woman who wrote the book that started this great war' – are the words, legend tells us, that Abraham Lincoln used to greet Harriet Beecher Stowe when he met her in 1862, ten years after she wrote *Uncle Tom's Cabin*, the second-bestselling book of the nineteenth century. (The bestselling book was the Bible, and if you're looking for other stories that changed the world, that one's a pretty good place to start.) Beecher Stowe's story of Uncle Tom, an African-American slave, brought the horrors of slavery to the public's attention for the first time. It caused an uproar in the America of the day, furthering the abolitionist cause in the north, creating an unstoppable wave of empathy. It angered southern slave-owners, increasing the tensions between north and south and, as Lincoln suggested, it might well have helped to push an already teetering country into full-blown civil war.

We perceive, explain and make sense of the world through stories. They are the stars we navigate by, and that's why storytelling is a universal human phenomenon, a vital aspect of communal life across all cultures and throughout the entirety of our known history. Around fifteen years ago, when I returned from America to my croft on the north-west coast of Scotland, I also returned to the practice of psychology. My lifelong love of myth and story, along with the fact that at the time I was completing a Master's degree in creative writing, led me to develop a specialisation in narrative psychology. This is a branch of psychology which holds that we humans use story as our primary way of making sense of our experiences – by telling stories (which we usually call anecdotes) about our experiences, by envisaging our lives as an evolving story, and by listening to and learning from the life stories of others, or the stories we are told at bedtime, or read in books.

You don't need to be a psychologist, of course, to understand that stories teach us everything we know. Their lessons are deep and rich. Anywhere, there may be a door to another world: learn to look for it. Always leave a trail of breadcrumbs to find your way out of the dark wood. Don't maim yourself trying to fit into the glass slipper which was made for someone else. Gold is never a good goal. Never take your skin off and leave it unattended.

The characters in stories are great teachers, too. They can be role models for our development, and as a child I think I learned more about ways of being in the world from characters in books and stories than from people I actually knew. I was usually uncomfort-able around other children (I grew up in a house where concealment was the foundation stone of our lives; I found the openness of others hard to bear) and so I found friends in stories before I found them in the real world. My preferred companions were the solitary hero-ines in books and stories who were strong enough to win through the tough times. I studied them carefully, thinking about what kept them going, how they cultivated resilience. I loved the prosaic 'just-get-on-with-it' attitude of the princess in the old Orkney tale of 'Peerie Fool', who casually outwits a giant, steals back the skins he flayed from the body of her sisters, so bringing them back to life, and finally, with the help of her mother, kills the giant by pouring an enormous pot of boiling water over him. Or Kate Crackernuts, who, through a combination of close observation and steely nerve, not only manages to restore her sister's head to her body (it had been replaced by a sheep's head) but finds a cure for a sick prince (whose brother, of course, she then marries) at the same time.

My friend Caitriona took to fairy tales to try to figure out how to create the endings she most desired. She was constantly exposed to stories during her rural Irish childhood – and repeat-edly, because she had many younger siblings. She tells me that fairy tales helped to build her sense of possibility, which she thinks has been critical to her own survival during troubled times. 'During repeated hearings of the same stories, while I was sitting there spellbound, I seemed always open to the possibility that the story might be re-made; I felt that somehow a story which had previously had a sad ending might be able to turn out differently. And I would wait in suspense for those stories with happy endings, to hear that ending unpeeled, again and again, and figure out how it came to be. I wanted to know, how do you make happy endings? I would be captivated, living and reliving every single bit of the stories as they were freshly revealed to me each time, fully in the moment. They helped me to imagine outcomes which otherwise I might not have been able to see.'

Stories can reveal to us longings that we never knew we had, fire us up with new ideas and insights, and inspire us to grow and change. A young princess marries a prince who has been trans-formed into a black bull. When he falls into the clutches of the evil witch who originally cast the spell on him, she spends seven long years working for a blacksmith – the only one who can make the shoes that will enable her to scale an impassable glass mountain. When her time is up she manages to cross the mountain and saves her husband from the clutches of the evil witch.

Fragments of a shattered magic mirror made by the Devil penetrate the chests of people all over the world, freezing their hearts and making them see only things that are bad and ugly. One boy's heart is pierced by such a splinter, and he is captured and then ensorcelled by the Snow Queen. The girl who is his closest friend searches the earth for him, finds him with the help of animal and human allies, and eventually melts the icy splinter in his heart with the warm tears she sheds out of her love for him.

These are tales of courage, endurance, and reward for loyalty and fidelity; the tasks which must be undertaken in these stories are stuff out of which souls, not just shoes, are forged. How could we not be entranced by them? They are founded on the challenges and concerns which make up our daily lives.

Working with myth and story

 Is there a particular myth, legend or fairy tale that you loved as a child? If so, what makes it so memorable? The plot, or a character, or an especially beautiful image? Did you see yourself in the story?

 Are there stories you particularly disliked – and if so, why?

Transforming stories

Stories, then, not only reflect us back at ourselves, but help us to reimagine ourselves. One of the ways that I used myths and fairy tales in my narrative psychology practice was to help people to remember and work with stories which already held some kind of special meaning, some iconic status, for them. These are the stories which we hold in our hearts for years, or for decades, and which speak to what really matters to us, or show us who we are or would like to become – because myths and fairy tales don't just bring into awareness what is repressed or unconscious: they also have the ability to reveal to us new goals and possibilities. Stories help us to unravel who we are, and to work out who we want to become.

When I was a young woman, one of the stories which captured my imagination was Hans Christian Andersen's 'The Wild Swans', and it still has a powerful hold on me today – as you can see from its appearance in Woman B's woodland experience, in chapter 1.

This, you may remember, is the story of eleven princes and their sister, Elisa. Their mother has died and one day, their father decides to remarry – but he marries a wicked woman who is also a witch. The queen hates her stepchildren, and soon turns the princes into swans (though they are allowed to return to their human form at night) and forces them to fly away. She tries to do the same to Elisa, but she is too good and pure, and the spell doesn't work. The queen then banishes Elisa, and her brothers fly her on their backs to safety overseas.

There, Elisa is told by the queen of the fairies how she might help her brothers regain their human forms forever: she is to gather stinging nettles from a graveyard and knit them into shirts – one for each of her brothers. When they put on the shirts, the spell will be broken. And so Elisa endures the nettle stings and her painfully blistered hands, and she accepts the vow of silence which she must also endure for the duration of her task, for speaking just one word will result in the deaths of her brothers.

The king of another land accidentally meets Elisa and falls in love with her. He offers her a room in his castle, where she silently and steadily continues her knitting. Eventually he asks her to become his wife, and she accepts. But the archbishop of that land is angry because he thinks the voiceless Elisa is a witch, and, when, one night, Elisa runs out of nettles and goes to a nearby graveyard to collect more, the archbishop is watching. Ghouls which feast on the bodies of the dead are also present in the churchyard, and the archbishop imagines that Elisa is in league with them. He reports the incident to the king as evidence of witchcraft, and orders that Elisa should be put on trial. Of course, she can speak no word in her defence, and so she's sentenced to death by burning.

Even as the cart carries Elisa away to her execution, she continues knitting, and this enrages the people. They are about to snatch the shirts from her and destroy them when her brothers, who have discovered her plight, fly in to rescue her. When Elisa throws the shirts over the swans, one by one, her brothers return to their human forms – except for the youngest brother, who retains a swan's wing instead of one arm, because Elisa did not have time to finish the last sleeve of his shirt. Elisa faints from exhaustion, and so her brothers tell the astonished people her story – and as they do so, the firewood around the stake at which she was to have been burned miraculously takes root and bursts into flowers. The king plucks the topmost flower and presents it to Elisa, and they are finally married.

I loved so many things about this story that I can hardly begin to list them. I loved, of course, that it was the girl who saved her brothers, rather than – as so often in fairy tales – the male who saved the female. I loved the fact that they saved her in turn, and, as an only child, the undying loyalty of the siblings captured my imagination as a new thing I hadn't conceived of before. I loved the idea that fabric could be spun out of something as common as nettles. The image of the brother who remained part-swan fascinated me, in good part because, as a child who was once described by a teacher as having something of a 'Mother Theresa complex', I felt such a sadness for the one who could not be completely saved. And yet, wasn't there something magical and wonderful, maybe, about being part-animal?

As a product of a difficult childhood, Elisa's forced silence resonated strongly with me too. This was the story of a girl whose story, quite literally, was stripped away from her – she was forbidden to tell it. There were strong elements of that in my own life, at the time. And then, above all, there was the strength of her endurance. Whenever life seemed difficult, for all the years afterwards, I've remembered that story – and seen in my mind an image of Elisa knitting shirts out of nettles while her hands were blistered and bleeding from the plants' stings. And in the end, the spell *was* broken. That image defines the story for me: a story which taught me that transformation is a gift which comes from the stinging, the thorny, the prickly. Tolerate the blistered hands, it whispered to me: the pain creates the magic. And no matter how close you come to the burning, help may still arrive.

Now, a nettle is never simply a nettle. It is a symbol of everything that is possible, even when all hope is gone.

This story, like so many myths and fairy tales, led me to explore some of the issues humans have been struggling with forever: the difference between good and evil, the power of love, the limits of endurance . . . such stories declare that there is more to life than we can ever possibly know, and reveal to us glimpses of the mysteries which lie behind the world, and which usually are hidden from us. And at the heart of all of these stories is transformation: they help us to believe in the possibility of change. Brothers changed into swans and then back again; the ugly duckling turned into a swan; Cinderella transformed into a princess. We come to see that there are other ways of imagining the world and our place in it – because stories can help us find our path in life. When we're lost in the dark wood, they can show us how to find our way back home – or our way forward, as we set off on a new adventure. Whatever journey we imagine ourselves to be on, myth and fairy tales can inform our sense of what is possible, and enable us not just to cope with life's challenges, but to live more intensely, and more richly, in the world. Because spiritual growth also lies at the heart of every archetypal tale: as the hero or heroine leaves an often-disturbing home to set off on an uncharted journey, and to face and eventually overcome seemingly impossible challenges, they are led ultimately to develop their highest potential.

We are often drawn to specific stories or characters, and if we explore the reasons why, deeper truths about our life and our character may emerge as a result. As I grow older, the stories that I love most are those which are inhabited by powerful, slightly dangerous and often solitary old women. The wild Cailleach of Gaelic tradition: the old creator-hag who made and shaped the land, and who fiercely guards the wild creatures from excessive human predation. Baba Yaga, the dangerous old woman in the Russian tradition, who is often portrayed as little more than a wicked witch, but who in the oldest stories embodies wisdom, and holds the power of life and death in her hands. These two characters are perfect examples of figures which psychologists call 'archetypal'. This is a term which derives from the work of Carl Jung, a Swiss psychiatrist who suggested that there were two different levels of the human unconscious mind. First, there is an upper level, which he called the 'personal unconscious', and which relates specifically to the individual. But beneath this lies a much deeper 'collective unconscious', which is universal, and 'constitutes a common psychic substrate of a suprapersonal nature which is present in every one of us'.

Jung called the contents of the collective unconscious 'archetypes': inherited potentials or forms which are transformed into universal symbols once they enter into the conscious mind. Archetypal figures include the great mother, father, child, devil, god, wise old man, wise old woman, the witch, the trickster, the hero; archetypal motifs include the apocalypse, the deluge, the creation; archetypal situations might include the battle between good and evil, the heroic task, death and rebirth. These images are shaped by our culture and our own personal history, so that they take on particular and unique meanings and associations for each one of us.

The presence of archetypal images and motifs in myths and fairy tales is one of the main reasons why they're so powerful: they are bridges between the personal and the universal. They are also, in a way, like keys – they are capable of unlocking our imagination, opening the door to the mysteries of our inner lives. In the vehicle of a fairy story, archetypes become more than mere images: they become energies, embedded with instructions which guide us through the complexities of life and show us what we may become – or how we may participate in the becoming of the world.

The Girl Without Hands

A few years ago in my house on the far north-west coast of Scotland, a woman who I'll call Helen sat in a chair in the book-lined study which also served as a consulting room, and wept. Helen, like me at the time, was in her mid-forties. She hadn't long moved to the area from England, and like so many of those who had fled north, driven by the pressure of some strange internal compass, or a more primordial instinct to head for the hills at difficult times, she was escaping from a life which had probably never suited her. Now, though, it had recently taken a greater toll, in the form of a stress-related disorder which had kept her off work for three months. On the day she'd been declared fit enough to go back to her job as the head of human resources in a food company in the south of England for the first time, she had walked out of the building three hours later, having handed in her notice for good.

'I just couldn't bear it,' she said. 'Even though I'd been ill, and not capable of very much in the way of deep analysis of my life, the time spent away from the stultifying routine and the wicked office politics and the long hours and the sheer, utter pointlessness of it all, made me ask seriously for the first time in years what on earth I thought I was doing. Was this really what it was all about? I had a strong sense of time passing, feared that I would just drift into death like this, and then what would my life have been for?' And so, two months later, she found herself in a rented cottage on the outskirts of the village where at the time I was practising a form of narrative psychology, along with hypnotherapy and other techniques for developing the creative imagination.

The move – the space it had created in her life, perhaps – had shaken something loose in Helen, and that something was a resurgence of trauma about a childhood experience of being serially abused by an uncle over a period which she thinks lasted for about three months. It was something she hadn't thought about for years, she said; in fact, she'd simply refused to think about it. Never told anyone, because of the shame. But something in the fragility of her mental state after the stress and the move had brought it all back again. And now, she couldn't sleep for thinking about it. She found herself crying uncontrollably at unpredictable times, and she was beginning to have some physical symptoms of panic. She couldn't understand why it had happened to her; couldn't seem to work her way through it. She couldn't tell me anything about the experience; she couldn't even say the words 'sexual abuse'. 'My uncle hurt me,' was all she could say. She could produce no other words.

And so, very carefully, I told Helen a story: a story which I thought might help. It was the story of 'The Girl Without Hands'. There are many different versions of this story scattered throughout the world, but the one I offered her was this: a man whose wife

Whatever journey we imagine ourselves to be on, myth and fairy tales can inform our sense of what is possible, and enable us not just to cope with life's challenges, but to live more intensely, and more richly, in the world.

has just died wants his beautiful daughter, who is the image of her mother, to marry him in her place. But the daughter will not. And so her father cuts off her hands, and casts her loose. The girl makes her way through the forest and, hungry, slips into the garden of a beautiful palace to pluck pears. But she is caught, and taken to the king – who falls in love with her, marries her, and crafts for her two new hands made of silver.

The new queen gives birth to a son while the king is away at war, and her wicked mother-in-law conjures up a plan to have her and the child cast out again, back into the forest. 'She is driven into nature,' Jungian psychologist Marie von Franz suggests in her analysis of the story: 'She has to go into deep introversion . . . The forest [is] the place of unconventional inner life, in the deepest sense of the word.'[52] The queen then meets an angel who leads her to a hut hidden deep in the woods, and there she takes refuge. Because of her purity of heart, during the seven years that she spends there alone with her child, little by little her real hands magically regrow. When the king returns home and learns what has happened, he comes to the hut in the forest to bring his family home – but the young woman insists that he pay court to her all over again, as the changed woman she now is, seven years on. The king does so, and of course they eventually return to the palace and live happily ever after. And so the Girl Without Hands' transformation is now complete: the wounded child has become a whole, healed woman.

The story had a profound impact on Helen. For one thing, it enabled her to find a different language for what had happened to her – a language that went straight to the heart. She wasn't a 'victim of sexual abuse' – words which she could never say anyway – she had metaphorically had her hands chopped off. She spent some time online and found several different versions of the tale, and she began to think deeply about the various elements of the story. She found herself drawing the Girl Without Hands, thinking and dreaming about her, letting the magic of the images in the story work on her. We talked together about the original image of handless arms; we worked with the image of silver hands; we thought about what it might mean to grow 'real' hands back again, and how they would differ from the artificial ones and even from the old ones. We thought about what it meant to spend time in the forest, and on the Girl Without Hands' gentle insistence to her husband that she had changed now, and shouldn't be taken for granted.

I'd seen this happen before, but whenever it did it was never anything other than magical: the act of simply finding a story – one which offered an extended metaphor for what had happened to Helen – changed everything for her. It allowed her to properly explore, in an imaginative way, something that was too painful to be approached head-on. But more than that, it allowed her to actively transform her own story into a story not just of endurance, but of self-determination. She was, she declared, growing her real hands back now. And over a period of several weeks of exploring that beautiful image, she was able to find enough stability to make some serious decisions about what she wanted to do with her life. The tears had been replaced by an unexpected, quiet expression of joy; and the decisions she was now making were based on a new image of who she was in the world: a wounded girl who had become a whole, healed woman.

Developing the mythic imagination

Find a fairy story which you particularly love, or relate to. It could be one which you loved as a child, but if you can't think of one, flick through any collection of original fairy tales, such as those of the Brothers Grimm, Hans Christian Andersen or Charles Perrault, and choose one which appeals to you. (You can easily find fairy tale collections online if you don't have easy access to books.) It's interesting, but not essential, to choose a story which reflects issues in your own life today.

Once you've found the story you'd like to work with, begin to analyse it and work with it by exploring the following questions:

- What is it about the *plot* of the story (i.e. what happens) which drew you to it?
- Which *scenes* in the story are important to you, and why?

❧ What is the *theme* of the story? When we think about theme, we are asking ourselves what the story is really about. For example, is it about the acquisition of power? About finding true love? Is it about an attempt to overcome an obstacle? Or a search for meaning? Is it about good triumphing over evil? Justice versus injustice? Wisdom coming through suffering? The themes of many myths and folk tales are moral in nature, and focus on lessons that must be learned. They are also designed to espouse particular values which are desirable in the society of origin, such as compassion, generosity, humility. Or, they may represent what are considered to be universal truths.

❧ What *archetypal characters* appear in the story? Do you see yourself, or people that you know, in any of those characters? Do any of them particularly appeal to you, and why?

❧ Is there an *image* or a *symbol* which particularly tugs at you? Myths and fairy tales almost always include powerful visual images, such as a glass slipper, a beanstalk, a spinning wheel, a poisoned apple, a magic lamp, a blue bird . . . these visual elements are among the things which give the tales their enduring strength. Some images have universally agreed-upon symbolism; others may convey different things in different cultures or to different people, and the meaning and emotions attached to them may be profoundly personal. What do the images in your story say to you?

❧ Can you identify any key *motifs* in the story? These are individual details within a tale: a kind of character, an unusual creature, a strange land, a striking occurrence – in other words, any of the elements into which a tale can be broken down. Typical folkloric motifs could include a helpful all-knowing eagle, a wise old woman who provides a critical piece of knowledge, a youngest daughter who

helps a hero prevail against her father, a series of tests
which are set for a hero, a poor hero who ends up rich . . .

🌿 How does the *setting* of the story affect the way you feel
about it? Setting is about both place (where the story is
set) and time (when it takes place). Many folk-tale settings
remove the story from the real world, taking the reader/
listener to a time and place where animals may talk, or
which is inhabited by witches and ogres, and where magic
is commonplace. Often the setting is referred to in vague
terms ('Long ago in a land far away . . .' or 'Once upon a
time in a dark forest . . .'). Some settings may reflect the
typical landscape out of which the tale arose. A story's
setting defines (or confines) its possibilities, and creates
atmosphere. Setting also impacts character (think, for
example, of Hans Christian Andersen's 'The Snow Queen').

🌿 Work with your story creatively in whichever ways seems
nourishing to you. Think about writing or journaling
about any of the elements we've considered above. If
these are activities you enjoy, think about painting, sewing
or any other craftwork . . . or simply meditating on the
story and the images within it.

Living in a storied world

> *It is by such statements as, 'Once upon a time there was*
> *a dragon,' or 'In a hole in the ground there lived a hobbit'*
> *– it is by such beautiful non-facts that we fantastic human*
> *beings may arrive, in our peculiar fashion, at the truth.*
>
> Ursula K. Le Guin, from 'Why Are Americans Afraid of Dragons?'[53]

F*adó, fadó.* Long ago, long ago – the Irish storyteller's equivalent of 'once upon a time'. Whatever the language we speak,
we only have to hear the ritual opening words to a story, and we

are ready to be caught up in its spell. Our fascination with myths, fairy tales and folklore is evidence of our longing for enchantment. It's all around us, reflected in movies based on new visions of old fairy tales – movies which aren't just for children, but for adults, like *The Company of Wolves*, a classic retelling of the story of Red Riding Hood, or the more recent *Snow White: A Tale of Terror*, or *Maleficent*, a new take on Sleeping Beauty. We see it in our persistent fascination with the legends of King Arthur, evidenced in movies like *Excalibur* and *King Arthur: Legend of the Sword*. It's there too in fantasies set in other worlds which are like our own, but which have a strong mythical element, like the hit TV series *Game of Thrones* or Neil Gaiman's *American Gods*. Folkloric stories, themes and characters are constantly being reworked in contemporary children's books (think J.K. Rowling's *Harry Potter* books and Philip Pullman's *His Dark Materials* series) and in drama and pantomime. Historian and mythographer Marina Warner, in her book *Once Upon a Time: A Short History of Fairy Tale*, wrote that fairy tales are 'stories that try to find the truth and give us glimpses of greater things' and, she suggests, 'this is the principle that underlies their growing presence in writing, art, cinema, dance, song.'[54]

It's not just about myths and fairy tales, though; folklore of all kinds is becoming fashionable again. And maybe just in time, as a recent study into the future of traditional British folklore by Center Parcs, the company which runs a holiday village at Sherwood Forest – famous home of the legendary hero Robin Hood – suggested. Their research revealed that nearly a quarter of the people surveyed couldn't name even one story from folklore. When presented with a list of stories, 80 per cent of people were familiar with Robin Hood – no doubt due to the many films based on the character – but when presented with a list of other classic folklore tales and characters – with King Arthur, Jack the Giant Killer and the Loch Ness monster among them – on average those questioned could only recognise just two. Almost two-thirds of people said they didn't intend to pass on the stories to their own children, and one in five couldn't remember the tales to retell them in the first place, which undoubtedly contributes towards the problem. On the other hand, two-thirds of the people surveyed agreed that traditional stories, myths and legends help develop children's imaginations, and almost half thought they help teach children valuable lessons. As many as 70 per cent strongly believed that folklore still plays a part in our society.[55]

This concern about whether specific stories are being forgotten comes at a time when folklore seems nevertheless to be alive and thriving among some segments of the population – certainly among those involved in the creative arts – and is enjoying a resurgence even on social media sites such as Twitter. If you search for #FolkloreThursday, for example, you'll discover a remarkably popular weekly hangout space in which hundreds of people from around the world share snippets of old stories, images of mythical creatures, photographs of folkloric sites, old folk beliefs and local legends.

Dee Dee Chainey is one of the cofounders of #FolkloreThursday, and she told me that they've seen an enormous increase in folklore in the two years since they first began. 'We still find the hashtag trending most weeks,' she said, 'and we now have a Twitter community of almost 16,000 people. We've been hugely excited to see people spending all week researching folklore from around Britain, as well as globally, and asking their parents and grandparents about their old traditions, just so they can come on Twitter that week and share them.'

Like #FolkloreThursday's many followers, Dee Dee is in no doubt about the relevance of folklore today. 'Folklore is not just something old and dead,' she said. 'It's is very much alive, and it includes things like the ways that we think about the food we eat – the food our grandparents taught us to make at the kitchen table, and that we now pass on. It includes the customs we teach our own children, the songs and games our children learn from their friends in the school yard, and the little traditions each family observes at their festivals – whether that's kissing under the mistletoe, or having something old, new, borrowed and blue at a wedding. These are the things that remind us who we are, and the long line of people that we came from. And traditional tales still help us reflect on what it means to be human.'

There is a trickier side to the issue of folklore and identity, though, as Dee Dee explained. 'Folklore is often used to restore a sense of tribal identity based on quite a selective view of the past. Often this can be positive – tying people to the land around

them, providing a sense of environmental responsibility and producing a social cohesion that leads to supporting others in the
community. But it can also be very damaging, and used for ill:
to exclude anyone that doesn't conform to the tribal identity, or
to make a clear division between those who "belong" and those
who are "other".'

A lack of knowledge of traditions and customs is often quoted
as one of the problems people have with those settling into a new
community; it's a problem that many asylum seekers face today.
And yet, Dee Dee believes, folklore can help in these situations,
promoting an understanding of how similar we all are, as well as
an appreciation of our diversity. 'First,' she told me, 'we know that
many folktales and fairy tales have common roots, and undoubtedly spread across the globe because they resonate with the most
basic humanity within all of us, carrying symbols and themes
that we share irrespective of culture, society or personal beliefs.
Each community that receives a tale internalises it, and finds the
threads within it that hold meaning. These threads are rewoven,
and then flow back out into the world as the story is retold, with
added meaning, and added relevance to the new place and different people. Yet they still hold the original themes – the true essence
that makes the tale itself.'

In 1932, a researcher called Stith Thompson (building on the
work of another folklorist, Antti Arne) published a six-volume
Motif-Index of Folk-Literature, which identified common story
elements in traditional stories across the world. These include
characters, objects, actions and events – things like 'theft of fire',
or 'marriage of person to animal', or 'werewolf'. But although
these motifs are remarkably consistent across different countries
and cultures, Dee Dee suggested, the individual tellings highlight
our diversity. 'They show how each community, and each person,
takes a theme or idea and reimagines it. We add our own reference
points: the meal the characters are preparing becomes one we're
familiar with; the stories are embellished with details of the local
clothes, colours, smells that bring the tale alive for every listener,
providing reference points that make the tale their own.'

Dee Dee believes that, for asylum seekers, or others who
struggle to integrate themselves into a new community, exploring
traditional stories together can help foster understanding. 'They

encourage us to think and ask questions about the teller and their lives,' she said. 'A tale might evoke a place and a way of being that is unfamiliar to us, but it offers a doorway through which we can step into this new place and understand this unfamiliar community – because we can navigate it through the points of reference that we do understand. The young protagonist on a journey, as many of us have been; the evil adversary, a symbol of the difficulties we've all faced – we can all relate to these themes, and we find them in different guises in our own traditional stories. And so discussing folk and fairy tales, as well as sharing food traditions, local crafts, traditional music or dance, allows us an inside look at how a person from another culture experiences the world.'

Once upon a time, on an island far to the north of here, on a Saturday evening in summer, a small handful of crofters from neighbouring townships trickled down the road and into an enormous steel barn. This barn, which normally provided winter housing for pigs and a milk-cow, had been transformed with the help of a few bright rugs and hangings into a temporary theatre. Inside that theatre, the audience watched with smiles and faces alight as two travelling storytellers acted out the old Russian story of 'Ivashko Medvedko' ('Little Ivan, Bear-Child') to the accompaniment of an accordion. That, you could say, was proper magic.

The shed was ours, and the wielders of magic were Tom Hirons and his partner Rima Staines. Born and raised on the Suffolk–Norfolk border in England, Tom went on to study theoretical physics but, suspecting that the end result of his studies would be a career watching a computer screen, he took up the trade of leatherworking and focused for a time on crafting beautiful, striking masks. Now, his trade is storytelling and poetry. When Tom and Rima (an artist with a large online following who specialises in uniquely beautiful and distinctive mythical paintings) came to stay with us on the Isle of Lewis, they had only just conceived of these storytelling performances, and were travelling around with their dog Macha in an old red Post Office van, visiting friends and trying it all on for size. But in 2015, they successfully crowdfunded a project which they called Hedgespoken. And Hedgespoken, Tom tells me, is a travelling, off-grid storytelling show, based in a 1960s converted Bedford truck.

It sounds as magical as it seems unlikely. 'It's a dream we're making real,' Tom says: 'to travel slowly up and down this land and beyond, working with enchantment through story. By telling tales and producing theatre and puppetry, and showing that there's a power abroad in the imagination that's there not for the taking, but for the living.'

Their surprisingly successful crowdfunding experience allowed Tom and Rima to convert the Auxiliary Fire Service vehicle into a beautiful tiny home for their small family. But the Hedgespoken truck also has a drop-down stage on the side, making it fit for outdoor performances of many different kinds. 'It was a massive project for us,' Tom tells me, 'with many steep learning curves, made even more intense by the birth of our first child in February of 2015. But part of the impetus behind Hedgespoken was to create a life in which our boy can grow up steeped in a world rich with imagination, nature and wonder.'

The 'nature' part of the equation is especially important to Tom and Rima. 'Having a home on wheels means that the worlds of indoors and outdoors are not as firmly set apart as they can be when living in a settled way. And having that home also function as a theatre and venue for storytelling and music gives us the chance both to support our family as we travel, and to be a centre of creativity as we go. We'll travel from late spring to autumn, and there'll be a stable place in our community here on Dartmoor to return to after the touring season is over.'

Although they believed in its appeal from the beginning, Tom and Rima have been astonished by the way Hedgespoken seems to have captured the imaginations of so many people. 'As soon as work began on the truck, word of Hedgespoken spread far. We've been stunned by the goodwill shown to us in correspondence from all over the world. It seems there's a great hunger for what Hedgespoken has to offer. Something in what we are doing seems to be needed in these crazy times. And the times are crazy – we know it. Everywhere we've gone for years, the conversations around fires, around dinner tables late at night, on long walks across mountains and moors – they're all about the craziness. Where did it come from? What can we do? And how do we live with the grief, the hopelessness, the anger and the fear for ourselves, for our children, for generations to come? How can we best act in these times?'

Tom met Rima in 2010, and he tells me that they began dreaming together very quickly. 'We still have the sketches we made in the first months of our courting, imagining a travelling show even then, a magical wonder-happening. The thing is,' he says, 'we both really believe in stories – we believe they're important. It's essential that they continue to be told. A world without stories is not only as unthinkable as a world without music, but it is a world of death.'

Tom talks a lot about stories as magic, and I ask him what he means by that. What kind of magic? He laughs and shakes his head. 'It's hard to explain in words. There's a power that changes the world in ways that I don't understand. It's as if there's a way of action that strikes or strokes the fibres of reality in such a way that they sing, or resonate, or dance . . . and where there might have been the usual tangle of life, there is instead a symphony or a harmony. Good storytelling can make those fibres sing. For me, that thrum, or hum, or strum is what I live for. It's what we've tried to bring to our storytelling and to our other creative work. That's what we want to propagate with Hedgespoken.'

That's certainly what they propagated on that sunny August evening in our farm shed in the Outer Hebrides. Tom nods. 'That was what we always wanted,' he says: 'to create a theatre that really was of-the-people. We're both romantic – we believe that there's something essential and powerful about arriving unheralded one evening, to perform a single show to a small (or large) audience, and then to leave. Certainly there's magic there – the magic of the village green, the wayside show and the unexpected visitors – and that's what Hedgespoken is really powered by. There's a great tradition, all across the world, of theatre-of-the-people – not the high-brow stuff, however glorious that might be, but a theatre that's accessible, vital, powerful. The stories and shows that travel with Hedgespoken are of necessity revolutionary in flavour – sometimes in subtle ways, and sometimes not. These are the times we live in.'

I ask Tom what's on the cards for Hedgespoken in the future. Are there any plans to expand the nature of their offerings? 'We have big plans,' he says, with a characteristically wide smile. 'Wonder-shows at festivals and fairs, yes, and humbler storytellings along the road as we travel. But there'll be some subversive puppet theatre, for example – we've enlisted the remarkable Howard Gayton as our artistic director, bringing his wealth of experience with Commedia dell'Arte, street theatre, puppetry, mask-work and travelling shows. We're slowly, quietly, assembling a team of performers and creators to travel with us and help us bring something remarkable into the world.

'We also have plans to use Hedgespoken as a vessel for social inclusion – there are so many ways that storytelling and theatre and music can be used for social healing, and our thoughts turned some time ago to the possibilities of using our travelling stage as a way of helping give voice to temporary and excluded communities such as migrant workers, refugees and Gypsy and Traveller communities, and participants in temporary convergences such as protest camps.'

Tom and Rima's way of life – its simplicity, the passion they show for their art, the way that it verges on the folkloric – has captured the imagination of huge numbers of people over the years. Rima's popular and long-running blog, Into the Hermitage, has for many years now made it clear that you don't have to have much in the way of possessions in order to create a life that is rich in beauty.[56] I ask Tom whether inspiring people to live differently is part of the plan.

'In years to come, I think there will be many, many more of us living in the margins,' he agrees. 'And we intend to show that it can be done not just adequately, but beautifully, with triumph and power. In a time of mass movements of populations and mass extinctions of fauna and flora, learning to live in the margins without being crushed is going to be a primary skill we might well all need to learn. Certainly our son won't have to suffer a fear of it all falling apart – he'll grow up well-versed in the art of living with uncertainty in an age of insecurity. But if you're going to live outside the parameters of the mainstream, you have a lot to prove. One way of doing that is to inspire amazement. The human capacity for wonder is without end. Hedgespoken looks amazing, and it is amazing. Driving the lorry back to Dartmoor after our first proper outing, we felt as if we were travelling in a bubble of joy, because everyone who saw it began smiling. In the midst of the craziness, there is the possibility of amazement, and for a moment, something extraordinary becomes possible.

'We're not sure,' Tom says, 'but, here in this old and beautiful Bedford and the thousand dreams it's made of, we think we might have found some kind of Grail.'

In 1962, the French philosopher René Guénon suggested that we live in 'degenerate times', at the end of a long age during which important spiritual truths have been forgotten, the ancient centres of wisdom have been destroyed and the guardians of that wisdom have been dispersed. At such times, he said, a safe repository for spiritual truth can be found in folklore. He suggested that knowledge which is in danger of being lost passes into the symbolic code of a folk tale, and then is passed on to the people. They will perhaps only be concerned with the stories' surface meanings – but they will at least preserve them, and pass them down to their children. Then, in better times, people might once again appear who understand the code, and who will penetrate the symbolic disguise to the wider meaning behind.[57]

Whether or not they contain the encapsulated wisdom of ages past, what is certain is that myths, fairy tales and folklore offer us a world imbued with *participation mystique* – a world in which humans are fully enmeshed. In this world, animals always have something to teach us, trees and plants can save or cure us, wise old men and women are waiting in the dark woods to help us, and a well may be a doorway to another world. Myths and folklore can put us back in touch with the seasons and turnings of the year, and they can restore our acceptance of the necessary cycles of life. They can also remind us that we have a responsibility to future generations, and to the planet as a whole. If we approach myth and story in non-human-centric ways, it places us more firmly into the wider life of the world: our personal story is enmeshed with a greater story of which we're a part. That sense of awe, of connection, of belonging to a mysterious world which has many depths and layers to explore, is missing in so many people's lives today.

Perhaps one of the reasons for the particular resonance of myth and fairy tales these days is the fact that we are inhabiting a world in transition, and a world which seems to be so often in crisis. And crisis is what many myths and almost all fairy tales have at their heart. In most fairy tales the hero or heroine not only survives, but overcomes a monster or other adversary; or escapes from an impossible situation in the face of incredible odds. 'Jack and the Beanstalk', 'Hansel and Gretel' – and my own personal favourites from the Western Isles of Scotland: the many and varied stories of the cattle-tending girl who outwits and escapes from the *each-uisge* – the water-horse – who would drag her into the dark, icy depths of the loch to be his wife. In most versions of this story, the *each-uisge* transforms himself into a handsome young man to make the girl fall in love with him – but she notices the waterweeds dripping among his long dark locks, and realises what kind of creature he is. She persuades him to sit down with her, and then to rest his head in her lap; after he has fallen asleep, she carefully places a moss-covered stone under his head to make him believe she is still there. She runs for her life. Stories of this kind give us insight and hope, as well as teaching us a good strategy or two for our lives.

Dreamwork and the mythic imagination

British scholar Angela Voss has described 'imagination' as 'the mode in which the soul reveals its nature through the language of symbol and metaphor'.[58] The development of an active mythic imagination – an awareness of myth, of symbol and archetype in our everyday lives – can enhance our understanding of who we are and our place in the world, as well as enriching and enchanting every day that we're alive.

Dreams are redolent with archetypal images and motifs, and so dreamwork can be a fascinating way of exploring and building the mythic imagination. If you are not accustomed to remembering and working with your dreams, the following techniques, offered by dreamworker Toko-pa Turner, might be helpful to you:[59]

1. Before going to bed, set the intention to remember your dreams. You may want to re-read some of your previous

dreams to strengthen the waking/dreaming bridge, or meditate on a question you'd like answered.

2. How you wake up is fundamental. Avoid using an alarm clock. Train your body to wake you up instead – you'll be amazed by how accurate the body clock can be.

3. Keep your eyes closed and remain in your waking position. The dream can easily be dislodged (especially by your to-do list), so stay present with the dream, as if carrying a fragile creature across a rickety bridge.

4. If you remember just a fragment, try not to judge or interpret it. Just hold that fragment (be it a scene, image, character or feeling), and 'rehearse' it in your mind several times until it feels solid.

5. Keep a blank journal by your bed and write down everything you remember. Dreams are like lovers; they'll blossom if you pay attention to them and abscond if you ignore or invalidate them.

To develop your mythic imagination through dreamwork, try the following:

- Record your dreams in a dedicated journal.
- Write down the images and symbols which occur, and especially those which recur from dream to dream.
- Are there any archetypal characters, motifs or situations in those dreams?
- Are there any recurring themes?
- Do they remind you of any myths or fairy tales?
- Imagine other ways of working with the images and symbols in your dreams: write about them – prose or poetry, paint them, draw them, knit them or bring them into other art and craftwork you pursue.

The myths we live by

Do the stories live in us, or do we live in the stories? Do we tell the stories, or do the stories tell us? And if they're telling us, then what are they telling us to be? We'd be wise to think a while about that one, because stories shape the way that we see the world, and our place in it. They shape the way we view the nature of our civilisation – why it exists in the first place, and what we should do with it now.

We've always told stories which explain how things came to be. Since the dawn of human history, groups and communities of humans around the world have sat around campfires, or gathered inside royal halls and humble huts, to tell stories to each other about how – and why – the world is. This particular kind of story is called a myth. Myths tend to deal with weighty matters: gods, heroes, the creation of the universe, the purpose and meaning of life; they provide the foundational narratives for entire civilisations, incorporating and organising their beliefs and morals. Which makes it all the more curious that the word 'myth' is often used to convey something quite different today: a belief or idea which is false.

All cultures, all civilisations – all tribes and groups of human beings – have their unique guiding mythology, whether or not it is overtly recognised as such. And these stories which civilisations tell about themselves are the stories which determine the overall shape of individual and communal lives. They determine our worldviews: the assumptions we hold about why things are the way they are, about how things work, about what is valuable and about what is possible. And in turn, these assumptions underlie the choices we make, large and small, every day of our lives.

It's impossible to overstate how profoundly religious stories in particular have changed the world. Wars have been fought because of them, and people put to death because of them. Moral codes and systems of justice have been founded on them. Religious stories are the ultimate example of the ways in which stories can define our existence: if we are believers (and sometimes even if we are not), then based on what happens in them, and based on what their characters say and do, we make our most significant decisions about how to live and die.

There are, of course, other guiding mythologies at work here in the West, as well as religious ideologies; here are a couple of those which seem to me to define the nature of our civilisation, and the nature of the problems we face. Step back for a while, and think about what those cultural mythologies are telling us. How do they actually impact our daily lives?

The myth of more

The myth of more is a myth of progress. Behind it is a belief in the idea of the triumphant journey of an all-conquering mankind towards deathless perfection, as we leave our animal natures behind and launch ourselves on a one-way, linear trajectory towards a perceived mastery of the planet – if not, preferably, of the entire universe. This, we are told, is progress, and progress means more of everything. We must always be striving for more in everything that we do and are: more territory for humans, even to the stars and back; an ever-increasing lifespan; we must constantly be striving for physical perfection and, ideally, for eternal youth. Progress means never sitting still, never counting our blessings – always wanting more, more, more. In order to be fully human, we must want to progress; it's one of our defining characteristics. Otherwise, we're no different from animals.

The myth of more generates the fundamental law which pervades the lives of all of us who live in capitalist countries, and which is a given in all of our societal stories: we must always produce more. More, more, more. And we must buy more of the stuff that is produced, because a) that will make us happy and respected individuals, and b) if we don't, 'the economy' will collapse. And the economy must always grow (though it's interesting to reflect on the fact that no one ever gives us a really good, slam-dunk reason why). In this (dystopian) story inside which we're trapped, all the characters are called consumers, and their value to the world they live in is judged by the level of their consumption. We are, quite literally, what we buy.

If that description seems a bit excessive it's probably because, as British journalist and activist George Monbiot wrote back in 2012, pathological consumption has become so normalised that we scarcely notice it.[60] While researching her film *The Story of Stuff*, Annie Leonard and her co-writers discovered that, in the past three decades alone, one-third of the planet's natural resources have been consumed – but of the goods which flow through our still-expanding consumer economy, only 1 per cent remain in use six months after sale.[61] As Monbiot suggests, 'So effectively have governments, the media and advertisers associated consumption with prosperity and happiness that to say [otherwise] is to expose yourself to opprobrium and ridicule.' And yet, a growing body of psychological research suggests that materialism is associated with anxiety, depression and broken relationships.

But what if we stepped out of that cultural narrative for a moment, and asked ourselves whether this is the story we really want to be in? What if, instead, we chose a different economic model to live by – one which didn't depend on despoliation of the planet for its success? What if, rather than slavishly following the dictates of our global leaders, we laughed at the ads which try to tell us that we need a new smartphone every year, or that we should assess our self-worth by the size of our car? What if we stopped buying the cheap shirts made by children in Bangladeshi sweatshops, or picking up from the supermarket shelves the carefully packaged, factory-farmed pork from pigs who have never seen outside in their lives? What if we found different myths to live by, and what if those myths taught us to truly value what we have, rather than always striving for more? What if they taught us to value enchantment rather than exploitation?

We can be heroes, just for a day

The intense competitiveness of the capitalist model which dominates Western societies is likely to be responsible for the equally intense sense of personal ambition which festers inside so many of us, and the constant striving for individual recognition which we're taught to see as normal. Parents push their children to be the best at everything – at sports, at academic subjects, at the musical instrument they so badly want them to play – pressing them so hard that levels of anxiety, stress, anger and emotional withdrawal are sky-rocketing among children who feel a constant pressure to perform.

This striving to be the best or the greatest is reflected in our cultural worship of the hero: the individual who rises above all others. The most popular books and movies today are profoundly heroic in nature. Look at the storylines of the most successful Hollywood movies: all too often, they can be reduced to the formula: swashbuckling, swaggering hero – male or (increasingly) female – conquers all and ensures that American values prevail. These are the characters that we're supposed to look up to, and aspire to emulate – and among the most popular movie heroes of the past few decades are characters like gun-toting Dirty Harry, ex-soldier Rambo, and fist-flourishing Rocky Balboa. And when common-or-garden heroes aren't enough for us (more, more, more) then there are always the superheroes to help us out: we don't seem set to lose our taste for Batman, Spider-Man and Captain America (or even, improbably, Ant-Man) in a hurry. Vampires, of course, are the new superhero, and teenagers all over the world are falling for them like flies.

Several decades ago, American mythologist Joseph Campbell developed his well-known outline of the 'Hero's Journey'. In his book *The Hero with a Thousand Faces*, Campbell suggested that the world's most important mythological stories share a common framework: they all involve a hero – who happens to be a person of exceptional gifts, which may or may not be recognised by his society. He, or someone he loves, or the world in which he lives, suffers from a symbolic deficiency (in a fairy tale, for example, it might be a missing ring of power, or a bucket of water from the well at the world's end). He must then set out on a great adventure to find the missing treasure and bring it back to the world he left.

The notion of the Hero's Journey is linear, all-conquering and world-saving. It's derived from the intensely individualistic, human-centric cultural mythology that has us firmly in its grip. What, then, would a post-heroic journey look like? The stories which storyteller and narrative consultant Geoff Mead[62] refers to as the 'stories [we would] tell if we considered our purpose to be neither destroying nor saving the world but learning to live more beautifully in the world that we have'?[63] Mead argues that, unlike the classic Hero's Journey, post-heroic stories begin not with a call to adventure but with a fall from grace: something going wrong that

Today's mythical misfits
are rejecting a culture
which values neither
intuition nor imagination,
which values neither
the living land nor its
non-human inhabitants.

causes us to lose our way. 'To find the way back, the post-heroic protagonist must stay constant to what he [or she] really loves and endure long and difficult labours without the aid of magical interventions. Such are the soulful quests of the second half of life,' Mead suggests: 'they take us through the wilderness that lies beyond "happily ever after" to a place of strong, compassionate, maturity where we have found our calling and have learned to be true to what really matters in life rather than obey the dictates of others or the voices of our egos telling us how we ought to behave.'

Most of us, of course, don't think of ideas like progress or heroism as 'guiding mythologies' for our civilisation; we just take it for granted that that's how the world is. The truth is, we have no idea how much we've been conditioned. Our social, economic and political institutions – as well as our own daily lives – are so embedded in this story that it's hard for us to imagine there is anything outside it. That's how dominant cultural narratives (the ones which tell us how we must live) gain their power over us.

It's also interesting to ask who these people are who define and refine these stories for us, and you don't have to think for very long before realising that they're the people with 'authority'; the people who always seem to have their voices heard. They're scientists, politicians, interest-group lobbyists, economists, the heads of major corporations and their spokespeople, and members of the media . . . all these groups, and more, determine both the shape and the content of the dominant narrative which is presented to us. Just as important, they also determine the narratives which are *not* presented to us. Equally fascinating is that they do not present their offerings as stories at all – and certainly never as the foundational myths of our culture – but as definitive and unassailable explanations of how the world simply is.

But the way the world *is*, according to these stories, doesn't seem particularly well-designed for anyone other than the wealthiest and most powerful segments of the human population. It's not designed for the starving human masses in the desert countries, and it's not designed for the vanishing non-human species which comprise the Sixth Mass Extinction of life on this planet. There is no doubt, as theologian and cultural historian Thomas Berry argued several decades ago in his essay 'The New Story',[64] that humanity needs a new story to live by, and a new paradigm for what it means to be human. Berry proposed that such a story should incorporate an 'integral vision' in which '[h]uman persons bear the universe in their being as the universe bears them in its being'. In other words: one in which we see ourselves as an intrinsic part of the world around us, not as separate.

But there's the interesting thing: what if, searching for new stories to live by, we actually looked back at those old stories again – the fairy tales we loved as children, and the myths which entrance us still as adults? What if we could find some clues there – in the stories which tell us that we are part of this living, breathing world around us? The stories which taught us and inspired us for millennia – the stories which, today, are largely dismissed as primitive, and relegated to the domain of children. Like the old Irish tale of the great cow of plenty, the Glas Ghaibhleann (pronounced 'Gavlen'). She was a great cow whose milk flow was so abundant that she could feed multitudes, and she travelled the land, giving her creamy milk to anyone who needed it, filling whatever vessel they carried, no matter how large or how small. But when a wicked person tried to take more than her share by placing a sieve under the cow – which enabled her to fill many buckets placed underneath the sieve, because of course the sieve never seemed to be full – the magical cow disappeared forever from the earth, offended by such greed. Or like the rich body of old European stories about the quest for the Grail, in which the question the adventuring knight must ask in order to gain the Grail, heal the wound of the Fisher King, and so heal the Wasteland, is a simple, pointed, empathic, 'What ails thee?'

These are the stories which offer us a more enriching set of values to live by. They show us that the greatest treasure of all is a kind heart; the most powerful magic always is made from an act of love; and no life-saving or world-changing goal can ever be achieved without the help of a community of others – human and non-human alike. These are the stories which remind us that, tucked up in the rambling, roundabout lines between once upon a time and happily ever after, lie all the secrets for a meaningful, sustainable life.

The mythical misfits

The stories we tell about ourselves – our personal myths – are intimately related to these collective myths; our own individual stories develop and are played out inside the wider stories of our time. Jungian analyst D. Stephenson Bond, in his book *Living Myth*, used the phrase 'falling out of myth' to describe what happens to us when we can't live by the dominant myth of our culture any more – when the ways of life that previous generations pursued, when the values they espoused and beliefs they held, become intolerable to us.[65] A cultural myth contains the collective visions, hopes and fears of all the individuals who are born into that culture. It is alive and thriving when it offers up a way of life which inspires us, nourishes us and satisfies our need for meaning. But when the heart bleeds out of our cultural myth and it grows arid and lifeless, we in turn become alienated and rootless. Our lives are lived outside of any meaningful context; they become in a sense 'unstoried'. In his book *The Cry for Myth*, psychoanalyst Rollo May wrote about the ways in which the loss of myth in contemporary life has led to a sense of rootlessness, restlessness and loneliness. 'The person without myth,' he said, 'is a person without a home . . . The loneliness of mythlessness is the deepest and least assuagable of all. Unrelated to the past, unconnected with the future, we hang as if in mid-air.'[66] Because myth is many things, but above all myth is meaning. If we fall out of myth, we fall out of meaning.

In every generation there are people who fall out of the dominant cultural myth, but today it seems that there are more than ever before. And that's because our cultural myth is dying. If we cast aside the veil we habitually wear to shield us from our unendurable everydays, and look around with clear and wide-open eyes, it's not a thriving, vibrant Western civilisation that we'll see, but rather the consequences of the increasingly rapid disintegration of a morally degenerate guiding mythology. We might be richer, but we're certainly not happier, and the world around us is rapidly going to hell in the proverbial hand-basket. I don't need to talk about all the ways here: every one of us knows it, and the evidence is stacked up high for us to see in every media outlet, on the streets of every village, town or city, in every forest and field in the world.

The world is warming, animals are dying, crops are failing, people are starving and our 'leaders' are still fiddling while Rome burns. That's what we've achieved, with all our fine myths of progress and superiority. Cultural values and morals once taken for granted are dissolving at a frightening pace.

In *Ragnarök*, A.S. Byatt offers up a twenty-first-century retelling of the old Norse myth about the end of the world and the death of the gods. These gods deserve to die, Byatt suggests in her Afterword, for they are just like we are now. They have abandoned the Earth. They are 'limited and stupid . . . They are greedy and enjoy fighting and playing games . . . They know Ragnarök is coming but are incapable of imagining any way to fend it off, or change the story.'[67] Our story needs to change, and it needs to change before it's too late – before we perpetrate our own, rather less picturesque, version of Ragnarök. There'll be no happy ending possible in that story – neither for us, nor the Earth.

Change begins with individuals, and it begins with imagination. It begins with a different story which succeeds in capturing the imagination more effectively than the now-crumbling old story. And if the dominant cultural myth is failing us and failing the planet, then we need to transform it. Why not? After all, humans have always been mythmakers. Carl Jung wrote that when the myths of earlier generations fall into decline, the mythmaking process resides in individuals. The birth of a new personal myth in the imagination of a single individual, or a group of individuals, he said, might lead to the rebirth of new (and more functional) myths in the imagination of the culture.

It's the people who I think of as the 'mythical misfits', then, who kickstart the transformation of the world, and who begin to imagine more sustainable and meaningful ways of living. Today's mythical misfits – among them, many of the people who are scattered through the pages of this book – are rejecting a culture which values neither intuition nor imagination, which values neither the living land nor its non-human inhabitants. They're deserting the stagnant institutions, and creating communities which celebrate life rather than destroying it. When the great blazing bonfire of a culture goes out, what remains are a few individual flames. When those individual flames come together, we can kindle a new fire.

That fire's name is enchantment.

Which are the cultural myths you see operating in the world around you, and in your own life?

 Can you think of any old myths and fairy tales which offer up more ecologically aware, community-focused values to live by?

The Magic
of the Everyday

7. Coming home to ourselves

Everything is Waiting For You
After Derek Mahon

Your great mistake is to act the drama
as if you were alone. As if life
were a progressive and cunning crime
with no witness to the tiny hidden
transgressions. To feel abandoned is to deny
the intimacy of your surroundings. Surely,
even you, at times, have felt the grand array;
the swelling presence, and the chorus, crowding
out your solo voice. You must note
the way the soap dish enables you,
or the window latch grants you freedom.
Alertness is the hidden discipline of familiarity.
The stairs are your mentor of things
to come, the doors have always been there
to frighten you and invite you,
and the tiny speaker in the phone
is your dream-ladder to divinity.

Put down the weight of your aloneness and ease
into the conversation. The kettle is singing
even as it pours you a drink, the cooking pots
have left their arrogant aloofness and
seen the good in you at last. All the birds
and creatures of the world are unutterably
themselves. Everything is waiting for you.

David Whyte[68]

THE TABLE IN my kitchen has never belonged to anyone else; it was newly made for me. It arrived, unnecessarily smothered in plastic wrap, ready to assemble: a five feet by three feet, pale, smooth slab of Finnish pine, with a tiny drawer set into one of the longest sides; and four neatly carved, thick, round legs. My first job was to wax it – because I'll freely admit, I've never been a fan of varnish or lacquer. Wax brings the wood alive, and allows it to breathe. You are nourishing your furniture with the rich secretions of bees, and as you apply it and carefully move the cloth across the surface, it is as if you are rubbing yourself into the table, helping it come to know you. *Look*, you are saying. *Here I am! What a life we'll have together!* After three good coats of beeswax my table was shiny and ready to be set in its place.

Eight years on, this table has scars. The physical scars are obvious: a dent or a deep scratch here, a bone-deep stain there, set in wood which has warmed and darkened through daily exposure to light. The other scars are harder for strangers to decipher, but I know they're there. This table has kept watch over all of our dramas, seen so many dreams unfold and so many dreams fade. When we moved back to Ireland four years ago after our ill-fated crofting days on the Isle of Lewis, I banished this table from my kitchen. I feared that it knew too much, and I wanted to move on. But I missed it, this solid, homely witness to my life. Because yes – that is where its magic lies: this table is my witness; there is little it doesn't know. It has propped up humans and sheltered dogs. Heard so many stories, old and new; so many conversations, day and night. It has seen love flicker and almost fade, it has seen tears, and anger, and despair. But it has shared our joys and celebrated our triumphs; it's offered up tea and wine, and participated in our feasts. This is the most multilingual of tables: it understands English, Irish and Scottish Gaelic, and it's intimately familiar with the French of Belgian chanteur Jacques Brel. Who knows me like this table?

The table has been restored, now, to my kitchen: a place-holder for life as it happens. Each guest who comes to the house is invited first to the table, and as we take our seats it is as if we are embarking on the oldest of rituals, crossing a strange communal threshold. Now we are in the sharing space, the sacred space of Irish tradition, where food and drink are offered always to strangers or to friends. Often we'll stay there for hours, for there is an intimacy in sitting round a table that I find to be absent from the distance of carefully arranged sofas and chairs. Across a table, you are looking closely and directly into another pair of eyes, meeting soul-to-soul, and the table invites you to reach out, touch a hand, engage. *Here we all are*, the table whispers. *What mysteries will we uncover and share together today?*

Here now, in our new Connemara home, a tall pine bench stretches along one side of the table, backed up against the yellow-ochre wall. This is where I like to sit, and after our evening meal is done, more often than not I'll stretch my legs out on the bench, lean back into the well-padded cushion at the corner, and David and I will talk into the night. He sits directly across from me, on a lovely light oak armchair with a high slatted back. Other chairs are brought to the table at need: old pine chairs from my days in America, with slightly frayed cream covers and brightly coloured rugs thrown over their backs. Each one has its history; every chair is loved and known, and carries some residue of all the friends who have sat on it and shared their stories around that fine and sturdy wooden table.

Yes, I have my own place at this table, just as I have my preferred, beloved, chipped old mug, and my favourite glass for wine, and an ancient jug with a glued-together handle that I can't bear to part with. All of these things are memory-carriers. All of them speak to me of *home*.

 What objects – things that you have found yourself, rather than those which have been inherited or passed down from your family – speak to you of home? What is it about them which makes them special?

What is home? The answer may be different for each of us. Home is a container, and the container may be large or small. As large as the planet, or as large as a country – the land that we came from, or to which, for whatever reason, we feel we belong. Home is family: the humans and other creatures we share our lives with. In my case, it's a husband, three collie dogs, a little black cat and an unexpected orange tabby kitten – home has more than its fair share of legs and tails. Home is a quality of the things you carry through life with you: a many-scarred table, or your hands cupped around that favourite mug. Home for me includes a set of books that has travelled with me around the world; until my books are unpacked and set on their shelves, I never fully feel as if I've arrived.

For all of us, though, home begins with the building we live in: the place we return to, to sleep each night. Home means shelter – but sometimes it shelters sorrow. Home isn't always associated with good memories. Our childhood homes may or may not have been safe places; they may or may not have been places where we flourished. There was a room in a red-brick house on the rough edgelands of a council estate in the north-east of England where I remember waking up for the first time. It housed an enormous dark wardrobe which might, one day, have led me to Narnia if I hadn't been too fearful to open its door. There was another house with too many cockroaches, and another with too few hiding places, and I do not believe that I ever felt truly at home until, at eighteen, I left it.

I dreamed about 'a home', though, as a child: one which would be safe, and beautiful, and wild. When I was six or seven years old, I found the home I had dreamed of in a book. The book was by Enid Blyton, and it was called *Hollow Tree House*. Susan and Peter, the main characters, were going to be placed in a children's home by their cruel aunt. And so they ran away, and set up home in the huge hollow trunk of an enormous tree that they had discovered in the heart of a forest. They filled it with very simple furniture, a clock, a painting; they adopted a red squirrel for a friend, and made it into exactly the kind of home I had always wished for. It was utterly perfect: a safe space, a most unlikely and hidden place, a place far away from the treacheries of adults, in the midst of the rich, loamy life of a wild green wood.

I never did get to live in a tree, though I've occupied many different buildings since. Sometimes I think I've had too many homes,

Once I lived in a
house which refused
me . . . When I left it,
I felt as if I were running
for my life. A house is a
living being, and it isn't
always benign.

but every room, apartment or house I have chosen to live in during my adult life has challenged me or cherished me, and reflected back at me a fragment of who I am – or who I run the risk of becoming. A tiny room of my own in a hall of residence at the University of Liverpool, reverberating with all the uncertainties and inadequacies of my first year cast out into the world, alone. The bay-windowed bedsit in a quiet street in Muswell Hill where I finished up my PhD and had my heart properly broken for the first time. A Parisian apartment in Montmartre which, for six months, was altogether too beautiful to be true. The first place I ever owned: a tiny, characterless terraced house in east London, where I never could find the remotest of ways to feel I belonged. The perfect refuge of a dilapidated Connemara cottage which saw the crumbling of my first marriage and which never, ever let go of its hold on my heart. A beautiful but impossible old farmhouse in the hills of Kentucky, a lonely lakeside house in Georgia, a croft on a heartbreakingly bleak island at the farthest western reaches of the British Isles. Each of these buildings, and too many others to mention, has gathered into its walls a piece of me. I am scattered in fragments through a multiverse of homes.

Make a list of all the houses and/or places you've ever lived. How would you describe, in just a sentence, what happened to you in each of those places? What parts of yourself did you leave behind in them?

A confession of faith in stone

The house shelters day-dreaming, the house protects the dreamer, the house allows one to dream in peace.

Gaston Bachelard, from *The Poetics of Space*[69]

Our houses contain us, for better or for worse, and as we travel on through the years it is not just our relationships with people which define us, but our relationships with the buildings in which we dwell. They may wrap us up cosily in warm, welcoming walls or they may shrug us off – but whatever we imagine, they are rarely just passive backdrops to the drama of our all-too-human lives. At fifty years old, on the Isle of Lewis, I lived in a house which refused me. Marriages had ended there, lives had been taken and people had gone mad. That house (and that place) challenged me and almost broke me. When I left it, I felt as if I were running for my life. A house is a living being, and it isn't always benign.

When I was a small child I began from time to time to experience a very strange sensation which I took to calling 'The Twilight Zone', after the spooky and unsettling television series which was being shown at the time. It was a distinctive and deeply unpleasant feeling which began somewhere in the region of my stomach, travelled up through my throat, and ended with a kind of hollowed-out, or maybe slightly spaced-out, set-apart emptiness in my head. If I were to try to characterise it now, I'd think of it as a curious feeling of profound *unbelonging*. A perception of being entirely in the wrong place; a sense of loss intermingled with a strange kind of silent keening. It only ever happened when I was somewhere I couldn't make any sense of, some place in which I couldn't find any sense of myself. It never happened outside; it only ever happened in houses, and almost always in houses which belonged to other people.

That occasional but oddly distressing feeling of unbelonging followed me into adult life. It happened to me in student accommodation, and in the dreary, all-too-temporary London bedsits I flitted in and out of during my early academic years. It happens to me still sometimes in the houses of others – even people I'm close to. It's one of the reasons why I find it so hard to sleep in the homes of my friends. Perhaps it's a kind of claustrophobia, an oversensitivity to the mental and emotional 'emanations' of the people in those houses, caught and held tight inside the walls. And perhaps that's why, in all of the places I've lived in, I've always found it necessary at the earliest possible stages to put as much of myself into them as I can. There is no house I've ever moved into where I haven't immediately and feverishly painted over every wall, every piece of woodwork, the inside of every cupboard and hidey-hole – as if, by quite literally painting myself into the house I am painting over whatever might have happened there before, painting over the residue of others, making the place mine: tranquil and safe. It's the only way I can ever begin to relax into a new home.

That yearning for a place to escape to which reflects our own needs, and our own personality, becomes especially critical for those of us who lived in shared spaces. No matter how much we might love our partners or our children, there is always some longing for a room of our own – a place where we can be entirely ourselves, indulge in our passions (no matter how messy), or create a haven of tranquillity on the fringes of a busy family home. This undoubtedly explains the boom in 'posh sheds' for women, which are beginning to make solid gains on the man-caves that have existed for decades, if not centuries, in our garages or back gardens. The interior design magazine's portrayal of the classic woman's shed is stereotypically feminine: clean white walls and floral prints – but just as many are brightly coloured, chaotic havens for fledgling artists and crafts-people. Lately, I have begun longing for what I insist on calling a 'Baba Yaga' hut: a simple wooden shed in a hidden corner of our land, preferably among the trees. There would be no electricity there, no 'mod cons', nothing much to separate me from the outside. I would fill it with feathers and fleece, with found bones and bundles of herbs. I don't really know what I would do there, other than to sit sometimes, and pretend that I might one day grow into a magical old woman who lived alone in a wood. But whatever form these sheds and huts that we long for take, they are above all sacred spaces: places where we can fully express our imagination; places for creativity, solitary reflection and relaxation.

In my home in Connemara, I am fortunate enough to have a large and light-filled, dedicated room for my writing and other creative work. It is situated on the far side of the main house, with its own entrance, and so it is easy for me to shut the door and lock myself into a world of my own. Every item in this room has meaning for me; nothing lasts long in it which does not. On every surface there are fragments of things recovered from the natural world, and of the creatures which have a special place in my imagination. The skull of a fox; the fractured shell of a heron's egg, the wing feather of a raven. A rattle made from the hide and rib bone of a horse. A mermaid's purse, driftwood, smooth pebbles from a Donegal beach. Paintings of wolf and bear, of the Cailleach who shaped the land of Ireland, and of Morgan, the Lady of the

Lake. There are bright splashes of colour here, layers of textile from travels around the world, rough wood and stone. One wall is completely lined with books. It is entirely lived-in, and a little chaotic: beautiful to me in a quite different way from the perfectly coordinated, sanitised, over-designed homes that magazines and television programmes tell us we should aspire to.

In one way or another, our homes are mirrors of the people we are and the things we care about. As French philosopher Gaston Bachelard suggested, the house is 'the topography of our intimate being', both the repository of memory and the lodging of the soul. Our homes embody us: the nature of the building, the way we decorate and furnish it, the objects we bring into it. Think of the houses in fairy tales, which are never simply houses: they are symbolic dwellings which offer a glimpse into the souls of the people who inhabit them. The too-sweet, too-good-to-be-true Gingerbread House which Hansel and Gretel find in the woods – a sticky fly-trap, if ever there was one. Baba Yaga's frightening hut in the heart of the woods, which could run on chicken legs and was surrounded by a fence of skulls. Or Rapunzel's high tower, unscalable and impenetrable . . . These houses are no mere backdrops: each one of them contains potent and archetypal symbols which reflect the psyche of the character who lives in it. And each of us contains inside of us a beautiful palace hidden behind a wall of thorns, a dark, dusty room filled with the bones of dead loves, a fire-filled cave in which the most beautiful tapestry in the world might be woven.

In 1923, when he was forty-eight years old, Carl Jung began to construct for himself a two-storey stone tower in the village of Bollingen, on the upper shores of Lake Zürich. He built the tower over a period of four years, making his own paintings on the walls, carving the stone and digging a well. He added to it slowly for the next twelve years, and spent large portions of every year of his life living there. Jung was very clear about his reasons for building his stone tower: he intended it, in some way, to externalise his psyche. He imagined that the spontaneous, undesigned creation of this very personal dwelling-place would reveal to him some essential aspect of his own nature which all of his writings had failed to make clear. 'Words and paper,' he said, 'did not seem real enough to me; something more was needed. I had to achieve a kind of representation in stone of my innermost thoughts and of the knowledge I had acquired. Or, to put it another way, I had to make a confession of faith in stone.' For Jung, in the end, the tower was more than just a symbol of psychic wholeness: it was the place where he felt he was most deeply himself. 'At Bollingen,' he wrote, 'I am in the midst of my true life . . . There is nothing in the Tower . . . with which I am not linked.'[70]

> 🌿 In what ways does your home, warts and all, reflect core aspects of the person you imagine yourself to be?

> 🌿 How can you make your home reflect core aspects of the person you would like to become? What objects, artwork, symbols can you bring to it which will remind you of this? How can you declutter, and clear away the things which have become obsolete or unnecessary – which you've maybe outgrown?

> 🌿 If you could have a hut or shed as a sanctuary, what kind of place would it be? Or if you already have such a thing, what makes it a sanctuary? What deep longings would/ does it satisfy in you? What part of your soul would be/is nourished by it?

Most of us, of course, do not have the luxury of constructing dwelling places like Jung's tower; we are constrained by what is available (or what we can obtain planning permission to build) in the places where we live and work – and critically, of course, by what we can afford. But more and more people are seeking radically different ways of being at home. The trend towards 'tiny houses' is one of those, and it is deeply responsive to the times we're living in. The tiny house movement consolidated itself in America, and brought together a variety of very different people who, for one reason or another, wanted to 'downsize' their living spaces. The average American home currently stands at around 2,600 square feet, but the typical tiny house is under 500 square feet, and may often be as small as 100.

People take to tiny houses for a wide range of different reasons, including the obvious financial benefit – they cost significantly less to construct and maintain than standard houses, and don't require enormous mortgages which take a lifetime of slavery to pay off. But the tiny house movement also reflects a desire which seems to be growing in more and more people for a life which is simpler, less cluttered, freer – and which carries with it a much lower environmental burden. In this, it flies in the face of a society which tells us that bigger is always better, and which conditions us to want more and more *stuff* in an endless pursuit of status, and the self-defeating goal of 'having it all'. Tiny houses thumb their noses at such excess. *We are enough*, they proudly declare – and indeed, their tininess seems to encourage innovative, well-crafted and often surprisingly beautiful design.[71]

For those who want to find ways of living which are more in tune with the needs of the planet, but who find the idea of tiny houses challenging, the growing trend for 'ecovillages' might offer a way to go. The Global Ecovillage Network[72] defines an ecovillage as 'an intentional or traditional community using local participatory processes to holistically integrate ecological, economic, social, and cultural dimensions of sustainability in order to regenerate social and natural environments'. Ecovillages, they say, are living models of sustainability, which 'represent an effective, accessible way to combat the degradation of our social, ecological and spiritual environments'. They consist of urban or rural communities of people who want to integrate a supportive social environment with a low-impact way of life. And so they're founded on commitments to grow as much of their own (organic) food as they can, to use local and eco-friendly materials for building their houses, to protect the biodiversity of their places, and to preserve clean soil, water and air through proper energy and waste management.

But whether or not we are suited to life in the community of an ecovillage, the ethical and environmental choices we make in building the houses of the future are critically important if we want to change the prevailing narrative of the way we should live in the world. A 'good' house – a house which is responsive both to environmental needs, and to our own human needs for

deep engagement with and a sense of belonging to our homes –
doesn't have to be the perfect example of vernacular architecture.
It doesn't have to be hewn out of wood or stone – but it is a building which in some sense blends into and reflects back (or which, at
a minimum, isn't inimical to) the landscape where it is situated. A
good house is a dwelling which is eco-friendly, and which, where
possible, uses natural materials for construction, furnishings and
decorating. This is the foundation for enchantment in the places
we call home: enchanted homes are places where the artisanal, the
handmade, rather than the mass-produced, is valued; places which
are not crammed full of miscellaneous *stuff*, but in which (whether
it is in the minimalist tradition or more in line with country clutter)
every item is carefully chosen, loved and valued.

Her desire to create a home which sat lightly on the planet meant
that these were exactly the kinds of issues and choices which
Joanna Gilar grappled with, when she and her husband Eurik
decided to build a little house in the corner of her mother's garden
in Sussex, in the south of England. Joanna is a writer, academic
and storyteller,[73] and she told me that she wanted to build a home
which honoured her 'entanglements with the earth'. 'I had fantasies
of a small, basic, straw-bale house in the space at the very back of
our land,' she said, 'where little else sits but trees, wild rabbits and
Himalayan balsam. I wanted a house that would fit in: that would
exist as just another word in the endless babbling conversation of
that field.'
But the complications of the English planning system meant
that they would have had to spend years fighting for permission
to build such a house. After seeking advice, they stumbled across
another option: to build a kind of static caravan which would sit
close enough to Joanna's mother's house that it would be classified as an 'adjacent dwelling' – effectively, an external extension.
They wouldn't need planning permission for this, just a legal cer-
tificate which would be much easier to obtain. Because Joanna
had just discovered that she was pregnant, and they now had a
strong sense of needing their own space, they decided to go ahead
with this faster route to having a home of their own. They found
a company which specialised in the kind of house they would need
to build, and which seemed able to build them rapidly, efficiently

and ecologically. Just two months before their son was born, the building process began.

'Although we'd had to sacrifice our field-hobbit-house for the sake of getting things done,' Joanna told me, 'I was still passionate about creating a house that was not only beautiful, but that addressed my concerns and questions about the way we live now. But it wasn't easy to achieve: instead, the building company besieged us with catalogues of glossy perfection, of floors and doors and stylishly rustic windows. And although all of these met modern regulations for things like energy usage, they were "ecological" in the box-ticking, bureaucratic sense, not in the sense of stopping and asking – are they really needed? Because I was very much aware that for every five houses built in the UK, the equivalent of one house goes to landfill, and I didn't want to be part of that.'

Joanna found herself, then, in continuous negotiation with the builders about possibilities of doing things differently. 'I was constantly asking questions. Is cement a necessity? (Yes.) Are there ways of making it more gentle, less pernicious? (Yes.) Are there things which may come into our house from junk yards and not factories? (Yes.) How much and how many? Can I source them? Can we use them? The builders were open-minded, but the impulse and planning had to come from me, and I'm a storyteller with a doctorate in fairy tales – I had no idea if I could create something solid and lasting in this utterly different realm, and I feared both for my sanity and the house.'

The groundwork, she said, was one of the most challenging struggles that the couple faced. 'I found it extremely difficult to give the go-ahead to cut down the trees and clear the space for the work, and to pour cement on what was once a patch of earth and wild bluebells. But given that we had to, I wanted the most ecological option possible, which I'd discovered was cement mixed with potash, created from factory waste, so part-recycled. This was the option recommended to me by a company which specialised in low-carbon building, but unfortunately they couldn't tell me where to get it. I spoke to countless ground-workers, none of whom had any idea what I was talking about. I spoke to multiple suppliers, who were utterly flummoxed that a confused pregnant woman who had no idea how to speak the language of the building trade was asking about the percentage of potash in their cement supplies. I finally found the one builder in the whole of Sussex who could help us. He was a gentle tradesman who arrived with a beagle puppy in the back of his van. While his puppy dashed about our garden, he considered the space and its beauty, understood absolutely what I was talking about, and agreed to supply us with potash cement with no issue and a great price.

'The next week he emailed me to say he'd been offered a larger contract and would have to pull out. I emailed him to ask if he could let me know at least where to get the cement, but I never heard back. It was at this moment, with a building schedule that wouldn't wait, that I held up my hands. Come on, I said to myself. It's just cement. The world does not revolve around how much recycled content you have in your cement. The house will not stand or fall because of it. So we went with the ground-worker recommended by the building company, who dug up the trees with efficiency and covered the space with absolutely normal concrete.'

But for every lost opportunity, Joanna insisted, there were plenty of successes too. Disregarding the scepticism of the building company, who had suggested they should buy new roof tiles and then cover them with yoghurt to make them look vintage, they found a salvage yard which could supply enough reclaimed tiles to cover the roof and more (the leftover tiles, she told me, smiling, were passed onto a friend in exchange for six bottles of prosecco). They found their floor on eBay; it had once been a squash court. They found reclaimed internal doors on the Gumtree classified ads website, and stones for the front steps in another reclamation yard – but they are clearly proudest of their kitchen. 'I wanted to buy a second-hand kitchen,' Joanna explained, 'but Eurik didn't, and so instead he found David, an artisan carpenter in Brighton, who agreed to gather up all of the abandoned scaffold boards that had accumulated around the building site, and craft them into a kitchen.'

The process of building the house was, Joanna said, a constant conversation – not just between herself and Eurik, but with the people who were building the house. 'Once,' she told me, 'David the carpenter said to me, when we were arguing about whether or not we needed to buy freshly felled wood for the inside of the kitchen cupboards, or could instead use some old plywood which would otherwise be thrown away: "Surely, at the end of the

Above all, open the
windows wide: break
down the barriers, and
let the inside out, and
the outside in.

day, you just want the best kitchen." But I didn't, I wanted to say. Not in the sense of the factory-line perfection which creates great lumbering shadows of trash to be hidden away in other places. My kitchen should not only be a beautiful *presence* in my house, but a beautiful *absence*, carving a space out of the massive accumulation of things we no longer need or want.

'These dialogues were exhausting, but they weren't empty. One of the most moving moments of the build was when I stepped into our half-built kitchen building site, carrying my son in a sling on my chest, and David said to me: "I've had the most wonderful idea." He'd been struggling with how to make the handles for our kitchen cupboards, and his plan was to use the rusty poles from the fence of a tennis court that was being dismantled behind our house. I said: "Er – maybe . . ." And Eurik said: "Is he joking?" But David arrived in the morning, a bit dishevelled, to tell us that he'd taken a few home to experiment with and they had worked so well he'd stay up all night to finish them. Somewhat alarmed, we all trooped down to the kitchen. They hadn't been painted or altered, only lacquered, so that all of the moss, peeling silver paint and rust was preserved. He was right. They were perfect. Later, he said to me that he appreciated working on our build because there was space to be creative. It was moments like this that made the constant negotiations worthwhile.'

When I asked Joanna what she learned from the experience, and what advice she would pass on to others who were similarly struggling with limited time, budget and resources, and yet who wanted to build a house which was responsive to environmental concerns, she told me that there are two things she would do differently. The first relates to community. 'I would choose with far more care and mindfulness who we worked with to create the house. We did this later on, but not at the beginning. The decision at the beginning was made for the sake of efficiency, the illusive but seductive excitement of rapid production. We did our best with the building materials, but there are things – saving energy, avoiding the use of toxic substances – that didn't get done, because we didn't call up the right people to join in. Building the house made me realise just how dependent we are on the community of workers, traders, suppliers and others in which we are enmeshed. This build was a confusing and difficult process, and it made me realise that change has to come by making things different together, so that the whole world looks up and says: "Okay. I felt that."'

The second thing she would do differently, she said, is to remember to enjoy it. 'One of the hardest times for me was the week when my mum's beautiful garden turned into an ugly maze of ditches, cables and pipes. It felt like a symbol of exactly what was so difficult for me about building the house – that invasive feeling of making such a mess in a world that is straining to contain our turmoil. And I think I got so involved with working to allay this that often I forgot what an amazing thing it was that we were doing. Although acknowledging our crisis is absolutely fundamental, I also think that, whatever we might do to balance or answer to our ecological guilt, if we don't do those things joyfully then they don't have creative heart. And it's creative heart which changes everything.'

But Joanna believes that the way you build a house is only one aspect of engaging fully and deeply with the place you intend to call home. 'One of the problems with the way we live now is that we think too much about big steps, and forget the small ones. Of course, how you build a house is crucial to your relationship to it. But I think perhaps more important is how you *tend* it. Our house now is a wonderful place: the combination of our stubbornness for creative reclamation and the builders' more traditional efficiency and experience has created a place which is unique and beautiful. But I didn't properly feel this until I began the continuous engagement of care for it. What we are in relation to the house, and what the house is in relation to us, is something not static, but constantly becoming. I think what's crucial to me is that we have built a house in which the mundanity of the domestic is also creative. And I think I'm excited to see what else the house and we will create together.'

Joanna's sense of relationship to her house – a commitment to the process of growing, changing and becoming in relationship with it – is fundamental to the art of living in a state of enchantment. The houses which shelter us and nurture us and our loved ones are worthy not just of our attention, but of our devotion. They are intrinsic to the fabric of our lives, and deserve to be fully inhabited, loved and filled with beauty. They deserve too to be filled with life: save a corner for the odd family of spiders; cherish the bats that have chosen to make their home in your attic. Put away the chemical weapons and allow a little 'good, clean dirt':* our bodies were made from it and for it. And above all, open the windows wide: break down the barriers, and let the inside out, and the outside in.

The enchanted garden

> *We have strayed off course and need to find our way again.*
> *An old pathway, overgrown and forgotten, is waiting*
> *impatiently to lead us back home.*
>
> Mary Reynolds, from *The Garden Awakening*[74]

Home is a building, but home for the most fortunate among us might be a garden too – though if you had asked me, when we first moved to our new house in Connemara in the early spring of 2017, I would have told you that it was surrounded not by a garden, but by a bramble thicket. There I sat, like some wistful, ageing Briar Rose in a sea of thorns – ensorcelled not in a palace, but in the run-down, long-neglected grounds of a dilapidated 1970s bungalow. But after watching through weeks of relentless growing and greening, I would have told you, by midsummer, that I lived in a wood. It is a small wood, covering less than half of a strangely shaped one-acre plot, but it is a wood nevertheless.

There are silver ladies in my wood: tall, stately birches, their ageing bark deeply scored with black. Birch is the first tree in the old Ogham tree alphabet of Ireland: the tree of beginnings, of rebirth. There is willow too, and holly, and a scattering of baby rowans fetched in on some fitful breeze. This is a witching wood: dark green ivy wrapped around hawthorn; white-faced bindweed snaking through the brambles which guard the threshold to the wood-world beyond. It is a healing wood, too – with yarrow for

---

* The phrase comes from Thomas Hardy's *Far from the Madding Crowd*, in which a guest is offered food at a country inn: 'And here's a mouthful of bread and bacon that mis'ess have sent, shepherd. The cider will go down better with a bit of victuals. Don't ye chaw quite close, shepherd, for I let the bacon fall in the road outside as I was bringing it along, and may be 'tis rather gritty. There, 'tis good clane dirt; and we all know what that is, as you say, and you bain't a particular man we see, shepherd.'

your wounds, mint for your digestion, sweet violet to ease the breaking of your heart.

I am in love with my wood: the night-calls of the stalking fox and early morning encounters with the badger at the gate. It is haunted by magpie and crow; it's a breeding-ground for robins and goldfinch. Four hives of honeybees work hard at its edges, and half a dozen hens scratch their way determinedly round the clearings. We tread carefully on the winding path that we have forged through it, because of the clouds of speckled wood butterflies which dart up from the wildflowers, just inches away from our feet. We tread even more carefully off that path, because everywhere we look we see baby hollies, baby rowans, baby birches and a very occasional pine – a remarkable effusion of new and continuing life.

In the beginning, the stories say, was the Wood. 'When I was but a young lass,' said the Cailleach – the divine old woman of myth who made and shaped this land – 'the ocean was a forest, full of trees.' This wood into which I, seed-like, have blown is on its own path of becoming: a path which grows thicker and greener with every year that it is not cleared or 'managed' – for this place was not always a wood: I have seen photographs of it, from a decade or so ago, when it was a neatly manicured, well-kept garden with a few sedate trees. But, abandoned for years to its own devices, it has grown into a wood – and I am reminded of the words of my wise friend, activist and garden designer Mary Reynolds, who told me once that *all* land, left to its own devices, wants to become wood.

Mary is an unlikely garden designer: she really ought to be called a garden *un*designer. She's something of a local heroine in Ireland: in 2002, at the age of just twenty-eight, after somehow managing to talk her way into the competition, the then completely unknown landscape gardener won a gold medal at the prestigious Chelsea Flower Show. To everyone's astonishment, she not only beat Prince Charles (who came away with a silver), but other much more experienced designers.[75]

Mary's entry represented something of a gardening revolution: the other competitors' gardens reflected the fashions of the times, and so were heavily manicured, structured, extravagant with brightly coloured flowers. In contrast, Mary brought together a team of traditional craftspeople, drystone-wallers and native plant experts, and presented a naturalistic mini-landscape which managed to retain a feeling of wildness without presenting itself as undisciplined. 'Tearmann Sí – a Celtic Sanctuary' was profoundly Irish, but utterly unsentimental. It was based on themes and symbols from old Irish traditions and mythology, and yet wasn't in the least bit 'twee'. Mary's approach to gardening wasn't just new to the world: it was, at the time, quite new to her. Formerly, she had been a fairly conventional designer, accepting pretty much whatever work came along. Her change of heart came after a particularly vivid dream in which she found herself taking the form of a crow, flying over woods and hills. She could hear her name being called, she says, and soared over the landscape looking for the source of the voice. The voice grew louder, more determined; it seemed to be coming from a wood. She flew through the trees and saw a figure, sitting on a log, apparently waiting for her. The woman, leaning on a stick and smiling up at the crow, was painted blue – and as Mary-as-crow flew closer, she realised that the woman was herself. 'She didn't say a thing to me,' Mary told me, 'but it was as if a key turned in my head, and when I woke up I knew all at once that I wasn't going to make any more "pretty gardens".' At the time, gardening had become the 'emperor's new clothes', she said: something was wrong, but no one was willing to say what. 'So I decided to say what. It was that dream which took me to Chelsea, and after Chelsea I focused entirely on this new way of working with the land.'

After Chelsea, the BBC and RTÉ invited her to do TV garden makeovers, and the British government commissioned a garden to promote biodiversity at the Royal Botanic Gardens, Kew. For that one, she chose a selection of plants which would naturally grow together in the same soil type and microclimate: in other words, what she calls a selection of 'compatible weeds' – plants that almost everyone else works hard to eliminate from their gardens. Her inspiration for the overall design came from W.B. Yeats' poem 'The Stolen Child', which she had pasted to the wall above the desk in her bedroom when she was a child:

> *Where dips the rocky highland*
> *Of Sleuth Wood in the lake,*
> *There lies a leafy island*
> *Where flapping herons wake*
> *The drowsy water rats;*

There we've hid our faery vats,
Full of berries
And of reddest stolen cherries.
Come away, O human child!
To the waters and the wild
With a faery, hand in hand,
For the world's more full of weeping than you can
    understand . . .

'Weaving atmosphere into a piece of land is a bit like telling a story and putting the listener under a spell,' Mary said. 'And I believe that by holding the atmosphere of a particular poem or story in your head when you're designing a garden, you can create the same atmosphere in the land when it's done.' In the finished garden at Kew, a path led to a moss-covered island shaped like a sleeping fairy woman. 'Fairies, to me, embody the spirit of the land,' she told me. 'And now I wanted, in all my future work, to lead people back to that place.'

In her book *The Garden Awakening*, Mary describes the kind of gardens she once designed as 'like still-life paintings; controlled and manipulated spaces . . . Somehow, somewhere along our way, gardens had become dead zones.' Although people take to gardening because they want to feel more connected with the natural world, she suggests, the practices they use have the opposite effect. 'They're actually at war with nature, and what I wanted, after that dream, was always to work in harmony with nature. And so I had to re-examine all of my work. To maintain most gardens, you have to control, to stop things that want to grow from growing. But now, I wanted to learn what nature's intentions were on each individual plot of land I worked with. And so I set about finding out how to work with this energy, rather than against it. I stopped designing gardens for people who didn't want to participate in the process, or to form a relationship with and take responsibility for their land.'

What Mary is describing is what I think of as an enchanted garden: one which, like the most enchanted of houses, works with, rather than against, the landscape in which it is situated. It is not a rigidly designed, carefully manicured space, but rather a place with wild edges where the patterns and energies of nature can seep through. A little like my own gone-to-seed woodland, which lies beyond a flat green lawned area where the dogs can run and fetch balls.

Mary believes passionately that it is only by forming deep and reciprocal relationships with the land that we can really begin to address the environmental crises we're facing right now. 'Sometimes the world seems so messed up; people have become so disconnected, and I wonder how long it can go on for. But I have to have hope; I think we can begin to fix it – but only if we work with the land. It begins with healing the land and bringing it into balance. It's about letting nature express her true self in those spaces. If we focus in on how that might happen, we can genuinely interact with the land, and come into relationship with it. It's as if a magical doorway opens for us, and a garden can become a place of safety, abundance, peace.'

For Mary, too, that sense of magic is something we all know when we're children – the trick for us as adults is to recognise and then reclaim it. 'Yes,' she nodded. 'I knew that magic as a child – but like most people, I forgot. Maybe you have to forget, to be able to grow up in this world. It's as if you arrive with the knowledge but then you have to do a full circle and come back to it. That's what I feel I did. I came back to what I had always known, but had simply forgotten. And now, it's as if I've come home to the world. To the land.'

It's that sense of coming home to the land's magic which Mary promotes now, in her ongoing garden design practice. 'There's a vibrant energy in wild natural landscapes that we suppress in over-designed spaces. Places where the life force of the earth flows freely, and you can feel its power and vitality. I want to awaken that energy, so that people can find it in their own gardens, no matter how small.' And yet, Mary isn't suggesting that we let the land revert to wilderness. 'The soil would heal itself,' she said, 'and all the wild creatures would come back to the land. But if we're to survive on this earth, we need to be part of that process too. There's a place for true wilderness, of course. But human interaction with the land is a different form of magic, if it's done well.'

That struck me as a particularly Irish approach to the culture of nature, and she agreed. 'I think the energy of the land is particularly strong in Ireland. The country is littered with sacred places.

'All land, left to its
own devices, wants to
become wood.'
Mary Reynolds, activist
and garden designer

And even if some of the land seems tame, the wildness is there, just beneath the surface. That's true of the Irish too, and I do believe the land we live on in some ways shapes our character.'

In *The Garden Awakening*, Mary offers a practical, step-by-step manual for bringing the land back to life over the long term. How do you begin, I asked her? 'By taking off your shoes and socks and going outside!' she told me – wherever you happen to be. 'I know that not everyone has a big piece of land. But everyone can work with the land somehow. My book is based on designs even for really small spaces. Even in cities, everything is connected. Just find a place and get the rubber away from the soles of your feet so you can touch the ground. The only thing that has ever made me feel better at impossibly difficult times in my life was to take my shoes and socks off and walk on the earth. And if you work with land, I believe that you yourself begin to get well. It's about becoming who you truly are.'

Mary believes that the land creates a bond with the people who work with it. 'All of us can find that relationship with the land, if we take the time to build that bond. Gardens can become our teachers, if we are patient and choose to listen.' To that end, she is hoping to be able to create a garden and educational centre on a five-acre field which her parents gave to her a few years ago. Her dream is to convert it into a magical place, a centre for her ideas, and she is currently looking for funding to make that dream a reality. 'I'm a single parent,' she told me, 'and in recent years I've chosen to limit the work I do so I could be home to raise my kids. But now, I see that as my way forward. I want to teach people how to connect with land, work with land, heal the land.'

For someone who has achieved so much, and who still has so much to teach us, Mary is a disarmingly modest woman. It's hard to persuade her to acknowledge the uniqueness of her gift – or even to acknowledge that she has one. But eventually, it slipped out by accident, when we were talking about the internal changes which accompanied the change in her approach to work, after the crow dream. 'It's as if,' she said hesitantly, 'I've become that energy I'd lost, that wild energy I was chasing without even knowing that I was chasing it. I woke up. I woke up to the land. And once you've woken up, you can't go back to sleep.'

- If you have a garden, or a patch of land, can you allow part of it to grow wild? Or plant a few medicinal or culinary herbs or wildflowers, instead of geraniums, in a plant pot on your balcony?

- Walk around the place where you live, whether it's in a rural or urban location – because all kinds of plants push up through the cracks in city streets, and grow in parks and on verges. Look at the plants that are growing wild there. See if you can identify them, and then begin to investigate what they are (or might once have been) used for, and any other beneficial properties they possess. Could you pick the leaves and flowers and dry them for tea? (Be very sure that you've identified plants properly before you think of consuming them!) Can they be used to dye fragments of cloth? What folklore is associated with the plants and trees that surround you?

- In *The Garden Awakening*, Mary Reynolds suggests that the environmentally sound future of planting design involves producing our own food within a balanced, self-sustaining ecosystem. How can you grow some of your own food in whatever garden, courtyard, balcony or windowsill is available to you? If you are lucky enough to have a garden, can you sacrifice some lawn space for raised beds in which to grow herbs or vegetables? There are many beautiful old varieties which will enhance the look of your garden, as well as being exceptionally tasty, and which will also increase plant diversity.

- What symbols and images can you incorporate into your outside space which have meaning for you? Among those in Mary's beautiful designs are a spiral easily marked out with stones, and with a wishing tree in the centre; a star shape (also constructed from simply laying stones on the ground) enclosed in a circle to indicate protected space. Mary suggests that, if you have a garden, you include 'intentional spaces' in it: a quiet or hidden place for silence and meditation, for example; a wishing tree, or a fire pit.

8. An ear to the ground

Tell me the landscape in which you live,
and I will tell you who you are.

Attributed to José Ortega y Gasset

The places we are

I F I WERE a place, I would be an island. I've lived on islands; I
know how they are. I know how they get under your skin, and
I know how it is that some of them can flay that skin right off
you, leaving you naked and exposed in ways you never imagined
you could possibly bear. I lived on such an island once: a land of
sea and stone. A wild, inhospitable beauty that would break your
heart – and it broke mine, for sure. That island shaped me, and
the memory of it shapes me still. I'll carry it with me always, for
some places will not permit their forgetting. The island I would be
carries the possibility of that wild inhospitality. Its weather would
of course be affected by the day on which you approached it, but
it would depend much more on the kind of vessel you came sailing
in. Come in a simple wooden coracle, and it's yours for the taking.
Come in a pirate ship, or a flashy rich-man's yacht, and it'll wreck
you on its beaches without a second thought.

My island's edges might be fraught with danger, but its interior
would be lush and green. You'd have to scale the mountains to get
there – mountains forged from age-old gneiss, carved and curved
like the secret folds of an animal's pale-grey brain. These are dark
mountains, not easy to cross, but behind them you'd find the treasure you sought: hidden green valleys loud with tumbling water, and
the thick oak forest where the old gods still dwell. Follow the river to
the heart of the wood: a woman lives there, in a cottage whose walls
are studded with shells. A fox sleeps by her hearth, a raven roosts in
a dark corner, and a sealskin hangs on the back of her door.

This is the island I would be.

We think of ourselves as 'in' landscape, but sometimes we forget
that landscape is also in us. We are formed by the ground we walk
on: that which lies beneath our feet. That which holds us, supports
us, feeds us. *Ground* is where we stand, the foundation for our

lives. Whether it is hard and cold or warm and soft, ground is the foundation of our being in this world.

Ground is the safe place at the heart of us; we 'go to ground' when we are trying to hide or escape from something which is hunting us. We 'hold our ground' when we stand firm against something which challenges or threatens us. We 'have an ear to the ground' when we are properly paying attention to what is going on around us. To 'keep our feet on the ground' is to be realistic, not to get too big for our boots. Without ground, we are nothing.

Some pieces of ground are also 'places'. To find our ground, then, is to find our place – but what makes 'ground' into a 'place' is so much more than just a defined (or confined) location. Places have their own distinct names, features, landforms, environmental conditions – but places are more than just physical: they are reflections of the human cultures which are formed from them and belong to them. As human animals who are inextricably enmeshed in the world around us, it is hardly surprising that the nature of our relationship with our places is critical to our ideas about who we are, and what it might be possible for us to become. We construct the daily textures of our lives and our systems of meaning in relation to our places: they are part of our existence, intrinsic to our being; they are more fundamental to us than the language we speak, the jobs we hold, the buildings we live in and the things we possess. It's in our places that we come face to face with (or sometimes, perhaps, choose to turn away from) the bright face of the Earth to which we belong. The need to make sense of, and find meaning in, our relationship to the places we inhabit is a fundamental and universal part of the human journey in this world.

To put it quite simply, we cannot be human without the land. Our humanity cannot exist in isolation: it requires a context, and its context is this wide Earth which supports us, and the non-human others who share it with us.

Every ecology, every community of plants and animals and soil, has its own particular kind of personality, or intelligence, which affects the people who live in it in many different ways. We all know it; we feel it in the places we live, and we feel it especially as we move around the planet. Modern science might use different words, but it tells us exactly the same thing: the topography of a place, its geology, its weather, the flora and fauna which inhabit

it alongside us – all of these aspects of a place contribute to the
character and sense of identity of the people who live there. The
experience of inhabiting high, bare granite hills bears little similar-
ity to the experience of inhabiting lush, grassy, chalk downlands;
to occupy a city, with its manufactured concrete floors and walls,
shapes you in an altogether different way.

Psychologist Carl Jung called this process of shaping 'the con-
ditioning of the mind by the earth': every country, he said, along
with the people who belong to it, is characterised by a collective
attitude or state of mind called the *spiritus loci*. 'The soil of every
country holds . . . mystery', he wrote. 'We have an unconscious
reflection of this in the psyche.'[76] The unique mysteries of each
unique corner of this Earth express themselves inside each of us in
a perfectly unique way. In his 1993 book *Look to the Mountain*,
Tewa writer and educator Gregory Cajete preferred to use the term
'geopsyche' for the imprint which a landscape makes on the psyche
of the people who inhabit it.[77] When you live in a landscape for a
long period of time, Cajete suggested, you begin both physically
and psychically to mimic the characteristics of that landscape – and
it is from that process of shaping ourselves to the landscape that
'landscape archetypes' are born.

The archetypal qualities of landscapes, like other archetypes,
are somehow both universal and diverse. The archetypal island
symbolises boundedness: a sense of being set apart, a feeling of
being sufficient and somehow complete. 'No man is an island,'
John Donne insisted, but if we live on an island, we might well
imagine that we are. For some of us, that separation suggests safety
and refuge; for others, confinement and the impossibility of escape.
A thickly treed forest conveys darkness and mystery – something
to fear and retreat from, or a welcome doorway to an enchanted
world? A desert suggests clarity and the silent vastness of open
space. A welcome light shone onto your world, or an agoraphobic
feeling that there's nowhere to hide? However we may feel about
the archetypal qualities they convey, the landscapes we live in not
only shape us: they are metaphors for the people we imagine ourselves to be.

When I lived in America many years ago, I fell in love with
the poetry of New Mexican poet Pat Mora: one of a long line
of Hispanic women poets who identify intensely with the

south-western landscape, and particularly with the desert. Mora's poem 'Desert Women' typifies this:

> *Like cactus*
> *we've learned to hoard,*
> *to sprout deep roots,*
> *to seem asleep, yet wake*
> *at the scent of softness*
> *in the air . . .*[78]

Mora's desert women are indistinguishable from their distinctive landscape, both reflecting it and incorporating it. I have lived in several countries and spent time in many different landscapes during my life, and each in its own way has left its mark on me. Inside me is that island at the end of the world on which I once became stranded, castaway; on which I merged so deeply with the oldest, hardest rock on the planet that I feared petrification. But inside me too is the gentleness of the rain-haunted west of Ireland, and the dense silence of a misty early morning bog. There is a stripped-to-the-bones south-western American desert, fierce sun laying bare all my imagined inadequacies; there are lush green oak-groves in an ancient Breton wood where Merlin sleeps still, trapped in a tree. I am a collection of all the landscapes I have loved.

I have never been rainforest, though, and I could never be jungle – there is nothing of me or mine in those humid, colourful, shouting places. And isn't this true for so many of us? That there is a single kind of landscape in which we feel a sense of homecoming; a particular kind of landscape in which we feel so much more whole? For the lucky ones among us, those are the landscapes in which we finally have come to rest; for others, they're the hauntingly vivid landscapes of the imagination which never quite let us go. What surprises me still, perhaps, is that so many of us can resonate so deeply with a landscape we've imagined, but to which we've never actually been. In his masterful book *Space and Place*, geographer Yi-Fu Tuan offers the example of C.S. Lewis, a lifelong devotee of the far north. As we can clearly see from the vividly portrayed winterlands of his Narnia chronicles, Lewis loved the idea of 'northernness'. It was, Tuan says, a vision of huge, clear spaces hanging above the Atlantic in the endless twilight of northern summer which drew him, and which appealed to something very deep in his psyche.[79] But not only did Lewis never live in northern lands – he never even travelled to the extreme north.

We think that we imagine the land, but perhaps the land imagines us, and in its imaginings it shapes us. The exterior landscape interacts with our interior landscape, and in the resulting entanglements, we become something more than we otherwise could ever hope to be. We take on and begin to express something of its mysterious, earthy qualities; in turn we offer it our stewardship, our poetry and our songs. We offer it too our breath, blood, bones and endless flakes of dead skin. Each place has its own identity, each place deserves to be approached carefully, and with respect. Here are some of the ways that the land teaches us: a mountain range teaches us to come to terms with immensity; a cave teaches us to go deep; a river teaches us about flow. The land teaches us something about what it is to be human in this world – and sometimes, the most challenging places teach us the most. But above all, the landscapes we inhabit teach us that, in every way that matters, we and the land are one. To welcome those entanglements – to become in them and through them something both greater and infinitely more interesting than a single, isolated human life – is to be enchanted – to be *sung into* – indeed.

Archetypal landscapes

What do you think of when you think of these places? What images and moods do they conjure for you?

- A deep, still pool.
- A dark cave.
- A stormy sea.
- A small island far out at sea.
- A desert.
- A high mountaintop.
- A rocky chasm.

🦋 If you were a landscape or an element of the landscape, what would it be? Write a short piece from the perspective of yourself as an element of landscape, just as I did at the beginning of this chapter.

The place of belonging

The opposite of true belonging is nostalgia: a longing for a place which no longer exists – or which maybe never existed at all, except in our imagination. How many of us have returned to a place we grew up in, or lived when we were very young, only to discover that the image we have clung to no longer exists? I've never really suffered from place-related nostalgia. I certainly never loved the place I was born; I could never make any sense of it. Although I have always hankered after the western Atlantic coastal fringes of Ireland and the British Isles, I was actually born in the north-east of England, in the small seaside town of Hartlepool. In those days, Hartlepool was famous for one thing: it was the place in which, during the Napoleonic wars, a group of townspeople found a monkey wandering on the beach, and hung it because they thought it was a French spy. Curiously, you could buy postcards in the shops in those days, proudly declaring 'We hung the monkey!'

In spite of the long dune-covered beaches which fringed its edges, I found it hard as a child to love Hartlepool. I saw a town founded on docklands and shipyards, surrounded by chemical works, steel works, chicken-processing factories and sugar-processing factories, each of them spewing clouds of chemical-filled smoke into the air. I grew up in and around one of the most deprived council estates in the country, and the people there seemed (unsurprisingly) always to be down-trodden and depressed.

I couldn't find a way to belong to the Midlands city of Coventry, either, after my family moved there when I was nine. Coventry had once been an important place with a long and distinguished history, both real and legendary, peppered with iconic characters like Lady

Godiva and King Canute, and the centre of a thriving textile trade. But the city that I came to know was characterised primarily by its dying car-manufacturing industry. The Specials' 1981 hit song 'Ghost Town' was written about Coventry, perfectly expressing the lack of hope felt in industrial cities in those days, with their soul-destroying urban decay and recurring violence on the streets. There was a sense of transience, of impermanence; of things lost and likely gone forever. How to belong, in such places and in such times?

At eighteen I moved to Liverpool to study psychology – and for all its difficult socioeconomic conditions, I related more to the city than either of the places I'd previously lived. The famous sense of humour, a leftover pride and vibrancy from the Merseybeat era, the significant Irish influence, or simply relief at the fact that I was in the north again? I'm not really sure. But although I felt enormous affection for Liverpool, when my three-year degree course was up I didn't consider staying there. I moved on again. A three-year period in London, to obtain my doctorate in the psychology and neuro-science of anxiety and panic. A postdoctoral period at the famous Hôpital Pitié-Salpêtrière in Paris – then back to London again, to another research fellowship at the National Hospital for Nervous Diseases. During all of these years I was busy, occupied – but I never had the feeling that I was in the right place, a place I could stay in, love and relate to, and where I could be part of its tribe. The truth is, I had never loved cities; it was simply that I seemed to be bound to them by my work. I had only ever felt the stirrings of possibility in far wilder places than that: in rural north Wales, where my mother moved when I was in my early twenties; in the Highlands of Scotland, where I spent a summer vacation working in a Loch Ness hotel.

I never had a strong, visceral pull to a specific place, combined with a feeling of being somehow in tune with the land, until I first came to Connemara at thirty years old – by which time I'd travelled around the five major continents of the world, and experienced a variety of beautiful and diverse landscapes. What was it that attracted me to this particular place, above all others? No doubt it was all tied up with an ancestral longing for the land of Ireland which had been with me since childhood. But it was more than that, because I hadn't been affected so deeply by any other place in Ireland, including the equally wild and beautiful Dingle and Iveragh peninsulas of County Kerry, in the south-west. 'Never casual, the choice of place is the choice of something you crave,' Frances Mayes writes in *Under the Tuscan Sun*.[80] And in that sense, the places we love reflect something – or someone – we wish to be. What did I wish to become that was reflected in that famously changeable west coast light? From the islands scattered like a broken necklace in its stormy seas, to its crystal-clear interior lakes; from its central ranges of folded granite mountains to its ubiquitous wide-open bogs – there was nothing in this place that didn't speak to me. The message was all to do with clarity, and integrity: the commanding, unrelenting presence of land that is entirely and fully itself – that couldn't be broken, couldn't possibly ever be made into something else.

Connemara was, quite simply, the place where I began to wake up. It's also the place where I have finally been able to return. I believe, too, that it's the place where I'll stay – because sometimes, like your first 'proper' human love, the place that you first truly love will hook itself deep into your heart and won't let you go. Sometimes, a place just claims you, right from the very beginning. *Mine*, it says. *Mine*. And nowhere else, not even remotely, will ever really feel like home.

Since I left Connemara back in 1996 I have lived happily in, and learned to sort-of-belong, in my own way, to some of the wildest, most beautiful and iconic landscapes along the western shores of Scotland and Ireland. But here's the thing about belonging: it seems that there's belonging, and *belonging*. I've always believed that you can learn to sort-of-belong to any place, if you choose – indeed, that there's a moral imperative to do so, because the land which bears us and nourishes us deserves no less of us. As I discussed in chapter 3, I know how to cultivate that kind of belonging. Learn the ecology, history, language, culture, mythology of your place. Go out into it for long periods of time, every day. Sit in the same place every day for an entire year, in all the seasons and weathers; talk to the land and listen to it, and maybe then you have some claim on belonging to it. And a feeling of being at home, for however long you happen to be in that place – because not all loves are forever; not all places are forever. Sometimes we have to leave. Sometimes we need to leave. But wherever I go, I feel obliged to *root*. I am a serial rooter, perhaps, but I try to root deeply into every place I've inhabited, to live fully in that place. It's the only sane way to live: to be fully present in the place where your feet are actually planted, right here, right now. It's also the only way to live that is deeply respectful of the earth.

That's one kind of belonging: the kind you learn to do, wherever it is that you happen to be living at the time. Then there's the feeling of belonging that comes with heritage: a sense of belonging to a place which you may or may not ever inhabit, which is encoded in your DNA. Those of us with Irish ancestry know this feeling especially well: no matter how many generations ago your people left, and no matter where they ended up, there's a part of you that will always feel Irish. No matter how beautiful the other places that I've lived, no matter how transformative my time there, I've never properly felt at home anywhere other than Ireland. In my case, a good part of that is genetic.

But maybe there's another kind of belonging altogether: the kind of belonging which happens when a place claims you – when it makes itself known to you, and you in turn open yourself fully to it. These are the places we've been to once, but can't get out of our heads; the places we can't seem to help but return to on vacation, year after year; the places which we look for as settings in the novels we choose to read. This 'claiming' kind of belonging is expressed perhaps in the beautiful old story of Gobnait, an Irish saint who lived in the early sixth century. Gobnait was born in County Clare, and when she was older she fled a family feud, taking refuge in Inis Óirr in the Aran Islands. While she was there, an angel appeared to her and told her that she must leave, because this was 'not the place of her resurrection'. She should, the angel said, look for a place where she would find nine white deer grazing. So Gobnait wandered through Waterford, Kerry and Cork. First she saw three white deer in Clondrohid in County Cork, and she followed them to Ballymakeera, where she saw six more. But it wasn't until she arrived in Ballyvourney, in the south-west corner of Cork, that Gobnait saw nine white deer grazing all together. That was where she settled, and founded her monastic community. That was the 'place of her resurrection', and there she remained: a beekeeper, and a woman who is now thought of as a patron saint of bees.

From the first moment I heard the story of Gobnait, it resonated with me, and with a life in which I'd been wandering, like her, from place to place, in search of who knows what. Learning to sort-of-belong to each of them, but always, sooner or later, feeling some sense of being driven on. In search of the 'place of my resurrection'? The place where the soul is happiest on earth, from where it will happily and freely leave the body, when the time comes? It's been rambling and rather peripatetic, this journey of mine. I've imagined time and again that I've found my final resting place, when in fact what I've found were beautiful but temporary sanctuaries along a path I didn't even know I was following – each place offering its own lessons, its own transformations. But these days, with the benefit of long perspective, above all I see my journey from place to place not so much as a form of restless wandering, but as the acceptance of an invitation – an invitation to delve more and more deeply into the holy mysteries of place. And I see myself undertaking that journey as pilgrims do, with rare and blessed humility, knowing that something is lacking, but not ever quite knowing what it was until they've reached their journey's 'end'.

So, here I am: not really a line but a meshwork of places. A unique web of placeworlds lives in me – informing, creating, teaching, as I've walked my own Dreaming onto the land. Places that made me – literally, contributing air and water and food; places where I've left parts of myself behind – contributing skin cells, hairs, body fluids, breath. But through it all, there has always been Connemara. Tugging, tugging. Nipping. Biting. Itching. *Come home*, Connemara called, and I did, and now I find myself wondering again about 'places of resurrection'. Is there really such a thing? Is there really, for each of us, the possibility of a place where we might be happy to stay forever, and never feel a yearning for any other place? A genuine place of belonging, where we can begin to fathom our place in the world, and break out of our feelings of estrangement from it? A place where we can finally enter into our own wisdom, and fully live out our calling?

🌿 Make a list of the landscapes and places you've lived in. What are their qualities, physical and archetypal? What aspects of those places did you relate to, and which did you not relate to? How have you been shaped by them? Take a large piece of plain paper, and draw your own Dreaming track onto it: your very own songline. Find images which

represent what you found in each place, and glue them on.
Or, if you prefer, stitch it onto fabric, or make a collage –
work with the idea in whatever way you feel comfortable.

- Is there a particular landscape you long for? Is it real or imagined? Why do you resonate so deeply with it?
- Does the idea of a 'place of resurrection' resonate with you, and if so, do you know where yours is?

Becoming native to our places

*We cast a shadow on something wherever we stand, and
it is no good moving from place to place to save things;
because the shadow always follows. Choose a place where
you won't do harm – yes, choose a place where you won't
do very much harm, and stand in it for all you are worth,
facing the sunshine.*

E.M. Forster, from *A Room with a View*

Whether we believe in a 'place of resurrection' or not, in order to be fully alive and present in this world, each of us needs to build some feeling of relationship with the place we are living in right now. American writer and agriculturalist Wes Jackson called this 'becoming native' to our places: going to a place, digging in and coming to know it as well as you possibly can – as well as you would if you had been born there.[81] But 'digging in' is a vanishing art. Martin Heidegger, one of the most influential philosophers of the twentieth century, wrote extensively about the rootlessness of the contemporary world, which he believed is the cause of much of the anxiety which plagues us. We need to learn to *dwell* on this earth again, he suggested: to make ourselves at home in a place, to nurture and preserve, and ultimately to enable that place and the things in it to be free to be what they are.[82] Carl Jung also spoke about this problem: 'Rootlessness', he declared, 'begets meaninglessness, and the lack of meaning in life is a soul-sickness whose full import our age has not yet begun to comprehend.'[83] To

Always look for the
small beauties beneath
surface ugliness — the
crows holding a colloquium
in the middle of a
busy, fume-filled
traffic island.

these writers, a feeling of homelessness is an inescapable feature
of the contemporary human condition, brought about by what
American philosopher Edward Casey called 'the incessant motion
of postmodern life in late-capitalist societies', which prevents us
from experiencing place in a satisfying or meaningful way.[84] Casey
referred to the consequence of this as a kind of 'place pathology',
involving 'disorientation, memory loss, homelessness, depression,
and various modes of estrangement from self and others.'

How, then, do we create belonging? How do we engage in the
process of what many geographers and anthropologists now call
'place-making' – which, according to most definitions, is both a
retrospective and a prospective phenomenon: a process of remembering the history and associations of a place, but also of imagining
our own place in its future?

In Europe, 'Everywhere we remain unfree and chained to technology,' Martin Heidegger famously declared in 1954 – and our
growing attachment to technology, he believed, in some sense con-
taminated our authentic ways of being in the world, and prevented
us from being able to properly dwell in it.[85] But it's a mobile phone
and the vehicle of social media which Dave Borthwick uses to
express his own individual acts of dwelling. Dave teaches environmental literature at the University of Glasgow's rural campus in
Dumfries, and has a personal interest in the art of place-making
as well as a professional one. As @BorthwickDave on Twitter, he
takes photographs of rural Annandale in the south of Scotland,
where he lives with his family, and posts them along with fragments of what can probably best be described as prose poems.
Today, two images side by side: one of a hare at dusk, the other of
a pink-sunsetted river. The accompanying prose: '& return to the
soft strangeness of the hill above the river, its dusktime shifts &
shadows, the shared place of convergings & passings.' An image
of a ramshackle metal shed in the middle of a green field, with
rainclouds gathering overhead: '& McRindle's shed at time of shifting fronts, decay surrounded with parched green open to rain, &
heavy spell closing to nail the roof down.' A tiny deer half-hidden
by a stock fence: '& surprise an acquaintance at topfield's edge,
lingering in the leavealone so I do.'

With one or more such word-image combinations posted on
Twitter most days, there is clearly a thread here, and so I asked

Dave to explain to me exactly what that thread is. What is it that he is ultimately trying to do? 'What I'm trying to do is impossible,' he said. 'I am trying to map place. I live on a working farm (though I have no role in the work of that farm) and it's an unsung spot, literally a backwater. But for all of that, it is immensely interesting. There's a mixture of arable farming, neglected areas down by the water and flood zones. The quality of light is amazing, and with no high buildings, you can see literally for miles in every direction. The river provides endless fascination. It's a corridor for wildlife which cannot be fenced, or walled, or roaded over. And so the birds and animals are huge in variety. There are small plantations nearby too, relatively left alone, and so there's a wide area to explore.

'And there is no way to be done in knowing it. Each season yields something I hadn't noticed before, and all I can do is record moments which are always revealing new things. Of course, the more you learn of a place, the more you see. The cycle of looking and recording is a feedback loop. That's why most of my tweets begin with an ampersand: it's a way of acknowledging that each new recording is an addition to previous ones. Trying to know a place is to accept it can't really be done, and to know there will always be another "&" – into infinity, I expect. All places are unique, and unique too from this moment to the next.'

I was curious about how it all began, and what it was that had set Dave off on this particular journey. He shook his head, unable to pinpoint a single trigger for the image-poem combinations. But he remembered that, back in 2013, a friend had suggested that he join Twitter. 'She said it was fun,' he said, 'and I needed that, at the time. But once I'd joined, I realised I had nothing to say. In truth, I'd been in a state of having nothing to say for quite a long while. Although I hadn't then sought help, it's clear now that I was suffering from depression. I would hazard that I've suffered from cyclical depression all of my life. But in 2013 it was somewhat worse. I've usually brought myself out of this "psychological weather" with creativity. I would write, or dream, or read books outside my usual line of thinking, and the weather would pass. But in 2013 I had gone beyond what I was capable of weathering, and the forecast was not set to change. None of the usual strategies were working. I was untalkative. I largely hid in my office at work, emerging only to teach classes. Off-duty, I had developed a kind of aphasia: nothing to say and no way of saying it.'

Dave and his family also had recently moved house, and he thinks this might have been a contributor to his depression. 'I genuinely loved the new place from the first,' he remembered, 'but for five years we'd lived in a cottage which is only about a quarter of a mile, as the crow flies, away from where we live now – but four miles by road, and on the other side of the river. That move, a short distance, but away from a place the whole family had loved – and into which two children had been born – was rather devastating. I felt that after five years of digging in we'd been dug up, and the shovel that dug us up sliced through the roots too.'

And so was this the reason for the words and images, I wondered? A way of trying to dig in, again, to the new place? He nodded. 'But also because one of the ways I have always weathered depression is walking. In our second week in the new cottage, our landlord – who owns an estate with several rented dwellings – softened to me after he learned that I taught literature, because he is a reader. He sort of gestured outwards at the fields and said: "You can go where you want." I did (I would have anyway), and as I walked I took pictures on my mobile phone. I wanted to show my wife where I'd been, so she could visit too, and to record some of the astonishing (to me) aspects of the new place. It was a way of retaining some sort of communication, I suppose.'

And then – a sudden impulse to put it out there on Twitter? Or a more clearly thought-through plan? He shrugged. 'Perhaps it was a careless moment, or I just thought I ought to try it out and here was a thing, but I started to post some of the photos of my walk. I had no "followers" anyway, so it didn't really matter. I felt I had to say something about the pictures, though, because I wanted to insist this was a place, not just a picture; a real landscape, not a generic one – and so I commented on some of the pictures and then posted them. I guess that was the beginning of whatever it is I am doing. I couldn't speak, and in a way I tricked myself into talking. I had nothing to say, but through insisting on being precise about place, I had to use words.'

Usually, when we think of technology today, we think of it as Heidegger did – something that contradicts, or at least competes with, an impulse to merge with place. Technology, and in particular the use of social media, is usually thought of as incompatible with a deep immersion in the land – something which takes us away from it, not which helps us dig into it. And indeed, an increased reliance on technology is associated with a primarily indoor lifestyle. A 2014 study reports, for example, that the average adult in the UK spent almost eight hours a day attached to electronic devices. It's a growing phenomenon in children, too: on average, in 2015, UK children spent six to eight hours a day glued to screens. And Irish statistics show that, even in this predominantly rural country, as a consequence of their attachment to their devices, children spend less than an hour a day outside. Other studies have linked a lack of outdoor time to increased stress, obesity and reductions in the efficacy of our immune systems.

Even more worryingly, recent studies carried out on millennials are beginning to suggest that the brains of people in this generation might be developing differently because of their almost constant interaction with technology. Neuroscientist Susan Greenfield has argued that heavy exposure to digital devices has a major impact on the microcellular structure and complex biochemistry of our brains. And this, in turn, affects our personality, our behaviour and our ability to think. In short, she says, the modern world could well be altering human identity. In teenagers today, attention spans are shorter, personal communication skills are reduced and there's a marked reduction in the ability to think abstractly.[86]

And yet – technology isn't going to go away, I said to Dave, and besides, isn't there something rather subversive about using it for this purpose? He nodded vigorously. 'My early Twitter forays were with a Blackberry mobile phone. It wasn't lost on me that it was a fine thing to be using something usually associated with corporate efficiency to document place and to post poetry on the internet. The technology was compatible and enabling. And at least it wasn't using the phone to check emails, to receive phone calls, to set the alarm for the morning. This thing I was compelled to carry (I still call it "the albatross", in reference to the one Coleridge's Ancient Mariner has to unwillingly carry around his neck) could be used for my own purposes. I like that still.'

So, I asked him, is there a role for social media in the act of creative place-making? Is enchantment possible in the digital age? 'After three years on Twitter,' he said, 'I know that others have had a similar idea. There is lots of "place" on Twitter. There are lots of people providing reports from the present about unsung places and neglected species. There is a lot of the local. In summer, for example, I can follow an ornithologist who is counting and ringing the young of pink-footed geese, some of which may well have passed over me this morning. I don't like the word "followers" particularly, but among mine are people who tell me what it's like where they are (and of course I follow them as much as they follow me).

'I think it's too easy to label the internet as a disconnection. In fact, it can connect. It's reductive to call technology bad, because it is simply a tool – like a pepper grinder is, or a shovel. Technology is damaging in the use, not necessarily in the function. "The internet" is not one thing. It's a series of nodes around which people collect. Place is a category there too.'

Dave's commitment to continually mapping, and so coming gradually to know his place, is reflective of a process which is intrinsic to the art of learning to belong to – *becoming native to* – those places we inhabit now, wherever we originally are from, or might one day hope to be. Becoming native to our places involves, above all, a commitment to doing the best we can to fully know them, and all their faces, through all their seasons. It's the kind of knowing which is shot through the novels of Thomas Hardy – who is one of the most popular English writers of the nineteenth century. Hardy's novels are full of people who live in rhythm with the natural world, and perhaps we value them so highly because we know in our hearts that we've lost this most precious of things, that we've become insulated from our places. In *The Woodlanders*, Hardy simply calls this sense of connection 'local habit and knowledge'; his characters' perception of the world is entirely shaped by their local environment, and by their lived experience of it as it happens. There is no division between human culture and local environment. This is contrasted starkly with the experience of Grace, who has lived away from her native rural environment in a smart city suburb; in the process she has fallen (as critic Jonathan Bate puts it) from a 'state of nature' to a 'state of civility'.[87] When she returns home, she has 'become well nigh an alien'. She has also acquired a new ability: she can imagine herself in a place other than the one she now is – and so she has quite literally become dis-placed.

How do we begin to acquire this sense of genuine belonging to our local environment? Well, by determining to love something about our place, wherever it might be. It's more important than ever when we're living in places we find difficult or challenging, because it can be all too easy to dissociate ourselves from those places, to pretend we're not really in them, to hold ourselves back from engaging with them because they're only temporary, and we're hoping someday for something better. But the places where we live deserve more from us, because those places literally make our existence possible. And not to fully *be* in the place where you fully *are* – it's a peculiar form of insanity, of which the human animal seems uniquely capable. So don't hold yourself back from the hurt or broken places, the industrial wastelands, the places which have been wounded by us, or by natural acts such as wildfires and tornadoes. Always look for the small beauties beneath surface ugliness – the seedlings popping up in the hurricane-devastated forest, the butterflies around the landfill sites, the crows holding a colloquium in the middle of a busy, fume-filled traffic island.

And don't just look for the beauty created by others – make it your life's work to create some yourself, whether it's planting seeds in your back garden, feeding the birds on your windowsill, or smiling at a stranger in your local shop. Because your neighbourhood is an extension of your home, and your home is the container for your life. The lanes or streets, the public and private buildings, the fields or the city parks – all of these form part of the ecosystem in which you are enmeshed. Accepting that you are a part of that ecosystem, and learning the ways in which you might be able to make yourself at home in it, are essential preconditions for knowing that you are fully alive in the world. Without which, disenchantment is inevitable.

Sometimes it's easier to imagine ourselves as part of an ecosystem if we live in the country, or in a wild place. Here, we can more easily identify the non-human others who inhabit it along with us; more clearly see the soil and understand the impact of the geology; more easily piece together the rivers, hills, fields and forests which are the building blocks of a particular, unique landscape. But urban areas are ecosystems too, and although it might not always be quite so clear to us, everything in them is just as interconnected: the weather, the waterways, the soil, the animals, birds and trees.

There is a tendency to imagine cities as alive only with the energy of humans, and to see city buildings as dead entities constructed from steel and concrete, possessing none of the 'soul' of vernacular architecture which is based on natural materials and local construction methods. And yet, and yet . . . Canadian literature professor Sean Kane, in his 1998 book *Wisdom of the Mythtellers*, quotes the following anecdote: 'The Aboriginal teacher Bobby Macleod said to Robert Lawlor, while walking through downtown Sydney, "With your mentality, these tall buildings are the result of the dreams and plans of architects, engineers, and builders. But the Aborigine also sees that the stones and bricks themselves have an inner potential – a dreaming to become a structure."'[88]

Whatever the environment from which it springs, local knowledge matters, because enchanted living begins with local living: genuinely understanding, and so living in harmony with the landscape you occupy. Enchanted living embraces the wider world, and acknowledges the value of respect and interdependence between richly different cultures – but it does so from the perspective of a deep grounding in its own locality, and in the unique bioregion which supports it. And this, of course, is more than just the acquisition of environmental knowledge, or awareness of local folk traditions and culture; it is about building communities which are rooted in, respect and take responsibility for the local earth they occupy, and which care about its health and integrity.

Know your place

- How would you characterise the *spiritus loci* of the place you live in today? What is its unique personality? Ask yourself these questions:

  - What is the geology which underlies your place? Is it granite or chalk? When was the land formed? Does knowing this change the way you think about it?
  - What flora and fauna can you identify in your place, rural or urban? How do the life cycles of the animals,

birds and plants impact on your own life? Teach
yourself and your kids the names of the weeds, the
trees, the birds, the insects in your gardens and houses;
observe them throughout the year, so that you come to
understand their lifecycles, and the role they play in the
life of your own particular ecosystem. Which insects
do the robins eat; which berries are preferred by the
blackbirds? Which plants attract butterflies and bees?

- What are the key reference points within your
  landscape: hills, rivers, parks . . .?
- What is the human history of this place – who are its
  original peoples, and what events have happened here?
  How do those events impact you still today? Who are
  the human inhabitants of this place now, and how did
  they come to be here?
- A landscape is not just visual in nature, but can also
  be perceived in the taste of its herbs, and the scent of
  its flowers. Can you find a course which will help you
  identify and work with local herbs, or make preserves
  with local berries? What wild foods are available to you
  in your place?
- Always know where the directions are – which way
  is north, south, east and west. What are the different
  qualities of those directions? Where do the winds come
  from, and the rain?

Local living

How can you develop your local awareness, and support
your local community?

- Identify sources of locally grown food, and locally made
  goods and services.
- Look out for traditional/seasonal foods in your area.

- ○ Shop in locally owned stores rather than multinational chains.
- ○ Where does your waste go, and what is the impact on your local environment?
- ○ Where does your water come from?
- ○ Where does your power come from?

The power of place, speaking

Mythtelling assumes that the stories already exist in nature, waiting to be overheard by humans who will listen for them . . . a myth is the power of a place, speaking.

Sean Kane, from *Wisdom of the Mythtellers*[89]

Once upon a time in the Twelve Ben mountains of Connemara, not too far from my home, the great Irish hunter-warrior and folk hero Fionn Mac Cumhaill would battle with another great warrior, Cú Chulainn. Fionn stayed on a mountain called Binn Ghuaire; Cú Chulainn stayed on the opposite side of the valley on a mountain called Dúchruach. One day, during one of their altercations, Cú Chulainn picked up a giant stone and threw it at Fionn. It narrowly missed him, and landed at an unusual angle in a field which is now part of the Kylemore Abbey estate. The shape of the stone resembles a traditional clothes iron, and so it's called 'The Ironing Stone'; children still use it as a wishing stone today.

An enchanted, floating island off the west coast of Connemara once was cast under a perpetual shroud of fog; two lost fishermen landed on the island and lit a fire on her shores. By bringing fire to the island, they broke its spell, fixing it in place and lifting the fog. As the air cleared they spotted an old woman chasing a white cow along the shingle beach. When she caught up with the cow she hit it with her stick, and it was instantly turned to stone. The island thereafter was known as Inishbofin: Inis Bó Finne, or the Island of the White Cow. The old woman and the cow are said to appear every seven years, or when there is a need to warn of impending disaster.

Ireland is steeped in place-lore, and every story about how a place came to be named, or how a feature of the landscape came to be there, has its origins in the ancient myths of this old country. Those myths and stories are still alive, and they're profoundly rooted in place. One of my favourite books on place-making, Keith Basso's *Wisdom Sits in Places*,[90] emerged from his anthropological research with the Western Apache people of North America. Basso traces the ways in which their place-names are linked with stories which not only convey the history of their ancestors, but which still inform their sense of communal identity today. What is especially fascinating is that many of the stories illustrate what are considered to be good and appropriate ways of living and being in the world. And so members of the Western Apache community tell Basso: 'The land is always stalking people. The land makes people live right', and 'I recall stories of how it once was at that mountain. The stories told to me were like arrows. Elsewhere, hearing that mountain's name, I see it. Its name is like a picture. Stories go to work on you like arrows. Stories make you live right. Stories make you replace yourself.'

This moral relationship with place clearly exists in our own native traditions, most notably in the ancient Irish lore of places, which is called '*dinnseanchas*'.[91] The body of tales which make up the *dinnseanchas* translate the land of Ireland into story. Like the two stories just related they are usually vehicles for explanations about the structure and naming of the local world. But in the *dinnseanchas* stories, just as in the stories of the Western Apache, there is often a strong moral component. There are cautionary tales about the consequences of seeking inappropriate knowledge, for example, as in the story which is told about a woman called Bóand, who went looking for the secret well of Nechtain. The well, it was said, would rise and pluck the eyes from anyone who came there – except for Nechtain himself and his three cupbearers. Bóand went 'through pride to test the well's power' and, declaring that it had no force which could harm her, she walked around it three times widdershins. But three waves broke out of it and engulfed Bóand, depriving her of a leg, a hand and an eye. Fleeing from it, she turned to the sea, where she was drowned at the mouth of the river which is now named after her: the Boyne.

When places and features of the landscape are tied to old stories, knowing and remembering those stories as we walk through the land can help to weave us into its history, connecting us to ancestral voices and raising our awareness of the continuity of human relationship with the place – so helping us to establish meaningful and enduring bonds with the land in which we live. Specific geographical features of the land take on symbolic importance, and, knowing their stories now, we find ourselves forming personal relationships with them. As Canadian explorer of oral traditions Robert Bringhurst tells us, 'stories are some of the basic constituents of the world' – and to know a place's stories – how it came into being, the history of human culture there, the stories of its flora and fauna, the legends and folklore which arose from it – is to begin to understand its basic constituents. Just like knowing the stories of a friend, we find that we can engage with the place in a deeper way, so that it becomes more personal to us, and more real.

For many of us today, though, our relationship with place has become demythologised – a fact which is both an explanation for and a consequence of our sense of alienation from the world around us. Exploring the mythology of place, then – remythologising our places – is not just an interesting intellectual exercise, but an act of radical belonging. Like any other species on this planet, we badly need to be grounded; we need to find our anchor in place, wherever we might happen to live. Stories can be our anchors.

Human mythologies and cosmologies have always emerged from the landscape – they don't just come out of our heads. They're a product of our immersion in the world, of our interaction with our places; in a sense, they're acts of co-creation between humans and the land. And to be firmly anchored in your place is to know the landscape around you as alive with image and symbol. Some of the most vivid examples of this way of perceiving the land can be found in Australian Aboriginal stories of the Dreaming, which are passed down through the generations to convey both local knowledge and cultural values. Most Dreaming stories are about the Ancestor Spirits, who came to Earth in human form. As they moved through the land, they created animals, plants, rocks and other features of the landscape, and they also determined the relationships between groups and individuals to the land and all the other creatures which occupy it. The stories tell how, after the Ancestor Spirits had finished creating the world, they transformed themselves into trees, stars, rocks, watering holes or other objects in the land. The Ancestors, then, remained in these places, which now are held to be sacred – and because they remained, the Dreaming never ends, and the sacred places link past and present, as well as people and land.[92] As Kakadu elder Bill Neidjie said: 'Our story is in the land . . . it is written in those sacred places . . . My children will look after those places. That's the law.'[93]

Ethnographer Deborah Bird Rose, who has carried out long-term fieldwork with Aboriginal communities in Australia, describes how they see a place called Jasper Gorge:

> [E]very trip is another iteration of the Black-headed Python, the great snake-woman who made this place. She formed the sinuous valley with her swervy action, and parts of the story can be seen along the cliffs. Over there is a large stone that is her coolamon: here the rock is split where she cut it with her hair belt, and up there where a ridge works its way along the side of a hill is another part of the snake track. The Black-headed Python walked in the shape of a woman as well as in the shape of a snake. Like many Dreamings, she was a shape-shifter, and her metamorphic power extended beyond her body to impress itself onto the country as well.[94]

Finding your stories of place

- What myths and folklore can you find that are already associated with your place?
- From those stories, what mythical/archetypal characters inhabit it?
- Do you know any broader cultural stories about the species of flora and fauna which inhabit it?

Re-storying the Earth

*You know, I think if people stay somewhere long enough –
even white people – the spirits will begin to speak to them.
It's the power of the spirits coming up from the land. The
spirits and the old powers aren't lost, they just need people
to be around long enough and the spirits will begin to influence them.*

The words of a Crow elder[95]

In Leslie Marmon Silko's novel *Ceremony*, Native American medicine man Betonie talks about the ceremonies and rituals which
all humans must perform in order to keep themselves and the world
happy and healthy. He stresses the need for them to change as the
world changes, in order to retain their power and to connect with
the world as it now is: 'In many ways, the ceremonies have always
been changing . . . only this growth keeps the ceremonies strong
. . . things which don't shift and grow are dead things.' In the novel,
Betonie's respect for the old traditions coupled with an awareness
of the new world enables him to create new ceremonies which bring
true healing, and which keep humanity in harmony with the world.

The same goes for stories. The stories which are located in a place
also change over time – it's a body of lore which is constantly recon-
structing itself, just as the world around us is in a constant process
of transformation. Whenever we live in a place we become part of
its story. We bring new possibilities to it, forging – if we are prepared to countenance the possibility of such enchantments – unique
relationships with it and with the plant and animal life around us.
The fact of our being in a place changes, or adds to, its story. And
so, although familiarity with the old stories of a place is an important part of coming to truly know it, to understanding how it came
to be the way it is, and the history ('real' and imaginal) of human
life in it – the storying of place doesn't end there. Places, and their
stories, are in a continuous process of becoming. And so, if we are
truly enmeshed within a place, a new and unique part of its ongoing
natural and cultural history, we'll go on to make our own stories. We
bring our own points of reference, and we will imagine new stories
about the place which are based on our own ways of experiencing it.

Beauty is a body bowed
from the weight of a life
fully lived. Beauty is hair
bleached in the light of a
life fully loved. Beauty is
the angular, bony edges
of a life fully risked.

*

Until I moved back to Connemara in 2017, I lived for three years in a tiny old riverside cottage in the hills of Donegal, in the far north-west of Ireland. We had moved there from the Isle of Lewis in the Outer Hebrides, where I had immersed myself in a land which was steeped in the mythology of the Cailleach: the wild and powerful old woman of Gaelic mythology who created and shaped the land. Just as they are in Ireland, mountains and other places all around Scotland are named after her; she is immanent in the land itself. There are many, many stories about the Cailleach which, in that part of Scotland, also relate to her sister (or in some stories, her alter ego) Bride, who presides over the light half of the year just as the Cailleach rules over the dark. Directly in front of our island home was a long, low mountain which had the shape of a reclining woman; as I learned more and more about the Cailleach's mythology and her association with high and rocky places, I began to imagine that she was present in the mountain, and to make up my own stories about how that came to be. The Cailleach-mountain dominated our village and the headland, and as I walked the land each day, through all the difficult times we had there, I spoke to her as if she was an old friend.

Although much of Ireland is also steeped in the mythology of the Cailleach, in the part of Donegal where we lived I could find no local stories about her, and no specific landmarks named after her. I felt curiously lonely and utterly cast adrift. Where was the Cailleach in this place? Where might I find her? How could I possibly belong to a place where there was no Cailleach, whose stories had claimed me so powerfully and dominated my imagination for the better part of four years?

On the hill behind our cottage there was a wood, and in the wood there was a heronry. Every day, we'd see herons flying along the small river which tumbled across stepping stones at the bottom of our garden; it wasn't that far to the sea. And sometimes in the early morning, as I walked with the dogs along the lane which led up to the high bog, I'd see a heron standing on a stone in the middle of the fast-flowing river, the still point in the turbulent birth of every new day. When you live in close proximity to such beautiful, iconic creatures – and especially if, like me, you are immersed in myth and story – they not only capture your daytime imagination, but begin to infiltrate your dreams.

In the Irish language, the word for the grey heron is *corr*; it also happens to be the word for crane. This is because, just around the time that the Eurasian crane became extinct in Ireland, the similar-looking grey heron arrived to fill its ecological niche. Heron and crane, then, are interchangeable in Irish mythology, and in those old stories, crane is a powerful and a liminal bird. She haunts the thresholds where water, land and air intermingle; she guards the treasures of the Otherworld and is a guide to those who wish to travel there. Perhaps because she stands upright, tall and thin, she is associated with shape-shifting in the feminine form – and indeed, most likely for this reason, eating a heron's flesh was once forbidden. The most famous story about a crane is the story of beautiful Aoife, who was turned into a crane by a jealous rival; she went then to live in the house of the god Manannán Mac Lir. When Aoife died, 200 years later, Manannán made a magical 'crane bag' from her skin.

Now, surrounded as I seemed to be by herons, I read as much about them and their crane counterparts as I could find. They are associated, I discovered, with longevity; in some of the old stories they are connected, too, to hags and old women. Thinking about this as I walked along the lane, one winter morning at dawn, I stood and watched as a heron flew up from the riverbank, shriek-ing. There was something oddly hag-like about her call, and all of a sudden, a character popped into my head: Old Crane Woman came to me, part woman, part bird. By the time I arrived home, she had taken possession of me. Springing directly from this place I lived in, rising fully formed out of my river, I had found the Cailleach in another form.

Sometimes, if you happen to be walking along a track within reach of water at dusk or dawn, you'll see her there, Old Crane Woman: a tall, gangly figure wrapped in a mid-grey cloak. Her legs and her arms are unusually long, and seem to bend in odd directions. Sometimes you'll find her stand-ing in the river, still as can be, on one leg; you'll know her by her long nose, her frayed grey and white dress, and her

*long, thin arms with the sharp, sticking-out elbows. Don't
startle her: she'll be gone in a flash.*

Throughout that December, I wrote a series of fragments about
Old Crane Woman, and published them on my blog. 'Grey Heron
Nights', I called them: a Celtic antidote to the mythical Greek
'Halcyon Days', which bridged the winter solstice. She seemed to
have her own voice, her own rhythm, incantatory, the rhythm of
place – or the power of place, speaking.

*Old Crane Woman is thinking. Sitting on her nest, thinking,
thinking. What is she thinking about? She's thinking about
beauty. Beauty? you laugh – Old Crane Woman? and Old
Crane Woman hears you, yes, she does. See how sharply she
turns her head? You think she's ugly, then, that Old Crane
Woman? With her sagging skin and knobbly knees, hair all
matted and tattered and grey? You think you know what
beauty is? The blandness of youthful skin, the softness of
plump young flesh, the innocence of bright young eyes?*

    *You go right on there, then: you go on and ask Old Crane
Woman. Ask Old Crane Woman about beauty, and she'll
laugh out loud. Can you hear Old Crane Woman laugh?
You want to know what beauty is, boy? Look over there
now – look at Old Crane Woman. See how she rises there
from her nest, stretching out her bony old arms, arching up
her long, thin neck. See how she stands, how still, how still.
See how her skin shines in the starlight – skin that is thin,
transparent, and worn.*

    *You want to know what beauty is, boy? Look again at Old
Crane Woman. Listen to Old Crane Woman's cracked, croak-
ing song. Beauty is a body bowed from the weight of a life fully
lived. Beauty is hair bleached in the light of a life fully loved.
Beauty is the angular, bony edges of a life fully risked. Look
into Old Crane Woman's cavernous black eyes: you'll learn
a thing or two about beauty. Listen to Old Crane Woman's
song: you'll learn a thing or two about beauty. Listen to Old
Crane Woman laugh in the long, cold dark. Listen to her weep
in the fragile light of dawn. Listen to her joy in the pain of
giving birth. Are you learning now about beauty?*

You think she cares what you think? You think she cares,
Old Crane Woman? Old Crane Woman is hatching an egg.
She's the watcher in the dark, the keeper of the tales. She's
the guardian of the gate, the crystal in the cave. Old Crane
Woman was here before you and she'll be here after you.
You pay your respects.

The figure of Old Crane Woman was new in the ever-transforming mythology of that particular corner of Donegal, but she emerged in the only way that is meaningful: not just out of my head, but directly out of the place itself, and the creatures that inhabit it. Old Crane Woman occupies the space somewhere between the grey heron, the river and my own imagination. She's an act of co-creation. This is how the land draws us into relationship with it. This is how we build belonging, and this is how we re-enchant the Earth.

Mapping your own story of place

On a large piece of paper, make a rough map of the place you live. It doesn't have to be a work of art, or to be drawn to scale: the point is simply to mark the major points of reference on a piece of paper. It doesn't matter how big the area you cover is, but ideally it should cover the immediate vicinity of your own home, as well as the places you go to regularly.

- If there are existing stories about your place, add a brief note about them.
- Now, write onto that map some of the things that have happened to you in those places. If there are places or landmarks that you have your own names for, add them too. If there are places which you imagine could be inhabited by mythical or archetypal characters, mark them down. Do you have an equivalent of Old Crane Woman, who was derived from a heron? What stories/

archetypal characters can you make from the animals and
birds who inhabit your place?

🌿 Now that you have the idea, think of doing something
else with your personal place-map. Make a collage, for
example. Use fabric, and stitch yourself a map.

🌿 Repeat the process for the most formative places in your
life – perhaps the place where you grew up.

Listening to the land's dreaming

*It being Dreamtime, the land and everything in it was
dreaming. Well might a person in those days say, there is a
Dream that dreams us.*

John Moriarty, from *Dreamtime*[96]

The land holds the memory of everything that has happened
there; its offers us those memories in the shape of stories. There
are layers of story under our feet, just as there are layers of rock,
and we are part of those stories which the land dreams. Our lives,
and those of our ancestors, have moulded the land we know today.
The monuments we created, the hedgerows we planted, the fields
we ploughed, the ditches we dug, the rivers we dammed, the stones
we pulled out, the roads we laid down . . . We're joined in this work
by the others who share the land with us – from the birds who
carried the seeds of the flowers which grow here, to the trees which
self-propagate in the wood; from the warrens of rabbits and setts
of badgers, to the ephemeral forms of the hare. But the land also
dreams in geological time: of glaciers and ice ages, of volcanoes
and metamorphosing rock. Of the days when the continents were
engaged still in their stately dances, holding fast to one partner
only to split off later and go their own way.

These are the stories the land holds: the stories which were
old before humans happened along, and the stories that we made
together. This is the Dreaming of our land, and it is as real here
as it is in the deserts of Australia. We've forgotten much of the old

Dreaming; it's time to scrabble amidst the rubble, and see what we can unearth. But more importantly than this, it's time to participate in the process of its never-ending becoming. If the stories are always alive and transforming, then so is the soul of the world – and so are we, held within it. The land is waiting for those who know how to watch and listen; for those who are open, and know how to dream. Listen to the whispers of the land. Be silent for a while. Watch the characters, see the threads. Weave them into a new tapestry.

9. Kinship and otherness

A Prayer to Talk to Animals

Lord, I ain't asking to be the Beastmaster
gym-ripped in a jungle loincloth
or a Doctor Dolittle or even the expensive vet
down the street, that stethoscoped redhead,
her diamond ring big as a Cracker Jack toy.
All I want is for you to help me flip
off this lightbox and its scroll of dread, to rip
a tiny tear between this world and that, a slit
in the veil, Lord, one of those old-fashioned peeping
keyholes through which I can press my dumb
lips and speak. If you will, Lord, make me the teeth
hot in the mouth of a raccoon scraping
the junk I scraped from last night's plates,
make me the blue eye of that young crow cocked to
me – too selfish to even look up from the black
of my damn phone. Oh, forgive me, Lord,
how human I've become, busy clicking
what I like, busy pushing
my cuticles back and back to expose
all ten pale, useless moons. Would you let me
tell your creatures how sorry

I am, let them know exactly
what we've done? Am I not an animal
too? If so, Lord, make me one again.
Give me back my dirty claws and blood-warm
horns, braid back those long-
frayed endings of every nerve tingling
with all I thought I had to do today.
Fork my tongue, Lord. There is a sorrow on the air
I taste but cannot name. I want to open
my mouth and know the exact
flavor of what's to come, I want to open
my mouth and sound a language
that calls all language home.

Nickole Brown[97]

THE ISLE OF Lewis – that long old island at the top tip of the Outer Hebrides – was a wild, remote and beautiful place where opportunities for enchantment came thick and fast. But sometimes, still, there were unexpected moments that could take my breath away.

Late one afternoon, just before dusk, I took a brief solitary walk out onto the headland by our old croft house. Mist enshrouded the entire land. The mountains behind me were invisible, and the presence of the sea ahead was apparent only from the sound of water slapping against jagged rock. (No matter how still the air, on those sharp island edges the Atlantic was never truly quiet.) As I approached the small hillock where I liked to stand to look out to the Isle of Scarp, the Monachs and (if the day was clear) the St Kilda archipelago, the shadowy shapes I noticed just ahead of me began to resolve into a group of stags. That in itself wasn't a surprise; in that part of the world, red deer were so plentiful that they could be a nuisance, and some years we saw gangs of stags thirty-strong roaming the township, grazing on the crofts that weren't deer-fenced.

I slowed down, but not before a couple of the stags closest to me had noticed my approach. They didn't run – you needed to have a dog or two in tow, or to be moving pretty quickly, to spook those deer; they were surprisingly resilient. They simply moved, repositioned themselves, and as I came to a complete halt and counted, I saw that nineteen stags were now ranged in a semicircle at the bottom of the hillock in front of me. They were part-animal, part-shadow in the thickening mist. And then a stag with a particularly impressive set of horns (a royal, for sure) broke out of the semicircle and took a few steps forward towards me. I stood completely still. He took a few steps back. Then a few more forward. The others stayed where they were, motionless. For a moment, no more, it felt like a threat, and I felt a sudden sharp lurch of atavistic fear, a curious reversal of the normal pattern of hunter and hunted. But it passed as suddenly as it had arrived, and I was overcome with wonder at what I was seeing.

This elder stag's strangely choreographed movement lasted for a good couple of minutes, and I stood there entranced, awe-struck, until I inadvertently set them all free by moving forward a step myself, as if longing to join the dance with him – at which point they finally turned and ran, nineteen shadows skimming the land through the fog, along the rock-strewn ridge that leads north.

It would have been all too easy to read more into this than it was – to look for 'signs', or to imagine some other significance. But here is the thing about enchantment: it doesn't require magic, but it certainly requires attention. Enchantment isn't about magical thinking; it is about being fully present in the world. And so it is enchantment enough simply to say that for a couple of minutes, maybe a little bit more, in a foggy out-of-time encounter with the leader of a company of nineteen stags, I was fully in that moment, and fully aware of myself simply as one animal facing another.

Aldo Leopold, one of America's most influential early conservationists, understood how an extraordinary encounter with a wild animal can utterly transform the way we see the world. When he was twenty-two, Leopold went to Arizona's Apache National Forest as an officer in the US Forest Service. He'd just graduated from Yale's School of Forestry, and this was his first job. After lunch one day, Leopold and the surveyors he was working with shot an old mother wolf and her six adolescent pups at the foot of a mountain. 'In those days we had never heard of passing up a chance to kill a wolf,' Leopold later wrote. 'We reached the old wolf in time to watch a fierce green fire dying in her eyes. I realized then, and have known ever since, that there was something new to me in those eyes – something known only to her and to the mountain. I was young then, and full of trigger-itch; I thought that because fewer wolves meant more deer, that no wolves would mean hunters' paradise. But after seeing the green fire die, I sensed that neither the wolf nor the mountain agreed with such a view.'[98]

Above, all, the kind of experience that I had with my deer, or which Leopold had with his wolf, reinforces our understanding of the animacy of the natural world. It suggests to us not only that the creature or creatures we're interacting with are alive, and sentient, but also that the land around us has mystery and meaning of its own – a meaning into which (if we tread very carefully) we might be invited, and a mystery that we might be enticed to explore.

But all too often – and especially when it comes to animals like wolves – we find ourselves inextricably entangled in old prejudices, and tethered by ancient fears. In the United Kingdom, that much has been clear from the fierce, years-long debate about 'rewilding', and from the response to suggestions that animals such as beavers, bears, lynx and wolves should be brought back to live on the land. Restoring such species, rewilding advocates argue, can lead to an increase in the diversity of other flora and fauna, help woodlands to expand, and at the same time encourage people to reconnect with the natural world. Significant progress in rewilding has been made across Continental Europe in recent years: Eurasian beavers are now found in twenty-five countries, European bison are ranging across Eastern Europe, and wolves have spread across much of the continent, being found now in Germany and France – and there's even been an odd sighting in the Netherlands. But in the UK, fears of attacks on people and livestock mean that rewilding efforts have mostly been limited to extensive plantings of rather tamer species, like trees.

Our fears don't just relate to the reintroduction of lost species and larger, occasionally intimidating animals; we find it hard to tolerate and live alongside the few undomesticated animals that we do have. Badgers and foxes are some of the few wild mammals that are left in Britain and Ireland, and it is an astonishing thing that so many people would rather see them gone. The controversial and appalling English badger cull is a reflection of that: in spite of the controversy surrounding the question of whether bovine tuberculosis has anything to do with badgers, it's so much easier to pull the trigger, just in case. We see the same attitude in the growing backlash against urban foxes, around 150,000 of which are estimated to be living in English cities today;[99] fox culls are regularly threatened in cities like London. For all that foxes have many passionate supporters, ancient biases are still very much at large, telling us that they are mere 'vermin', whether it be in the country or the city – and heaven forbid that any other creature should be allowed to inconvenience the masters and possessors of nature. We'd kill them rather than let them have the leavings in our dustbins. We'd live in barren, lonely sterility – wipe out entire species, create for ourselves a world occupied only by humans – rather than suffer such indignity.

John Lane, a professor of English and environmental studies at Wofford College in South Carolina, has written about a similar love-hate relationship which exists between human and coyote. When he and his wife Betsy heard two coyotes yipping and howling in the land behind their suburban South Carolina home, he was delighted. The sound of coyotes soon became their nightly music, and Lane set about recording them, trying to recognise individual voices. 'I saw some promise of wildness returning to our region,' he writes in his book *Coyote Settles the South*.[100] 'I saw the redemption of our landscape wounded and scarred by hundreds of years of human settlement.'

That promise of wildness personified by the coyotes led Lane to study them and to visit their territories – which, over a period of around fifty years, have expanded out from the American West and into the south-east, where they've settled in quite comfortably and propagated with surprising success. But he found that not everyone around him shared his pleasure at the arrival of this species which Americans have been at war with for over a hundred years. 'There's a lot of coyote hate out there,' Lane says. Most of the people he spoke to see coyotes as 'savage beasts, as fawn devourers, as rabies vectors, as slinky killers of pets and domestic livestock – even as potential murderers of children and old people.'

The tension between these differing perspectives was explored by Barbara Kingsolver in her novel *Prodigal Summer*, in which her lead character Deanna is a wildlife biologist who lives alone in the southern Appalachian wilderness, watching over the plants and animals there. When Deanna meets and begins a relationship with Eddie Bondo, a younger man who comes from a sheep farming family in Wyoming, conflict inevitably ensues from his radically different views on conservation, hunting and predators. Hating coyotes is his religion, Bondo tells her, as he determines to hunt and kill the coyotes whose den she is protecting because she values their contribution to the vitality and stability of the mountains' ecosystem. In the end, he agrees not to hunt the coyotes, but his rejection of their predation compels him to leave Deanna.

But in spite of this hatred, Lane argues, there's nothing more American than the howl of a coyote. They're part of the national identity – but they're more than that, too. 'What I do when I cast my imagination out to them is more like kin recognition,' he says. 'I share close to 75 per cent of my DNA with these canines.' Lane believes that, although wild animals like wolves might be more glamorous, and perhaps more easily tolerated because they exist far enough away from American homes that people mostly don't feel seriously threatened by them, we should care too about the animals who flourish in the margins of the lives we've created. These are the creatures which have lived alongside us since the very beginning: creatures like crow, mouse and coyote. And in the UK and Ireland, creatures like badger and fox. But mice are dirty, people say; crows are noisy, spiders are messy, bats are frightening . . .

All of these are trivial concerns that we ought to be able to live with – but our discomfort perhaps reflects a greater problem with the notion of 'otherness'. And our inability to tolerate what is other isn't limited to our relationships with animals; it's true of our relationships with humans who are different from us – in skin colour, sexual preference or religious belief. Unfortunately, otherness appears to be built into us: psychological research, for example, clearly shows that by the age of five, we have already come to prefer to socialise with people of our own race.[101] But such attitudes can be solved by education as well as experience, and most of us learn easily to trust and love people who are different from us. Both for their own sakes and the sake of the wonder we feel when we encounter them, we would do well to extend that ability to members of the non-human world.

The language of animals

We need another and a wiser and perhaps a more mystical concept of animals. Remote from universal nature, and living by complicated artifice, man in civilization surveys the creature through the glass of his knowledge and sees

thereby a feather magnified and the whole image in distor-
tion. We patronize them for their incompleteness, for their
tragic fate of having taken form so far below ourselves. And
therein we err, and greatly err. For the animal shall not be
measured by man. In a world older and more complete
than ours they move finished and complete, gifted with
extensions of the senses we have lost or never attained,
living by voices we shall never hear. They are not brethren,
they are not underlings; they are other nations, caught with
ourselves in the net of life and time, fellow prisoners of the
splendour and travail of the earth.

Henry Beston, from *The Outermost House*[102]

When I was a child, I loved all those old stories which began
with words like 'Long ago, when animals could talk . . .'
So many myths and folk tales from around the world tell us that
animals communicate with each other in a language that humans
can't understand – or, sometimes, in a language which we once
used to know, but have now lost. In those stories which feature
humans who understand the speech of animals, some of them are
born with the ability; others obtain it through trickery, magic or as
a gift from the animals themselves – usually as a reward for an act
of kindness. Here in Ireland, Fionn Mac Cumhaill gained the gift
of understanding the language of birds when he drank three drops
of a broth in which the Salmon of Wisdom had been cooking. In
Norse myth, the hero Sigurd drank some of the dragon Fafnir's
blood, and was rewarded in the same way. In Grimm's fairy tale
'The White Snake', a servant eats a mysterious dead snake, and
this gives him the power to understand the language of animals. A
lovely story about the Greek prophet Melampus says that he had an
oak tree in his garden which was inhabited by a family of snakes.
One day, the young snakes came to Melampus when he was asleep,
and cleaned out his ears with their tongues. When he woke, he was
able to understand what the birds around him were saying, and so
could foretell the future.

Myths and fairy tales apart, when I was seven or so I was given
a seemingly more 'realistic' book which had a profound impact
on me: *The Story of Dr Dolittle* by Hugh Lofting. The book was

about the adventures of a doctor who could speak to animals in their own language – and oh, I wanted to have that gift more than anything else in the world. It would have been one of my three magic wishes, if anyone had happened along who could offer them to me. Sadly, I never found a fairy godmother or a grateful genie to set free from a bottle – but, instead, I found a friend who can communicate with animals. It's something Moya McGinley has always done, and when she was a child she assumed everyone else could do it too.

'Mostly, at first,' she said, 'there was just a simple ease with animals. I could feel and sense them in many ways, and unlike humans they seemed uncomplicated to me, and clear. As I grew older, a few odd things made me realise that the way I was with animals wasn't the norm at all. When I was at university, for example, all the cats (and we had many of them!) would leave home during the week and come back at weekends just before I got home. My mother always commented on it. I remember visiting a country house once; they had horses, and one particular horse drew my attention, and I went up to it and stood with it for a while, stroking it. It was totally at ease with me and I with it, but the owner of the house couldn't believe what he was seeing: apparently the horse didn't let anyone near it. So little things like that would happen over the years, and I'd always be very aware of animals, but at the time I wouldn't have said I was communicating with them. I suppose I didn't really value what was happening. I was focused on other things.'

During her late twenties, a friend who had something of a menagerie, and who worked professionally with horses, noticed Moya's ability to connect with animals. 'During that time,' Moya told me, 'I was exploring my "sensing" abilities more deeply in other areas of my life. I made myself much more aware of the things I was picking up on, and so I became more skilled at connecting with animals. Then my friend started to ask me to see some horses with issues that they were having trouble figuring out – and that's how I began to work more formally with animals.'

As I mentioned at the beginning of this book, the constraints of my own scientific training – which affect me still, even now that I think I've shaken most of it off – turned me into something of a sceptic at a very early age. And so if anyone else had told me what

'I've learned to trust
that what I'm sensing
is correct.'
Moya McGinley,
animal healer

Moya then told me, I'd probably think they were making it up or, at best, simply imagining things. But Moya is not only a dear and trusted friend: she is as lucid, down-to-earth and bullshit-free as they come. No *woo-woo* here: not the remotest trace. So I found myself simply nodding sagely when she told me about the animals who started to intrude into her sleep when she first opened up to working in this way, as if I couldn't possibly imagine why they wouldn't. 'My sleep-time was inundated with visiting animals,' she laughed. 'Just random animals dropping by, poking me awake. I don't know how, but it's as if they could somehow sense me, and they came out of curiosity to see who or what I was. After weeks of broken sleep and exhaustion, one night out of frustration I said, "Right, you lot – I need to sleep, so leave me alone tonight!" And they did.'

Now, a lot of Moya's work is aimed at helping humans understand their animal companions: explaining things from the animal's perspective, and helping the human to be around their animal. 'First,' she explained, 'it's about making a connection. I call it a "heart" connection: finding a place of absolute presence, love, expansion, non-judgement, stillness and, above all, equality. There is no agenda, no expectation. It's a strange kind of movement towards another spirit; the most important part of it is keeping a blank mind. It's hard to describe it in words; it's not a head or a thinking connection, and it's a "listening" (or sensing) more than communicating. I'm listening to the animal's response to what their person is saying or asking.

'So when I place my hands on a horse – for some reason, I find horses easiest to work with – I can sense areas of injury or discomfort. I feel subtle changes through my hands: heat, tingling, throbbing. And also sensations of things like stuckness, imbalance, tension, shallow breath. Sometimes I feel a sensation in my body, or get an image, or hear a message of some kind (though it's very seldom in the form of anything you might think of as words). It's not always a physical thing; sometimes I feel emotions, or energy. Areas of injury are relatively straightforward to pick up: either a horse "stops" me at an area of injury, or I'm drawn to that area. Or I feel a change in a particular area. The horse can also show me how it affects him – so he might show me a jerky gait, or an imbalance, or that he has difficulty performing a particular action.

Sometimes I get a sense of "rightness" or "wrongness" – so, for example, an owner might be describing a particular thing that the horse is doing, and I'll get a sense from the horse of "No, that's wrong; this is what actually is happening". And the horse will explain things from his perspective. Gradually, I can build up a full picture.'

Sometimes, it's a more complex, non-physical problem that she's dealing with. 'One horse I worked with,' she said, 'had a whole interaction with me around our concept of ownership. And it wasn't something for sharing with his owner; he came to me after his in-person session. He was due to be sold. He didn't have an issue with changing his person, but he did have a problem with the concept of ownership, and being sold. He likened it to slavery: that he was just a commodity to be sold on. He believed that there should be no transfer of money.'

Although I've always been fascinated by Moya's gift, and can listen to her talk about the animals she works with for as long as she can bear, the personal value of it came home to me after our much-loved border collie dog Nell was diagnosed with lymphoma. Now eight, she had been with us since she was seven weeks old; David had trained her himself to work sheep with him in the days when we had a couple of small flocks of our own, and we both loved her more than anything else on the planet. We seemed to have caught it early (it was found by accident, not because of any symptoms) and so, after a great deal of agonising, we decided to try her on chemotherapy – without which, our vet assured us, she would be dead within four months.

Moya came to visit after Nell had been having the treatment for four weeks. Although dogs are given quite low doses of the chemicals compared to human cancer patients, and although she seemed to be tolerating it all remarkably well (full of energy, eating like a horse – you'd never know there was anything wrong with her), when I'd taken her for her weekly treatment the day before, she hadn't wanted to go into the vets' office and had shown other signs of anxiety. I was wracked with guilt, wondering what she must be thinking – how could she possibly understand that we were doing this incredibly unpleasant thing to make her well again, when she probably didn't even know she was sick? What must she think of us for persisting in doing this to her, every week?

And so I asked Moya to see if she could get some sense of what Nell was 'thinking'. As she sat quietly at the table in my office, Nell came up to her and stood wagging – unusually, because Nell doesn't much bother with other people who come into the house. I wanted to know whether she felt ill. 'No,' Moya said: 'there's just a sense of . . . heaviness from the treatments. And she's wondering if it's always going to be like this now, or if there'll be an end to it.' And so Nell was told that there would be an end to it, and Moya assured me that dogs can usually pick up on your intentions, so if you try to convey to them that what is happening is for their benefit, chances are they'll trust you. Afterwards, Moya told me, 'I just needed to tune into her. It's not so much that she was "speaking" to me, but I could sense her response to what we were saying, in the form of sensations or feelings, or images. So that heavy sensation is an energy that I sense from her in response to what we asked.'

A few days later, Moya emailed me because Nell had kept popping into her head, which was unusual. 'She keeps showing me a "toxic" feeling,' she said. 'Is everything okay?' Off to the vet we went – and sure enough, Nell was showing signs of infection. She was promptly given a short course of antibiotics, and three days later was her old self again, bouncing around like a puppy. The next time Moya 'heard' from her, a few weeks later, we were just discovering that the same thing had happened again (it's a consequence of what our vet colourfully called 'bone-marrow burnout' – a known side-effect of chemotherapy) and this time it was serious enough that Nell had to be hospitalised for four days.

Apparently this wasn't the first time an animal she knows or has worked with has come looking for Moya. 'A dear friend, Katy, has a very anxious cat called Kobe, and one time when I saw him he was looking for fish oil to "help him think properly". So I passed this on to my friend, who was supposed to have taken all he said on board. But then, about a week later, Kobe "popped in" telling tales. Katy hadn't got his fish oils – and when I asked her of course she had forgotten, and was completely mortified.'

Now, Moya is highly sought-after to work with horses in major stables throughout Ireland and Scotland. 'I've become much more confident in that "knowingness",' she says, 'and I know it to be true now, because areas of injury I've identified have been spot-on, behaviours have changed overnight following a session with an animal, and owners have confirmed information that the animal has shared with me privately. And so I've learned to trust that what I'm sensing is correct.'

I spoke about this to Siobhan, a dressage rider in Wicklow who is one of Moya's clients. She first met Moya a few years ago when she called her for help with a very anxious horse. 'Shiva was getting so stressed that she would colic,' Siobhan told me, 'which is serious and can lead to horses being put to sleep. Moya's intervention at that time helped me to understand what was causing this anxiety, and connect with Shiva in a more positive way to work through the stress, and help her become a much happier, more willing partner.' And so, when Shiva started to 'melt down' about a year ago, after checking her physical health and making sure that nothing had changed in her routine in the yard to cause her behaviour, Siobhan called Moya again. 'I described to her how Shiva had changed over the preceding weeks from being a pleasure to ride to becoming downright dangerous. She was box-walking, refusing to leave the yard to go to the field in the morning, refusing to go into the ménage, refusing to eat at times. She was difficult to handle, difficult to ride, very reactive to everything. Her anxiety was beginning to impact on the horses stabled beside her, and I was concerned that she would start to colic again.'

Moya quickly discovered that Shiva had been caretaking Siobhan for a few months; she now felt that she needed to back off a little, but was unsure whether Siobhan was ready. And so she was feeling unsure of their partnership, and vulnerable. 'After I'd picked my jaw up off the floor and thought about it,' Siobhan said, 'this all made perfect sense. I had been diagnosed with cancer three months previously, and had recently completed my treatment. As far as I was concerned, it was time to get back to normal, but some unconscious part of me was stuck in the shock of what had happened and didn't get the message. Shiva was reacting to this. Once I understood, we could start to dismantle the blocks between us, and I asked Moya to assure her that I was okay and that she could trust me to take back the reins.

'The entire experience was a humbling one,' she told me. 'Not just because I realised how sensitive and connected to me Shiva was, but because Moya could pick up on all of this from the other side of the country, when I couldn't see it in my own horse, standing there beside her. And Moya, of course, had no idea that I had been receiving treatment for cancer. It wasn't something I spoke about.'

Fascinated by the entire idea of all this, and still slightly obsessed with worry about Nell, I asked Moya to tell me what animals think – if anything – about death. 'One very significant moment for me,' she said, 'early on in my work with horses, was when I worked with a horse who was very unwell, and who was going to be put to sleep. He simply asked, "Is it time to go back?" And it was the feeling of "going back" that moved me so much: it was pure joy and know-ingness and peace and absolute rightness. There was no sadness or fear; no fight or wanting to live or not wanting to go. Animals have such a simple, beautiful way of seeing the transition of death.'[103]

Mythical beasts and sacred trees

Humans have always lived in close contact with animals; it's not surprising, then, that they should populate our myths and legends too. All kinds of creatures, from the fiercest of bears to the most fragile of butterflies, play major roles in our mythologies. Animals might take on human characteristics, as they do in many African and Native American Trickster tales, or in the fables of the Greek storyteller Aesop. They might act as the messengers of the gods, guard the gates to the Otherworld, or offer themselves as a guide to a druid or a shaman. Depending on the story, they can be helpful to humans or harmful, so representing the ambiguous, not-to-be-taken-for-granted power of the natural world.

Even the most cursory readings of the old myths and stories of Britain and Ireland make it clear that our ancestors believed that the borderlines between humans and other animals were much less clearly defined than we imagine them to be today, and more easily bridged. These tales had their origins in times when there were closer connections between humans and the natural world – and in the days when there was no differentiation between the secular and the sacred, because the sacred existed everywhere, in everything. You didn't need a special building to find it in, nor a special person to act as your intermediary; it was right there, all around you – in that tree, or that stone, or that fish. In those times, then, animals were very much more than simply creatures that we might hunt and eat: they were teachers, and allies, and sometimes they were even gods. Some of our oldest stories involve powerful animals who embody a kind of wisdom which is different from (but entirely congruent with) the ways of knowing that humans have. Animals, of course, can do things that we can't, and can sense things that we don't know about – and in these old tales, wild animals in particular were repositories for the kind of knowledge which we long ago renounced.

In our native mythologies, animals are inextricably intertwined with the lives of both humans and gods – so much so that the ability to shapeshift from one to the other is taken to be perfectly natural. Old Irish literature abounds with humans who can shape-shift into creatures such as swans, fish, seals, horses and deer, blurring the boundaries which we still imagine set humans apart from the rest of the natural world. There is the beautiful, ill-fated Étaín, who was transformed into a butterfly by a jealous druidess before being swallowed and reborn as a woman. There is Caer, the swan-maiden who was beloved of the god Óengus Óg. There is Sadhbh, the deer-woman who was taken as wife by Fionn Mac Cumhaill, and who gave birth to his son Oisín. There are tales of men who take on wolf shapes to go hunting, and of madmen like Sweeney who sprout feathers and turn into birds. There is the story of Fintan, who came to Ireland with Cessair, Noah's granddaughter; his companions were killed in the Great Flood, but he survived by transforming himself into a salmon. A year later, he turned into an eagle, and then he became a hawk – until finally, 5,500 years down the line, he resumed his human form.

The old goddesses of the Celtic peoples are often closely identified with carrion birds, especially with crows and ravens. The best-known of them is the complex of Irish goddesses associated with the Morrígan, the 'Great Queen'; in her crow form, she represents both death and rebirth. Some goddesses were linked to forest animals which were hunted, like Arduinna from the Ardennes, guardian of the wild boar, and Artio, from Switzerland, who is associated with the bear. The widely acknowledged Romano-Gaulish Epona is the most significant example of the Celtic horse-goddess, who is usually associated with fertility and abundance; then there is the Irish horse-goddess Macha, who gave her name to Armagh – Ard Mhacha, the heights of Macha.

Sometimes, specific animals took on immense significance for individuals or tribes, to the extent that they in some way overtly identified with them. Anthropologists usually use the term 'totemism' to describe the ways in which indigenous communities around the world consider certain plants or animals to be the patrons – or even the ancestors – of their people. In Ireland, some tribes adopted the names of animals as their protective totem: for example, the Artraige (bear-people), Osraige (deer-people), Grecraige (horse-people) and Sordraige (boar-people). Inscriptions on Ogham stones suggest that individuals sometimes had their own totem animal: there, we find references to people with names like 'Son of the rowan tree', 'Wolf-singer' and 'Raven Born'. This kind of totemism undoubtedly inspired Philip Pullman's fantasy trilogy *His Dark Materials*, in which dæmons are the external physical representation of an individual's 'inner self'. Your dæmon can change from shape to shape while you're still a child, but during adolescence will eventually settle permanently into the form of the animal which you most resemble in character. And so Lyra Belacqua's dæmon Pantalaimon first appears in the story as a dark brown moth, but his final form is a beautiful red-gold pine marten. Human and dæmon are in effect two entities sharing one body, and to be severed from one's dæmon causes death to the human.

Totemism of this kind is likely also to have been the origin of countless stories around the world in which an animal assumes human form – either voluntarily, or due to an enchantment – in order to enter into a relationship with a man or woman. Or vice versa. Once upon a time, there was a poor man who had so many children that he hardly had enough food or clothing to go around. They were all pretty children, but the prettiest was the youngest daughter, and there was no end to her loveliness. One evening, at the fall of the year, the weather was so wild and rough outside that the house shook. And then *something* gave three taps on the window-pane . . . 'Will you give me your youngest daughter? If you will, I'll make you as rich as you are now poor,' said the great White Bear who stood outside. So begins the old Norwegian story, 'East of the Sun and West of the Moon'. And so of course, to save her family, the youngest daughter marries the Bear – only to discover that, at night, the Bear is actually a man. Eventually, after many mistakes and adventures, in the castle which lies to the east of the sun and the west of the moon, the youngest daughter breaks the spell which has enchanted him, and he is permanently transformed into the handsomest of all possible princes.

In her analysis of these stories, artist and editor Terri Windling suggests that the animal bride or bridegroom represents 'the wild within each one of us. They represent the wild within our lovers and spouses, the part of them that we can never fully know. They represent the Others who live unfathomable lives right beside us – cat and mouse and coyote and owl; and the Others that live only in the dreams and nightmares of our imaginations. For thousands of years, their tales have emerged from the place where we draw the boundary lines between animals and human beings, the natural world and civilization, women and men, magic and illusion, fiction and the lives we live.'[104] These stories, then, affirm the kinship between animals and humans, while still acknowledging their strangeness and otherness – precisely the kind of paradox on which enchantment thrives.

Just like animals, plants and trees play major roles in our native folklore; here again, they are portrayed as allies and teachers. Plants and trees could, like animals, be clan totems, and they were personal totems, too. Members of the Fianna, Fionn Mac Cumhaill's companions, wore sprigs of plants as they were going into battle: Oscar with a branch of red-berried rowan, Diarmaid with a branch of curly yew . . . Trees were revered, and were specifically protected under the old Brehon laws, which prescribed hefty fines for people who unlawfully chopped them down.

Some trees, or groves of trees, were held to be sacred. In ancient Ireland, there were five great trees (*bile*) which were held to be more sacred than any others: Craebh Uisnigh, the ancient ash tree at Uisneach; Bile Tortan, an ash near Tara; Craebh Daithi, another ash tree in County Westmeath; Eo Rossa, a yew at Old Leighlin in County Carlow; and Eo Mugna, an oak at the mouth of the Shannon. Each of these trees marked an important royal or sacred site, and each has its own story, told in the old Irish *dinnseanchas*, or place-lore. And in Ireland today, certain trees are still treated with a good deal of respect: no one will cut a lone hawthorn tree, because they are known to be meeting places of the fairies. Roads have been diverted and building plans changed in order to avoid the bad luck which would follow after cutting one of them down.

Personal totems

🕊 If you had a dæmon, what animal would it be, and why? Which qualities or characteristics of the animal appeal to you?

  ○ If you were this animal, how would you see the world differently? How would it feel to be in its body?
  ○ Look for stories, myths and artwork which are focused around this animal.
  ○ If the animal is native to you, look for places where you might observe it.

🕊 Do the same exercises for a plant or tree.

Talking plants

To dwellers in a wood, almost every species of tree has its voice as well as its feature.

Thomas Hardy, from *Under the Greenwood Tree*

Although we might find it easy enough to accept the idea that animals can communicate with each other, the idea that plants can do the same thing is, in spite of a growing amount of scientific evidence to support it, still often regarded as rather 'lunatic fringe'. But it's now well established that plants engage in regular communication, continually adapting to the information they receive from other plants around them. They alert each other to attacks from bugs and herbivores, to threatening chemicals and impending droughts, and even seem able to recognise kin. Plants seem to communicate with each other in several different ways: via airborne chemicals, soluble compounds exchanged by roots, underground networks of threadlike fungi, and perhaps even ultrasonic sounds.[105]

Asia Suler takes this idea of plant communication a little further: she believes, as do many indigenous peoples around the world, that plants can communicate with us too. Asia is a herbalist, healer and teacher who lives in the southern Appalachian Mountains of the United States. It all began in her early college days, she told me, when she developed a condition called vulvodynia, a type of chronic pain that involves the inflammation of the muscles and nerves of the pelvic floor. 'Chronic illness is painful on more than just a physical level,' she said: 'it pretty much scrambles everything in your life and leaves you searching for meaning in the midst of seeming senselessness. For me, the experience inside my body was so uncomfortable that I began going outside. I sought solace in the small patches of woods surrounding campus, I lost myself for a time in the fields beyond the last buildings. I couldn't talk to most people my age about what it was like to be dealing with chronic pain, so I began talking to the trees. And that's when the most incredible thing began to happen – the trees began to respond.

'It was subtle, and it took a while to really begin trusting the feeling sense I had. But as my doctors began throwing up their hands and suggesting things like surgery to remove nerve endings, I began to walk past the horizon line of what I had been given to understand was medicine or truth. So, I sought the medicine of the out of doors, the medicine of communion, the medicine of learning how to listen to the natural world.'

Asia changed her diet and her belief system; she talked to plants, and she healed. She worked on a farm in Maui and took care of suburban gardens, and eventually ended up as a 'plant technician' in Manhattan, working to take care of office plants. 'Then,' she said, 'one day I woke up and just knew I had to go to school to study herbalism. I didn't even really know what that meant at the time, to be honest! But I followed my gut and ended up moving down to Southern Appalachia to study with the Chestnut School of Herbal Medicine. Once there, the mountains simply claimed me. And I stayed.'

We occupy a world
in which there are no
longer penalties for
cutting down a sacred
tree; instead, the greatest
of rewards can be
found in extinguishing
entire forests.

Now, Asia makes plant medicine – digging roots and brewing tea, stirring poultices and helping people to heal by bringing them into connection with herbs. 'My life is rooted in developing relationships with the more-than-human world, and learning how to distil what I've been given into the medicine of apothecary and word. I'm passionate about reigniting an awareness of "earth consciousness": what I see to be the central truth that fuelled our ancestors' hearth fires – the idea that we live in a world that is alive and full of medicine.'

And in the Celtic nations we do indeed have a long history of herbal lore which has been passed down through our ancestors. According to legend, the history of herbalism in Ireland began with the eighth-century Battle of Moytura. Dian Cécht, the healer of the Tuatha Dé Danann (the old gods) saw that his son Miach had developed superior healing skills; he killed him in a jealous rage. There were 365 plants that grew on Miach's grave, one for each of his joints and sinews. The herbs were gathered up by his sister Airmed; she laid them out on her cloak and began to classify them according to their different properties. Unfortunately, Dian Cécht saw what she was doing and mixed up some of the herbs, and so today we do not know all of their properties. But traditionally, there has been a great respect for herbs: the 'herb woman' was a well-known member of every Irish community, and there is a phrase, *creideamh i luibheanna*, for a belief in the efficacy of herbs.

The plant medicine which Asia practises honours scholarship, study and hard-won book learning, she told me, 'but it also recognises that our deepest and most ancient guide is our own intuition. Like so many others, I grew up in a culture where it was considered inane, unintellectual or just plain silly to do things like talk to plants or recognise sentience in the non-human world. So it wasn't until I was a full-fledged adult that I realised it actually felt great to hug a tree . . . and that it wasn't just a fantasy that they will hug you back.'

I asked Asia what advice she has for others who would like to connect to plants, but don't know how. 'Well,' she suggested, 'if you're new to the idea of consciously tending plant relationships, or engaging with plants in more than just a "your house plant looks great" kind of way, take heart! The plants are always reaching out to us. Humans evolved in direct connection with plants, and in this moment there is already a plant that wants to connect with you, a plant that is willing to help you to understand more about your-self. Finding this "plant ally", as we call them in the herbal world, can be as easy as simply reflecting on your own innate affinities. What is your favourite flower? Is there a particular house plant that you love? Think back to your childhood: do you have any distinct memories about particular trees or garden plants? Is there a weed growing in your neighbourhood right now that intrigues you? We often think there is some magic formula to making just the right connections in life, but truly all we need is just to follow the threads of our own natural curiosity.

'Scan your life, and you'll find there at least one or two plants that intrigue, comfort or inspire you. Like any good relationship, your connection with this plant will need tending. Once you pick a plant (or, as I like to say, it chooses you) spend time with it. Perhaps put a picture of it in your bedroom, or try growing it, or sit with it in meditation. Eat it if you can! The more intimacy you create, the more you will learn (just like in human relationships).

'If you want to receive an even more direct droplet of wisdom, try exploring the plant's doctrine of signatures. Originating with sixteenth-century alchemist and philosopher Paracelsus, the doc-trine of signatures is the idea that the key to understanding a plant's healing character can be found within its very habit of being. By examining how a plant grows, where it grows, its struc-ture, colours, tendencies and affinities, we can begin to understand the poetics of how its medicine might resonate within our own bodies, hearts and minds. For example, perhaps you will feel drawn to roses. Roses have both beautifully open blossoms and very sharp thorns; this might speak to you of rose's ability to help you feel safe and protected enough to open your heart fully to experience the voluptuousness of what life has to offer. Try engaging with this poetic mind-set when you interact with your plant.'[106]

All my relations

In her beautiful book of essays *Dwellings*, Chickasaw writer Linda Hogan tells of a sweat lodge ceremony undertaken to mend the broken connection between people and the rest of the world. The people in the ceremony say the words 'all my relations' before and after a prayer, and those words, Hogan says, create relationships with other people, with animals, with the land. 'To have health,' she writes, 'it is necessary to keep all these relations in mind.'[107]

There is all too little of that kind of health in the world today; here in the West, the days when animals and plants might have been thought of as our relations seem like an impossibly long time ago. Now, we primarily see the non-human others who share the planet with us as resources for our consumption. Although many of us will love and share our lives with 'companion animals' – our cats and dogs and horses – that care isn't always extended to the creatures of the wild. They're not part of our family, part of our tribe; we can't humanise them in the same way as we do our pets, and we don't really believe that they have purposes and meanings of their own. And so we might sometimes admire them at a distance, but if they get in our way, or look as if they might pose some threat (no matter how vague), it's fine to wipe them out. It's fine to cut down a community of old oaks in an ancient woodland to build a few more trinkets for the humans; all that malarkey about networks of communication in their roots is all a bit abstract, really – after all, it's not like they're actually *talking*.

In losing our respect for other life forms, we have also lost a sense of who we are. We can only be fully human in context, but our image of ourselves is that we are set somehow apart, oddly alone in a world which is brimming with vivid life. But that sense of separation isn't only detrimental to our personal wellbeing – it's detrimental to the wellbeing of the planet too. The effects of deforestation on global warming have been known for decades: the razing of tropical rainforests adds more carbon dioxide to the atmosphere than the sum total of cars and trucks on the world's roads, and yet the World Wildlife Fund estimates that some 46–58,000 square miles of forest are lost each year.[108] As a consequence of our push for endless economic growth, and for more *stuff* for a constantly expanding human population that we can't bring ourselves to control, we have perpetrated upon the planet what scientists are calling the Sixth Mass Extinction: a massive extinction event resulting in an estimated 140,000 lost species per year.[109]

This world does not belong to us. The world is a great dreaming being which shelters other beings, and we are just one among a countless number of species who live in her and of her. Once, we had contracts with the plants and animals who share this world with us. We would treat them with respect; like them, we would take only what we needed from this earth and no more, and they would share their wisdom and medicine with us. They'd be companions on our journey through a life that can sometimes be hard, but whose loads are always lightened by communion.

We've come so far from that old wisdom. We want to know the stars, to solve all the great mysteries of the universe – but we don't even know ourselves, or how to be in relationship with the land, animals and plants around us. Now, we occupy a world in which there are no longer penalties for cutting down a sacred tree; instead, the greatest of rewards can be found in extinguishing entire forests. We have created a world for ourselves in which the president of one of its largest countries can gleefully sign a law which facilitates the shooting of hibernating bears and wolf cubs, and large sections of its population actually applaud.* This is not a sane world. And as a consequence of our multiple insanities, this world we grew up in, which we have taken for granted, is not only changing – much of it is dying.

To alter that state of affairs, we need not only to act differently, but to be different. It's not enough to march against this and that, or to sit at our desks signing online petitions protesting against the destruction of more green places to indulge our avarice, or more heartless culls of wild animals to avoid inconvenience. All of these are good and important things to do, but to create real, permanent change we'll need to fundamentally shift the way we see the world and our place in it. If we can re-enchant ourselves – fall in love with this complex and mysterious, animate world all over again – then we might stand a chance.

Begin, if you will, with a tree. Congratulate a young, fragile willow on its summer growth. Watch the first turn of the leaves

---

* On 3 April 2017, President Donald Trump signed House Joint Resolution 69 (HJR 69) into law. The legislation rescinds the U.S. Fish and Wildlife Service's (USFWS) 2016 Alaska National Wildlife Refuges Rule (Refuge Rule). The Refuge Rule was enacted to protect native carnivores on Alaska's refuges from the state's Board of Game (BOG) predator management program, which allows practices such as the killing of bears with cubs and wolves with pups, as well as the hunting of animals from aircraft, among other things.

of an old ash, all scars and stories, as she begins to grow autumn-sleepy, just as you are. Feel the dreadful heave at the roots of the tall birch after the winter storm, and wonder what sense it is that tells you how the deep roots had nearly lost their hold, down there past the iron lick of the lower soil and onto the fractured rock. Do you hear the bruising of the deep roots, find yourself wanting to reach out and touch the bark of the tree that withstood the wind – knowing that you too have withstood a storm or two in your time? The graceful birch, that lady of the woods whose silver-white bark is like no other's, and you.

10. Hands on the clay of life

We have lit upon the gentle, sensitive mind
And lost the old nonchalance of the hand;
Whether we have chosen chisel, pen or brush
We are but critics, or but half create,
Timid, entangled, empty and abashed . . .

W.B. Yeats, from 'Ego Dominus Tuus'

FOR A FEW short years in the far Western Isles of Scotland, I was a shepherdess. On our remote croft in the desolate hinterlands of the Isle of Lewis, we kept and cared for two small flocks of pedigree sheep. The Hebrideans were David's loves: small, black, horned and feisty creatures who were perfectly adapted to life on the wild Atlantic fringes of these islands. Each of them had a name, each of them had a personality, and we loved them dearly – especially Little Horn, a strange and slightly fey ewe with a tiny body and stubby horns; and Wonky, who managed to break a leg within about two days of us first bringing her home from the island of North Uist, and who walked with a bit of a stutter ever afterwards. My loves were the Jacobs: large and gentle brown-and-white sheep who struggled sometimes in the harsh conditions, and clearly longed for warmer, greener fields. Dulse and Norma, Big Sister and Little Sister, Pirate (a sheep with a snazzy black patch across one eye and a great deal of attitude) – they had the run of the common grazing land on the vast unfenced headland, and across several thousand acres of the craggy, grey mountains which separated Lewis from the Isle of Harris.

Watching over those sheep taught us many things about the place we lived in, and opened me up to a way of seeing and interacting with the land that I had never before imagined. It arose from the (perhaps rather obvious in retrospect) fact that sheep *eat* the land. And as ancient, perfectly evolved grazers (with, in the case of the Hebrideans at least, a goat-like inclination to browse thrown in for good measure) they are remarkably selective about which particular bits of the land they choose to consume.

I sat often with the sheep, and with Nell, our sheepdog, on top of a dry, grassy hillock in front of the house where they liked to graze. I'd watch them pick out individual stems and leaves, and nose others out of the way. You have to look closely, all the way down there at the level of the sheep's head, on your hands and knees, to catch them delicately nibbling at the glowing embers of a sundew flower, severing the short stems of sunny, wide-open tormentil, stunted by the harshness of the westerly winds. Sheep, you see, are masters of detail, and they taught me how to look at the land as a herbivore might. Following them as they grazed, I watched, and learned many things about the warp and weft of this apparently bleak and homogenous black moorland. The rock, Llewissian gneiss, so recently (in geological terms) grazed by lumbering glaciers. The ever-present water, which determines both the lie of the land and the nature of the soil – often saturated and anaerobic, but here and there drier and merely acidic. All of it liberally seasoned with salt, supplied free of charge by the prevailing Atlantic winds.

But above all, I learned about the plants – the unlikely abundance of tiny, beautiful plants in the surprisingly varied habitats of our township. The succulents which seemed to spring fully formed from the cracks in the lichen-coated rocks down by the shore; seaweeds in every possible shade of green and brown. Waterlily, bogbean and iris in the lakes; rich red and bright green mosses in the bog. And wildflowers everywhere: spring squill, thrift, bog asphodel, lesser celandine, lady's bedstraw, all-heal, milkwort . . . It was the sheep who first taught me to pick out and then to identify the plants; it was inevitable then, perhaps, that I would think of bringing sheep and plant together in quite a different way when eventually I learned to spin their wool. After separating out the cream from the brown in the thick Jacob fleeces which David would sheer for their comfort in the heat of summer, I began to learn how to dye it with plants I could gather from the bog and the shore. Bog asphodel makes a lovely pale yellow; the lichen, which in the Hebrides is called *crotal*, makes a rare rusty red; nettle makes a pale green. Some of the fleece I spun undyed and unwashed, 'in the raw'; the rich, waxy lanolin smell would stay on my hands all day. There is nothing quite as grounding as the scent of another animal on your skin.

There was enchantment in that work, and the enchantment came straight from the land. It was a satisfyingly circular enchantment, as I sat there pedalling my wheel, and dreaming of the land which made the sheep, whose wool we then took to spin, dyeing it with precisely those flowers which had nourished the animals in the first place . . . That was land-magic, for sure: as different a process from knitting a sweater with wool bought in a shop, as growing your own peas from seed and picking them fresh for your dinner is from buying a can of processed peas in a supermarket. For me, spinning their wool was a way of creating something new and unique out of the relationship I had with my sheep, and it bound me to them more closely than ever, helping me to participate more fully and creatively in the ever-unfolding, alchemical process in which the land constantly makes and shapes us.

Folklore around the world accords great power, wisdom and magic to women who spin and weave. A woman on the tiny Sardinian island of Sant'Antioco is the last in a thousand-year-old matrilineal line who spin and weave byssus, or sea silk, one of the rarest and most coveted materials in the world. Sea silk comes from the razor-thin fibres growing from a gland in the feet of a highly endangered Mediterranean clam known as the noble pen shell, *pinna nobilis*. Chiara Vigo knows where to find them, in a secret location among the underground coves and grassy lagoons. She claims to be the last person on earth who knows how to harvest, dye and embroider sea silk, which was used by women in Mesopotamia to embroider clothes for kings, 5,000 years ago, and which was thought to be the material that God commanded Moses to drape on the altar in the Tabernacle. It is three times finer than a strand of human hair, and when the woven sea silk is exposed to ingredients which are known only to women like Vigo, it glistens like gold.

Like the twenty-three generations of women in her family before her, Vigo doesn't make a penny from her work: she's bound by an ancient 'sea oath' based on the belief that byssus should never be bought or sold. 'Byssus doesn't belong to me, but to everyone,' she has said. 'Selling it would be like trying to profit from the sun or the stars.' Vigo believes that the cloth she makes is sacred, calling it 'the soul of the sea', and she treats her craft as an extension of her religious beliefs. She prays twice a day at a deserted cove on the island. 'You have to be respectful to the place you live in,' she says. 'You are just passing by, these places are here to stay. And the sea has its own soul and you have to ask for permission to get a piece of it.'[110]

What is this strange magic which resides in objects that are made by hand? Is it the residue of ourselves which we leave in them? The moisture from our hands seeping into the materials, the thoughts and dreams we're weaving as we work? So much care and love goes into the creation of a handcrafted item – and those items feel alive in a way that mass-produced objects never could. They're alive with the spirit of their maker, and so to acquire something which has been handcrafted by someone else is a curious act of intimacy. Our longing for this kind of connection – a desire to know where they come from, these things we live with, wear or drink out of – is evident in the ongoing revival of popular interest in handcrafted products, and in the growing interest in preserving and practising traditional arts and crafts. It's an antidote to the anonymity of globalisation.

It's not a new trend, of course; it began in the nineteenth century, as the pace of life began to accelerate and mass-produced goods began to pour out of the new factories. In Britain, the designer William Morris, along with several of his colleagues – including the writer John Ruskin – formed the Arts and Crafts Movement at the end of the nineteenth century, as a reaction against what was happening. Morris's prescription for an authentic life was simple: 'Have nothing in your houses that you do not know to be useful or believe to be beautiful.' He blamed industrialisation for suffocating the creative spirit, and advocated a return to making things slowly and individually, by hand. Artisans who adhered to these ideas focused on traditional, pre-industrial methods, and the use of older, more folkloric, styles of decoration.

In Morris's day, this return to an artisanal way of production was welcomed as a connection back to kinder days – and if ever a reminder of gentler times were required, surely it is now. So it is that we're seeing a surge in traditional fairs and festivals such as Weird and Wonderful Wood, Wild Tree Fair and The Green Gathering, which cater for contemporary seekers for a less mechanical, more imaginative approach to living. And so too we're finding increasing coverage of artisanal skills and products in bestselling magazines such as *Country Living*, and a sudden upsurge in similar new magazines which celebrate a simpler, handmade life.

There is nothing
quite as grounding as
the scent of another
animal on your skin.

The remarkable success story of the online craft marketplace Etsy.com is more evidence of this flourishing trend. Etsy offers a platform for people who want to make, sell or buy unique products. 'Our mission is to reimagine commerce in ways that build a more fulfilling and lasting world,' they announce on their website, declaring their aim to 'enable a unique population of Internet-enabled creative entrepreneurs who are building businesses on their own terms – prioritising flexibility, independence and creativity.' Everything listed for sale on Etsy must be either handmade, 'vintage' (more than twenty years old) or a craft supply; it claims 1.7 million active sellers around the world, 28.6 million active buyers, and it declared gross sales of $2.39 billion gross in 2015.[111]

For those who are buyers rather than makers, the purchase of a handcrafted object is an investment – and a commitment to longevity in a world in which everything has become disposable and easily replaced. Our growing interest in the handcrafted reflects an awakening understanding that our excessive consumption is not only killing the planet, but killing our spirits. Those of us who value handcrafted things tend to buy less and, if we can, buy better. We're more likely to cherish a much-loved item of clothing which can be repaired and reused, rather than being thrown away, and which will gather into itself memories and meaning during the years we possess it.

For those who work at crafts and traditional trades, their choice often reflects their desire for agency, self-reliance and work which has meaning, as an increasing number of people around the world struggle to extricate themselves from the forces of the global economy, and to bring their lives back under control and back into their homes. Artist Hannah Willow earns her living by painting, drawing, and working with silver to create beautiful jewellery; she sells her work through an Etsy shop, as well as through galleries and her website.[112] But she used to work in a corporate environment, and, she told me, ended up 'suicidally desperate for change' in a life that felt superficial. 'I felt life was passing me by at a rate of knots,' she said, 'while I spent my precious time working in a job I hated, for a company I thought a waste of time, just to keep a roof over my head and pay my bills. Many of us feel like this, but are at a loss to know what to do – we're so bound up in modern life, mortgages, bills and jobs. It's as if we're trapped by our own lives, and trapped by our civilisation and all that it represents. In those days, I didn't feel any of the magical things I can now connect to. But I broke free fourteen years ago and now live very simply with my husband and pets, spending each day in my little wooden studio painting and making. Since I left, and began to work with my hands, I feel part of the world now, part of a timeline of people contributing to a long and beautiful story.'

Hannah's art and jewellery draws heavily on her connection to the land, and the entwining lives of the people, animals and birds who live on it. Her themes are deeply folkloric. 'Drawing inspiration from folklore, for me, is a way of connecting to an older way of thinking. I believe that, once upon a time, we used to work with the Earth and not against her. I believe that knowledge and memories are not only held within the land, water and air of this planet, but recorded and held within folklore – stories and rituals contain the hidden memories of how we used to know. Exploring folkloric themes for me is like seeing glimpses of a different time, a simpler, more connected place where all life was respected and not commodified. The magic is still there to be found – under the hedgerows, in the ditches and holloways, nests and burrows, the barrows, trees and animals, in the light of the full moon on the land. That's what I'd like people to catch a glimpse of when they see my work.'

Hannah agrees that the growing interest in the folkloric and the handmade is a reaction to the disconnection that so many people feel. 'In this modern synthetic age,' she says, 'people are reaching out to connect with something genuine, something simple and profound. Something that will activate our senses as well as our memories, and reconnect us with nature, peace and magic. Something elemental, pure and original.'

Land and hand

The longing to make things with my own hands first blossomed in me when I said goodbye to my corporate career in the early 1990s, and moved to Connemara. Somehow, that longing was all tied up with falling in love with the land, and the connection between the two has never gone away. Making things didn't come easily to me; as a child, nothing I knitted or sewed ever turned out well – though I had an eye for colour and design – and so whatever creativity I possessed had always passed into words. But when I came to Connemara, I had had enough of human language; I just wanted to use my hands. After years of spending my days in a laboratory or an office, focused entirely on what came out of my head, it seemed like the only possible way to heal. Good, honest work with my hands – it seemed cleaner, somehow, occupying a position on some imaginary line between reparation and redemption. The problem was that I had no idea what to do.

The answer came when a patient new friend taught me how to quilt. To my surprise, I found that I was competent enough, and could indulge that love of colour and design at the same time – and there was something in the slow, careful piecing together of the cloth which seemed to me like the piecing together of a life. Then, I was unquestionably piecing my own life back together; I was both in flight and in recovery, trying to create some kind of pattern with the faded, fraying, random bits of fabric I had at my disposal. This was precisely the kind of work I needed – both symbolic and very real. And, among the group of local women who began to come together and sit in each other's houses one evening each week to quilt and to sew, I felt as if I were becoming part of that long line of communal female sewing and spinning circles which stretched all the way back into mythic time.

After my marriage broke down, I went first for a while to America, where I put all of my yearning for home into the creation of a pale but warm quilt which I called 'Ladder to the Connemara Stars': a triple 'Irish Chain' pattern with an eight-pointed star at each intersection. I hand-quilted it with a complex Celtic knotwork design over a period of about six months, and after the trauma of a broken marriage and subsequent difficult divorce, it felt as if I were literally stitching myself back into the fabric of life. I stitched that quilt imagining that one day I would bring it home to Connemara – an act of creation which incorporated both intention and belief. Two long decades later, in April of the year which I spent writing this book, I laid my quilt out for the first time on a Connemara bed. One day soon afterwards, my former quilting teacher (who I had not seen for twenty years) came to visit. She fingered the quilt

gently, examined the stitching, smiled at me, and said it was a very
fine quilt indeed.

I had finally come full circle.

Quilting is a skill which needs to be learned, but I wholeheartedly
believe that everyone has the ability to make simple, but beautiful
and meaningful creations from things gathered from the land they
inhabit. Absolutely no special skills are required: just a willingness
to look and to imagine. Kate McGillivray is a constant source of
inspiration to me in this respect. When I first met Kate, in 2013,
she was living in a much-loved old cottage in the Galloway hills,
in south-west Scotland. She'd been there for a good many years,
along with her husband Tom, a variety of companion animals
and a community of wild bees who took up residence in a disused
chimney. In those days, Kate described herself as a wanderer of
the old tracks and hedgeways that criss-crossed the land which
she would walk daily – absorbing, observing and listening. As she
walked, she would pick up 'found objects' – scraps of wool, feathers, leaves, stones, thistledown, bones, skulls – and bring them
home to work with.

British psychotherapist Donald Winnicott coined the term
'transitional object' for the items that very young children use
to retain a symbolic link to their mother, while they gradually
move into a space in which they feel they are separate from her.[113]
Usually, the object is something like a blanket or teddy bear, and
it serves as a link between the child's imagining mind and the
external world. Similarly, 'found objects' which we bring home
to put on the mantelpiece, or to work with in the way that Kate
did, are a link between the human imagination and the natural
world. The process connects us in new, creative ways with the
land we live on.

In Kate's spare time she would craft her found objects – in the
company of a miscellaneous selection of fabrics, inks, crayons and
paint – into unique representations of her relationship with the
land: things like fabric journals or small wall-hangings. I have
something she sent me once as a gift: a long strip of tea-coloured
linen, frayed at all the edges. A sliver of a stag's horn is sewn on
at the top, and a strip of old lace hangs down one side, along
with a length of what looks like handspun wool with a wooden

bead attached to the end. Along the other side, a meandering path ending in a spiral is embroidered on it in a rusty red coloured thread, and the words 'walking with fox' stamped in ink, each letter individually placed. It's the simplest thing in the world, and the most perfect.

Kate particularly enjoyed working with pieces of what she called 'tatty linen' as the base for her creations. 'I enjoyed its tactile weave,' she said; 'and linen rots and frays so beautifully when it's subjected to the plant-dyeing process, or exposure to outdoor weather conditions, or ripping and bundling. I would boil the fabric up in an old cauldron in the garden, combining it with materials from my immediate surroundings – plants from my garden or found materials such as herbs, bark, leaves, rusted metals, lichen, stone and peat – to give it colour and character. Or sometimes I would wrap linen around a stone or a tree, soak it in bog or burn, fly it in the wind and sun. When it was ready, I would add random stitches as the fabric seemed to dictate.'

Stitching was a key part of her work, and she describes what she was trying to achieve as 'muted tones, rows of erratic stitch and a general shabbiness. My stitching was worked slowly, always by hand, and with an acute awareness of the environment in which I was working. I liked to think of the cloth becoming imbued with the prevailing south-west winds, bees buzzing in the disused chimney pots and over my herb beds, the Old Water in full spate, the rhythmic tick of a clock, three cats purring and the warning toc-toc of a wren. My stitched lines were rarely straight; I preferred to meander, allowing myself to be distracted. The fabric and dye-marks dictated the directions my needle would take across the surface, and I didn't disguise my work – knots and snags were part and parcel of the process and were, to me, intrinsically attractive.'

When she first began working in this way, Kate handcrafted a doll as a way of exploring her relationship with the place she lived. 'I wove her body on a handloom,' she said. 'She was stuffed with raw fleece which I'd gathered on walks across the Galloway landscape. Slightly dreadlocked hair hinted at her flamboyant tendencies . . . her head, scarf, cloak and a little bag were made using linen which I dyed with herbs and rusting metals gathered from my garden and the deep verges. Her name (which can't be revealed) was printed on a scrap of fabric tucked into her belt. Her bag carried a tiny, and very essential, stone. Tied on a nettle thong was a very old charm in the shape of a hare.' Each of these aspects of the work – the name, the nettle, the hare – clearly had a deep personal significance and meaning for Kate.

My own study is littered with found objects which have been altered or worked on in some way. I especially love a thing that David made me as a birthday gift, a couple of years ago: a small, strangely twisted and gnarly fragment of wood from a rowan tree, topped with a tuft of white fur from an Irish brown hare which he had found dead by the side of the road. He 'dubbed' (twisted) more fur onto a piece of cotton thread (this is a trick known to all fishermen who are used to tying their own flies) and wrapped it around the wood in two different places. Anyone else might think of it as a strange object of desire, but in order to understand why it is one of my favourite things in the world, you need to understand a little something of the symbolism. First, like Kate, I am a lover of hares. I'm fascinated by their beauty, their behaviour and by the fact that they can conceive again while they're already pregnant. I'm also fascinated by their mythology, and especially by the many and varied legends throughout these islands which say that they were the favourite animals for witches to transform themselves into. Isabel Gowdie, who in 1662 confessed to witchcraft near Nairn in Scotland, said that when she wished to shapeshift into a hare she would say a chant which began: 'I shall go into a hare/With sorrow and sych and meickle care'. And the rowan – well, it's a protective tree, in our mythology, but I love it most of all because it survives in even the most inhospitable environments, growing even in the shallowest cracks of boulders, where it's hard to imagine how its roots might find a path to nutrients.

Here, in a country of rowans and hares, this object ties me to the creatures which surround me. It sits next to my computer, and when I am indoors, pouring into a machine the stories and ideas which come out of my imagination, I'll reach out sometimes and finger it. It weaves me right back into all that is real and important to me: the remarkable land that is Connemara, and the mysterious and fascinating creatures I share it with.

Simple living is
often a more radical
choice . . . When we slow
down and live more
simply, we use fewer
resources - both our
own, and the planet's.

Crafting from the land

More often than not, when we think of working creatively or artistically with the landscape, we think of visual approaches to it, like drawing, painting or photographing. Instead of these practices, which in many ways seem designed to set us apart from the land as a spectator of it, try Kate's more immersive approach to working with simple materials from the land and found objects.

- Literally, immerse your creative materials in the land. Push a small square of natural fabric (like undyed linen, wool or organic cotton) into the roots of a tree, or into the earth around a large rock. Bury it under a stone in a stream, or in a bog, or a pile of seaweed on the beach. Or wrap it around the trunk of a tree which means something to you – a willow for flexibility and rebirth; an oak for endurance and strength.

- Whatever you choose to do with it, think also about the times and seasons and cycles you're working in. Will you be wanting the bright and blazing energy of a full moon, or the quieter, beginning energy of a dark new moon? Will you bury it at midsummer or leave it out to catch the May Day morning dew?

- What will you do with the fabric? Use it as the basis for a collage or embroider on it? Incorporate it into a piece of patchwork with fabrics similarly treated?

- Do you have found objects which you can stitch onto your fabric or make part of your collage? If you happen upon a feather while you're walking, how can you use it creatively?

How can you learn to see the artistic potential in everyday things? There are many books which show you how to work with found objects and/or collage. One of my favourites is by UK artist Cas Holmes: *The Found Object in Textile Art*.[114] Look for inspiration on sites like Pinterest. Try to make your work, as Kate does, a reflection of your relationship with a place; or have it mark an important transition in your life. Work intuitively, and try not to constrain yourself with expectations of perfection!

Slow dancing

The desires which motivate a handmade life are paralleled by the motivations that underpin a growing cultural trend which advocates slowing down the pace of modern life. This trend arguably began with the birth of the 'slow food' movement, which arose spontaneously as a protest against the ubiquity of fast food; the 'slow' epithet gradually then came to be attached to more and more aspects of our lives and culture. The term 'Slow Movement' was first coined by Carl Honoré, in his 2004 book *In Praise of Slow*: 'The Slow philosophy is not about doing everything at a snail's pace,' Honoré writes. 'It's about seeking to do everything at the right speed. Savouring the hours and minutes rather than just counting them. Doing everything as well as possible, instead of as fast as possible. It's about quality over quantity in everything from work to food to parenting.'[115]

The Slow Movement has much in common with two other thriving trends: 'downshifting' and 'simple living'. Although it's undoubtedly been going on for very much longer, downshifting first began to be widely spoken about in the 1990s, in response to a growing number of individuals seeking to escape from the 'rat race', and from the obsessive materialism, excessive work and stress which are associated with it. To downshift is to look for a better balance between leisure time and work, to stop thinking about everything in terms of economic success, and instead to focus life around the discovery of personal meaning and building fulfilling relationships. It is, more than anything, about eschewing the cultural dogma that bigger, or more, is better.

Simple living is often a more radical choice, and encompasses a wide variety of methods for simplifying your lifestyle. It begins with removing the clutter of unnecessary possessions, reducing reliance on technology, and increasing self-sufficiency – by growing some of your own food, or making use of alternative forms of energy such as solar or wind power. When we slow down and live more simply in these ways, we use fewer resources – both our own, and the planet's: above all, living simply is usually about living lightly on this earth. And living more lightly is the only way that we as a species might get through the current environmental crisis intact.

All of these choices about living differently have a few things in common: a desire for greater connection – with ourselves and the natural rhythms and cycles of our lives, with others in our communities, with the natural world around us; a belief in the value of living a more present and mindful life; and a striving for meaning and fulfilment rather than the acquisition of wealth or goods. The biggest obstacle to living in these more connected ways is, quite simply, being too busy. A friend's daughter who lives and works in central London tells me that people of her age (she is around thirty) are increasingly scheduling their weekend activities as well as their working days. They 'book themselves into' an activity as if it were a genuine appointment, and there's no spontaneity any more, she complains. If you meet a friend for a cup of coffee, they're constantly checking their watch to see if the hour is up, because they've scheduled themselves to be at the museum, or the gym, or probably even to have sex with their partner. And it's all too easy to access calendars and other scheduling software on mobile devices, she says. It seems to encourage us to fill up all the available slots, leaving people feeling oddly anxious if they see a blank space on their screens.

But research has shown that allowing ourselves to slow down can bring with it major benefits. In 2012 University of California psychologists Benjamin Baird and colleagues, for example, reported that our most creative moments occur when periods of intense focus are combined with periods in which our minds are quiet, daydreaming or allowed to wander.[116] Unfortunately, few of us are accustomed to making time to be still, and the art of doing nothing is slowly becoming a lost art. At work, we're required to be intensely focused on our job; during what ought to be downtime, we immerse ourselves in screens and gadgets and in an excess of activity and connectivity. All of these activities trap us at a surface level of consciousness, and stop us from engaging in the deeper dimensions of our lives. They stop us asking the big questions about who we are and who we want to become and what kind of world we really want to live in. They prevent us from listening to our bodies and fully engaging with the world around us – all of the things that we've considered, through the course of this book, to be essential to living in a state of enchantment.

Sometimes, though, slowing down can be harder than it seems. It's easy enough to create 'to-do' lists for slowing down – making slowing down just another of the busynesses we continue to perpetrate on ourselves – but the only way to make deep and meaningful change is through a fundamental shift in the way we approach our lives and the world around us. What's needed is a deep evaluation of what we really value in our lives; of what we are prepared to change, and what we are not.

Beginning the shift to a slower, simpler life

1. Think about the ways in which you might be caught in the cultural trap of wanting too much. Do you really need a bigger house, or a new car, or a clutter of clothes and other possessions? Do you really want to think of yourself as on a 'housing ladder' or a 'career ladder'? Why not just step off?

2. Do you live within your means? If not, how can you do so?

3. Take stock. Learn to discriminate what you really need in your life from the things you assume you need. Think of all the heroines in fairy tales who are set the task of sorting the wheat from the chaff, or who – like Psyche, for example – are required to sort a great pile of seeds into their various types. And then make a list of all the things you possess, and all of the things you do which fill

your days (work and leisure) – and determine what it is you really value, and what you can do without. Which of them cause you to feel stressed? What are the habits or relationships which weigh you down?

11. Life as if it mattered

The Way It Is

There's a thread you follow. It goes among
things that change. But it doesn't change.
People wonder about what you are pursuing.
You have to explain about the thread.
But it is hard for others to see.
While you hold it you can't get lost.
Tragedies happen; people get hurt
or die; and you suffer and get old.
Nothing you do can stop time's unfolding.
You don't ever let go of the thread.

William Stafford[117]

It was the movie *Baby Boom* which nailed it for me. I was thirty or so years old, and I had just written a letter of resignation and popped it in the internal mail to an unpleasant and borderline misogynistic boss. It was Friday. I went home, both horrified and petrified by my own action: I was throwing away a secure, well-paid job with 'prospects' in a multinational corporation, and was planning to move to a dilapidated stone cottage in the far west of Ireland. Where I would have no prospects at all, no savings, and no obvious way either of paying the bills or paying off the tiny loan which was going to allow us to renovate the cottage in question – but where I would have peace and quiet and views to die for, in the only country which had ever felt to me like home.

My friends and family thought I was crazy. My then-husband thought I was, too. We had a mortgage the size of a planet, the housing market was in the doldrums, and yet I knew that if I stayed where I was, I'd die. Sometimes, though, when you're afraid of actually living, a living death can seem like the safest option of all.

Sometime during an utterly horrible weekend, throughout which I felt as if I was standing on the edge of the gap of doom waiting to fall in, I turned on the TV and found myself unexpectedly engrossed in a light comedy starring Diane Keaton and an especially delectable Sam Shepard. In it, Keaton plays a successful Manhattan business woman involved with an investment banker – both of them obsessed with their work and the progress of their careers. But after a cousin dies and leaves her tiny baby in her care, Keaton finds herself slowly changing, and her priorities radically shifting. Eventually, finding life as a mother incompatible with her company's expectations of her, she throws away her high-flying career, leaves her unsympathetic partner, and moves to a remote and slightly dilapidated Vermont farmhouse. In financially dire straits, she starts to make and sell home-made baby food – and sales begin to boom. The crunch comes when Keaton's old company wants to buy the business for millions of dollars, distribute the product nationwide and promote her to an even more high-prestige job than she had when she left. Although life in Vermont has been far from easy, and although this new offer at first seems to be everything she has ever wanted, in the end Keaton realises that she can't possibly give up her quality of life, her new lover Shepard, and the daughter she now adores. And so she turns them down and gets on with her simpler, but infinitely more satisfying life.

When I went back into work on Monday, I was called into a company director's office and offered many inducements to stay. Higher pay, a nicer boss, a promotion – everything that once upon a time I might have thought I ever wanted. With *Baby Boom* firmly in my mind, I smiled politely and said no. Because by that time I'd very clearly figured out that, whatever I might have been born into this world to do, or whatever I might conceivably come to do that would make even the tiniest fragment of this world a richer or better place – sitting comfortably behind a desk in a multinational corporation couldn't possibly be part of it.

Apprenticeship and calling

In his bestselling book *The Soul's Code: In Search of Character and Calling*, archetypal psychologist James Hillman declared: 'Each person enters the world called.'[118] Each of us, in other words, has a 'calling': we came into the world in this particular place, at this particular time, for a purpose. Calling in this sense is neither 'fate' nor 'destiny', and – in my own view, at least – doesn't necessarily have anything to do with the job you do. It can, of course, if you happen to fulfil whatever purpose you believe you have in life primarily through your occupation – though this is arguably 'vocation', which is a subset of 'calling'. For many people, though, their sense of purpose is expressed by ways of *being* in the world rather than ways of *doing*.

Hillman's notion of calling wasn't original: it can be traced back to Plato, who expressed the idea in his Myth of Er. He suggested that before each of us is born, our soul selects a purpose for us to fulfil during our time on Earth. Each soul must pass under the throne of the goddess Ananke ('Necessity') – the mother of the Fates, and the one who, Plato said, helps establish what is necessary for each soul to do or be before it enters the world. After what we intend to accomplish has been confirmed, we travel to the Plain of Oblivion where Lethe, the river of forgetfulness flows; once we've drunk from its waters, we emerge into life completely ignorant of the fate we've chosen. But we're accompanied into this life by a 'daimon' – a spiritual companion who acts as a 'carrier of our destiny', and helps to ensure we fulfil it.

Hillman took up these ideas, similarly suggesting that before we are born, the soul selects the pattern that we live out, and that we bring into this world, and carry inside us, an innate vision – a kind of concealed invisible potential – which we express during the course of our lives. Although Hillman used many terms for this vision, including the daimon, my favourite way of imagining this is to think of it as an acorn: the acorn, like any seed, carries within it the image of, and the potential to become, the oak tree that it might eventually be – given the circumstances which would allow it to flourish.

This image or potential which we carry inside – whatever we might imagine it to be – guides us, prods us, helps us throughout the course of our life to remember what we're here for. Sooner or later, Hillman said, something calls us to follow a particular path – and what we must then do is be sure that we make the choices and take the path which aligns our lives with our calling, rather than another which might seem to be the path of least resistance. Although this all sounds rather fatalistic, Hillman is at great pains to point out that what we are working with here is very much a potential, not a predetermined pattern. We journey through life, he said, in continual, moving adjustments – not following some grand predestined design. But the paths we take will keep on trying to align themselves to our overall purpose or calling – and so, in other words, the journey which will ultimately lead us to fulfil our calling reshapes itself in response to the choices we make in life.

Hillman believed that we might find glimpses of our calling in early childhood – an idea which was also central to the ideas of American psychologist Alfred Adler, who wrote about 'guiding fictions': significant event(s) in early childhood that we turn into a kind of personal myth which we then use to guide our life. Our first childhood patterns and obsessions, our favourite stories or characters – all such things can give us insight into our calling. Other clues come in the images and symbols and archetypes we hold dear; in the mythic patterns we persist in living out; in 'big' dreams. The challenge is to look out for them, to constantly be asking ourselves what is the meaning and purpose of our lives. Why am I here? And why (in the difficult times) should I stay here?

Not everyone comes to understand their calling early in life, and I'm not sure that really matters. When I work with these ideas in the workshops and retreats that I run, I often find surprisingly young people distressed by the idea that they haven't yet understood what their calling might be – as if calling were a destination you needed to arrive at as soon as possible, rather than the lifelong journey to fulfil your greatest potential, to express your unique gift, which I believe it is. That sense of a desperate race to 'figure it all out' as soon as you can is surely a reflection of modern culture, which tells us constantly that the fastest solutions are the best. Who has the time these days to do the research, learn, reflect, make a mistake, try again . . . like Alice's White Rabbit, we constantly imagine ourselves to be running late for the rest of our lives. For some important date, some 'aha' moment when we can tick another box and say, well, that's that then. I've done calling. What's next?

For me, calling has nothing to do with religious beliefs; it is quite simply the work of a lifetime – it's about living life as if it mattered. It's beautiful work, because it's not so much about doing and accomplishing as it is about developing and expressing a vision for your life. And one of the things that is forgotten in a task-driven culture which has no appreciation of calling is that developing a vision takes time. Sometimes, it takes a lifetime – for it to emerge, and for it then to be developed and expressed in all the ways that are possible for us. Because to express our calling is to allow ourselves to uniquely express one mode of being, one facet of the creative life force of the universe – whatever you might conceive that to be.

It's this rush to do, to accomplish, which is one of the most pernicious aspects of contemporary culture: it robs us of our ability to fully participate in the process of our own becoming. We want to have achieved our dreams – but we don't necessarily value the work that must be put in to achieve them. We want to be writers, for example – but we don't want to spend the years learning the craft of how to write. We see the results all around us, everywhere we look: overnight celebrities, instant experts, pop-up personalities with more form than substance. This is not how it's supposed to be. In this race to some imagined finish line, we've forgotten the value of true apprenticeship.

As ever, we find the treasure we imagine we've lost hidden there in full view for everyone to see, embedded in our old myths and fairy tales. For at the heart of so many good fairy tales is precisely this critical concept of apprenticeship. In the old German tales of Mother Hulda (or Frau Hölle) a girl must plunge down a well and spend a year apprenticed to the old woman before she can return to the world above with the lost spindle she had been seeking – a spindle which now, as a result of her labours, has acquired magical powers. In a rare old story from the Isle of Skye, a girl who is lost in the Cuillin mountains must apprentice herself to an old woman and an old man who create the dreams of the world for a year and a day, before she is guided back down the mountain by fairy deer. There she finds the love of her life, and a mission to teach his people about dreaming.

The messages are clear: sometimes, you have to step off the path you're so determinedly striding along and learn a few new skills. And learn them properly – through your own lived experience, not experience copied from others; and by continuing to learn for however long is necessary, from someone who really knows. These stories tell us that sometimes it's okay to feel that you're not progressing, because, as we've already seen, the myth of progress is another of those profoundly pernicious myths which our culture forces upon us. Sometimes, it's okay to say that you don't know, you're not sure, you're still trying to figure it out for yourself – and to avoid like the plague the people who are trying to sell you ready-made solutions of their own.

To fully express our calling, we must be able to tolerate the idea of apprenticeship. To understand what we don't know, to do the proper research, to find the right teachers, to embody the neces-sary lived experience, before we imagine that we're ready to share our gift with the world. Apprenticeship requires humility: a little-valued quality in a world hell-bent on glory. All the best fairy-tale heroines knew it to be true: sometimes it's okay to say that you're not quite there yet. None of us are ever quite there until it's time for us finally to die – because when we imagine that our journey has come to an end, the truth is, our ability to live a seeking, authentic life has come to an end along with it.

Earlier, I suggested that our sense of overall calling or purpose may not necessarily have anything to do with our career choices. My friend Jeanette works in a tea room in a village in the south-west of England, and though she finds the job pleasant enough, it's no more than a pleasant enough way of paying the bills. Jeanette's sense of calling comes instead from what she does in her 'spare time' (and what a curious idea that is, that the time we spend not working is somehow 'spare' – implying that it's not so valuable, or necessary). Jeanette is a local advocate for natural beekeeping: she guides people who want to host bees on their land, and collects and rehomes swarms of bees which happen to stray into inhospitable territory. 'I can't imagine how I'd turn it into a job or an income stream,' she tells me, 'but that's not what it's about, to me. I do it for love of bees, and out of a sense that we must treasure them, and maybe even that we can learn something from them. And we rely on them as pollinators, of course: they're hugely important. I've been fascinated by bees ever since I was a child, and so maybe I've always known that this was the gift I could offer to the world. It gives me a feeling of fulfilment and, yes, a strong sense of purpose too. I could say it was a calling.'

This kind of separation of calling from occupation isn't unusual, but it can be very much more problematic when the occupation in question doesn't satisfy us, and when at the same time we have no other sense of calling or purpose in our lives to fall back on. While some professions and jobs are more likely to be associated with a sense of vocation, few people today claim a genuine vision for their lives – beyond the obvious things like financial security and good health. It's a recipe for alienation, for sure – especially when, as research carried out in the UK in 2015 by Investors in People suggested, 60 per cent of the workforce are actively unhappy in their jobs.[119] Back in 1974, writer and broadcaster Studs Terkel published one of many books in which he interviewed Americans about their daily lives. In his introduction to *Working: People Talk*

About What They Do All Day and How They Feel About What They Do, Terkel made the following comment: 'This book, being about work, is, by its very nature, about violence – to the spirit as well as to the body.' Work for most people, Terkel demonstrated consistently throughout the book, involves daily humiliations and 'scars, psychic as well as physical'. There are some, he says, who may enjoy their work, but these cases may 'tell us more about the person than about his task'.[120]

In his book *The Protestant Ethic and the Spirit of Capitalism*,[121] our old friend Max Weber suggested that very few people are motivated to work on the basis of a vocational calling; rather, we work because specific requirements of the culture in which we live coerce us to do so in order to survive. A powerful infrastructure founded in technical, administrative and market forces 'determines our lives'. What, then, if we focused more on work which we were genuinely called to do, genuinely loved or otherwise seemed fitted for and saw some value in? Weber also coined the phrase 'the iron cage' to refer to the despair which many people feel about the ever-growing constraints on the creative and expressive aspects of our lives, which he saw as an inevitable consequence of the fixed, hier-archical, rationalised routines inflicted upon us by the bureaucratic authorities which rule our lives. 'The bureaucratic organization,' Weber declared back in 1930, is 'in the process of erecting a cage of bondage which persons – lacking all powers of resistance – will perhaps one day be forced to inhabit.'

Close to a century later, I think that many of us probably feel that we are already there. A growing number of people feel that they are trapped within 'the system', caught up in 'the rat race', owned body and soul by a vast and impenetrable bureaucracy which verges always on the absurd, and sometimes is positively Kafkaesque. This great and growing existential crisis is reflected in the longings that so many of us have to 'escape the system' and determine the course and content of our own lives – and that was a good part of my own motivation for handing in my notice and running off to the mountains of Connemara back in the early 1990s. All I had ever wanted, since as a teenager I had fallen headlong in love with the writing of D.H. Lawrence, was to extract myself from the workings of what he referred to as 'the Machine'.

When I was growing up, in a working-class family in the industrial north-east of England, work was held to be something which not only paid the bills, but in some sense 'built character'. Not only that, but even the hardest labouring jobs gave some sense of meaning to your life – some reason to get out of bed – as well as providing structure. In the north-east, many of those jobs vanished in the 1980s, but today, they're under threat everywhere: Oxford economists tell us that almost half of existing jobs are at risk of death by computerisation within twenty years.[122] Love and work, Sigmund Freud declared, are essential constituents of a healthy human life – and although many of us today might long for more leisure time, it's hard to imagine what a world would look like in which our jobs were no longer the primary structural force in our waking lives. The threat of an end to work raises the most fundamental questions about what it means to be a human being alive in the world today. What then would provide us with a sense of purpose; where would we apply our creative energies?

An enchanted life, one in which these questions are at the very core, is a life in which we come to recognise, and pursue, our personal calling – in which we seek out and uncover the unique gift that each of us brings to this world.

Sarah West sits at my kitchen table late into the evening and describes to me how, just over three years ago in the woods of northern Ontario, 'calling' descended on her rather literally, with a fierce and telling physical blow to the head.

'I had taken a week off work,' she says, 'and was back home in Parry Sound. I was doing what I loved best – spending time in the forest and with family. One afternoon I was woodworking, puttering around in the workshop. I bent over to pick something up and stood up quickly, slamming my head right into a metal clamp. It hurt, but it didn't seem like an especially dramatic event. I carried on with my day. But twenty-four hours later the concussion hit me like a ton of bricks, and I knew something was seriously wrong. My family whisked me to the hospital, where the doctors downplayed its severity because I wasn't actually haemorrhaging. But I was completely debilitated and didn't know what to do.'

Apprenticeship requires
humility: a little-valued
quality in a world hell-bent
on glory. All the best
fairy-tale heroines knew it
to be true: sometimes it's
okay to say that you're
not quite there yet.

Sarah describes the effect of the concussion as a profound form of sensory overload. 'We all have a "veil" of sorts which acts as a filter, enabling us to comfortably feel and engage with what we sense internally and externally – light, sound, movement, touch. With a concussion, this "veil" drops, and everything becomes too much to process. For me, light, sound and movement were utterly unbearable. My head was so thick with fog I could hardly think or speak. My body felt like lead, and whiplash left me in constant pain. Even the smallest movement was like trying to run through water. I had no energy for anything; my emotions were in disarray. I lived in terror for two weeks before finding an athletic therapist who told me what was happening, what to expect, and how to care for myself.'

Before the accident, Sarah had led a very busy life. She was engaged in what she describes as a good and challenging career, was immersed in volunteer efforts, and had an active social life with friends and family. 'I was always on the go,' she tells me. 'I gave everything my all. I was living in downtown Toronto, constantly pummelled by the buzz of the city, "in my head" most of the time. I most certainly didn't care for my own wellbeing – physically, spiritually, emotionally. Eventually, I came to feel like I wasn't where I was supposed to be, or doing what I was supposed to be doing. I felt stuck and powerless, longing to be somewhere else but never seeming to be able to make a move. Often, periods of emotional darkness and deadening would wash over me. Life wasn't awful, and it was filled with beautiful moments, but overall it just eventually stopped feeling like I was in the right spot.'

Sarah had always had a deep fascination with her own ancestral heritage in Scotland and Ireland, but her life was too frenetic to allow her the time to really explore it. 'I dreamt about leaving the life that I led and being in the Celtic nations. As a "settler Canadian" working with Indigenous peoples in Ontario, I was deeply aware of the importance of the rich wealth of teachings and sense of rootedness that comes with connecting to your indigeneity. But I had constructed my life so that I couldn't live in the fullest expression of myself. The core elements of who I am were not integrated. I felt like two different people – the Sarah of the city and work, and the Sarah who was intensely passionate about being immersed in nature, making art, sharing stories.'

It was the accident which forced Sarah to stop, and to take stock of where she was heading. 'At the outset of the injury,' she says, 'my healthcare team recommended a period of complete darkness with no activity to ease the overload on my senses. To build up my resilience, I was to ever-so-slowly begin to expose myself to light, sound, movement, and to using my brain again. Unable to occupy myself with the high-energy busyness I was used to stuffing my life with, I was faced with simply . . . being.' Sarah describes that period of utter darkness and removal from normal, daily life as a profound experience. 'How often do we get to just stop? To sit with ourselves without distraction, see who you truly are? For me, it was a scary and wonderful gift. In the deep dark, I sat with all the things that terrified and frustrated me. My mind went into a deep dreamscape and was free to imagine the most incredible adventures and possibilities. The concussion created the space and time for me to address everything that had come before, as well. I relentlessly turned over, examined and eventually planned to change most elements of my life.'

Sarah decided that her primary focus would be on getting well, but then she would move out of Toronto and, ultimately, take the opportunity to travel. 'I very nervously asked for and was granted a year's leave of absence from work. I moved back home to the forest for six months and found nourishment for my soul among the trees, making art, studying folklore and being with family. Eventually, I felt it was time to go, and so planned a six-month "grand adventure" through Wales, Ireland, Scotland, the Faroe Islands and England.

'It was always going to be more than just a tour,' she tells me. 'It was about stepping out in faith, in a willingness to do whatever it took to be well and explore my purpose in life. I gave shape to my odyssey by deciding to root in places for long periods of time, rather than skimming the surface and trying to see everything. I focused the journey around my passions: story, plants and art. I chose locations based on teachers and places of folklore that I felt called me.' And that, in fact, was how I came to meet Sarah: one of her first stops was to attend a myth- and story-based creative retreat for women which I was running in North Wales.

'Once I hopped on that plane and started connecting with the land and people, incredible new opportunities emerged in a way I could have never imagined. As I went along, new challenges and teachings arose, and I kept on working through them, continuously testing my strength and resolve. I kept having to release and shed unhelpful habits and patterns. During one beautiful moment after hiking the Crow Head peninsula in Ireland, I slept on a cliff's edge. I was suddenly acutely aware that my former unhappiness and injury had passed. The incredible people I'd met and experiences I'd had as I travelled had acted like a mirror, continuously challenging me to rethink how I approach myself and the world. I met new mentors, friends and teachers who showed by example how I could integrate and weave all my passions into my life. I was able to re-envision what my life could be. I've become aware of the unique gifts I have to offer. And best of all, I have the health, energy and support to give shape to this new vision.'

Looking back, Sarah believes that the concussion was an immense gift. 'It literally knocked me back into shape,' she says, 'and onto the path I need to be on. It forced me to confront living a life I knew wasn't quite right, and gave me the time and space to be restored. It's also left me with an intense sense of responsibility: to use this blessed gift of wellness and clarity to continue to give back, bringing healing into our wounded world. Label it what you will – a "calling" or "purpose"; it's been with me since childhood. And now I've found the strength, support and perspective to pursue my path.'

Thinking about calling

Taking up the ideas of James Hillman on how we might discover our personal calling, think about the following questions:

- ❧ What were your earliest loves and obsessions? Do any of them contain the seeds of a calling? Some things may be very obvious – as a child, for example, I was always inventing stories – but some may be subtler.
- ❧ Is there a particular story, or archetypal image or character, which strongly draws you? I have always, for as long as I can remember, been drawn to the image of the

Wise Old Woman in the woods. It represents to me an idea of wisdom that is deep but quiet, that doesn't shout out its own cleverness, but waits to be found. The old oakwoods are deep and beautiful; there is light and dark in perfect balance. The old woman is self-contained and values her solitude – but welcomes those who happen to find her. In some senses, that image represents the essence of what I believe is my own calling. What would be the equivalent for you?

- What really nourishes you and makes you feel whole?
- What do you love? What makes you get out of bed in the morning, even when times are hard? What would sustain you if you were to come home and find everything gone? What are the constants, the things that are truly essential to you, the things that reflect your values and help you to grow? How can you find more ways to honour those things that are essential?
- What is the great thing for which you would sacrifice your life?
- Conversely, what can't you tolerate?
- Who are the people you most admire? What are the qualities you admire them for?
- Who are your community, or who do you wish were your community?

The ritual life

A ritual, according to the Oxford Dictionary (when the word is not used simply to mean a 'habit'), is 'a religious or solemn ceremony consisting of a series of actions performed according to a prescribed order'.[123] As the field of anthropology defines the word, rituals are generally undertaken for a specific cultural purpose, such as marking the transition from childhood to adulthood. A ritual consists of a set of usually predetermined actions which have intentional symbolic meaning, and their function is usually to reinforce social bonds in the community.

University of Virginia religious studies professor Vanessa Ochs has spent much of her career studying and writing about rituals, both old and new. According to Ochs, one of the reasons why we find rituals useful is because they 'offer ways for emotion to be contained and channelled' – in other words, they help us to negotiate the difficult emotions that come with major life events and transitions. Rituals also give us a sense of belonging. 'Rituals connect us to groups, they connect us to the divine, they suggest a deeper world of meaning beyond the mundane habits of the everyday,' Ochs says. 'They can transcend time, connecting us to our ancestors and to those who will come after us.'[124]

In contemporary Western societies, we undertake rituals or ceremonies to mark certain events in our lives or certain days of the year – baptism, marriage, funerals, acts of worship or celebration on holy days – but they are generally few and far between, and often seem lifeless, archaic or even irrelevant in the context of our day-to-day lives. And we are remarkably selective in the events which we choose to mark: we tend to recognise events which are seen as life-enhancing, like marriage, but we have no rituals or ceremonies to mark the more painful passage of separation and divorce. We celebrate births, but we have no accepted rituals to help us through the process of dying. We have no significant rituals to mark key transition times or turning points in our lives: adolescence, midlife and elderhood. In other words, we've lost the art of creating meaningful and appropriate rites of passage.

Ethnographer and folklorist Arnold van Gennep was one of the first scholars to seriously study rites of passage, at the beginning of the twentieth century.[125] In indigenous cultures, he suggested, rites of passage have three phases; he called them separation, liminality and incorporation. (Later scholars have almost universally tended to label these three stages separation, initiation and return.) In the first phase, people withdraw from their current status or role in the community and prepare to move to another; there is often a symbolic detachment from, or 'cutting away' of, the former self. The liminal phase represents a time of transition; this is usually a time of learning and instruction of some kind. In the third phase (incorporation) the transition is completed, and the individual can assume his or her new identity or place in the society. Most rites of passage involve some kind of symbolic death and rebirth, and in most indigenous cultures they're seen as being fundamental to individual growth and development, as well as to socialisation into the community. More generally, they create a sense of movement through life, an acknowledgement that there are important thresholds which must be crossed, and that life involves a series of transformations which are both inevitable and worthy of celebration.

In many traditional cultures around the world, the passage from adolescence to adulthood (for men, at least, if not always for women) involves a journey of the kind which some Native American peoples call 'vision quest'. These journeys usually involve going out into a wild place, alone, and usually without food and drink; their purpose is to induce a vision or dream which will ultimately help participants to shed some light on a big question which they take with them. The Australian Aboriginal 'walkabout' tradition is a male initiatory journey which marks the passage into adulthood. Walkabout takes place in remote areas such as the outback so that those undertaking the journey can create a connection with their traditional, spiritual roots – following the dreaming tracks, for example, which link sacred sites.

In the West, we lack these traditions – but increasingly people are beginning to create their own. At the age of twenty-three, American Andrew Forsthoefel headed out of his home with a back-pack, a voice recorder, books by Whitman and Rilke, and a sign that read 'Walking to Listen'. He had just graduated from college and was ready to begin his adult life – but, he said, he didn't know how to go about it, and nor did he have anyone who could serve as a guide. He was expected to follow the well-mapped path which was common to the American middle classes, and he was comfortable enough, and secure. But he felt something was missing on that course, and it had nothing to do with money or achievement: it was about the mystery of people, and the ways they chose to live their lives.

So Forsthoefel decided to take a cross-country quest – one in which everyone he met would contribute something to the guide he was lacking. 'I wanted to learn what it actually meant to come of age, to transform into the adult who would carry me through the rest of my life. Who was he? What did he know? How would he finally become himself, and where did he belong? . . . I needed information and experience, some kind of rudder that would help me navigate whatever lay ahead.' And so Forsthoefel travelled across the country, asking people what were the things they knew now which they would tell their twenty-three-year-old selves, if they had the opportunity to do so. He recorded the stories of several hundred people during the course of his journey, and its end was marked by a ceremony offered by friends from the Navajo Nation.

What did he learn from the experience? 'The people were like my footsteps', he writes: 'Every one of them was necessary . . . We were inextricably bound together, giving and receiving, speaking and listening, seeing and being seen. We were all walking, side by side . . . What a way to live, to live *for* others, experiencing light and dark and every shade in between so that the experiences might be an offering for someone else someday, so that my life might serve something greater than just myself.'[126] It sounds to me like a perfectly beautiful note on which to enter into an adult life.

Mark Sipowicz is a Jungian wilderness guide in Colorado who helps individuals – mostly men – to engage in rites of passage work. He came to this work, Mark tells me, after embarking on a 'vision quest' in Death Valley almost a decade ago, when he was forty-four, and which he says changed everything for him. 'I had a successful small business in a field that I loved. I had a loving wife and two bright and beautiful boys, and was surrounded by meaningful and longstanding friendships. But I also knew in my heart I was in trouble. Something was missing. I was afraid to die – maybe I was afraid to live in some way I had not yet lived; I was haunted by questions about quality, mortality, fate and destiny.

'When I discovered modern practices which are based on ancient ways of walking alone out into the natural world, with those "big" questions in hand – I felt I could finally properly address these questions, find some relief, some answers – ultimately ask some better questions, and find a way forward – all in a very physical way; outside, in the wild landscapes that I had loved since my youth.'

Now Mark's work is centred around helping others to work with ritual journeys. 'My mission is to help others who have heard a knock – or maybe even only a faint scratching – at the door of their consciousness that can no longer be ignored. People who are searching for deeper meaning in their lives, or longing to live a life that feels more authentic, or who have a sense of calling that they haven't yet tended. I take them outside, into the wisdom of the hills and valleys, the green forests and the wild rivers, where we usually discover that the answers are always closer and more natural than we think.'

One of the offerings at Mark's organisation, Soul and Stream, is a three-day wilderness retreat – a kind of vision quest – for men which is designed to help them re-vision their lives.[127] Mark and a fellow guide take participants to a wild camp in the foothills of the Rocky Mountains, where they spend the first day preparing – working with story, poetry, dreams and somatics – and thinking about what they want to take from their experience. On the second day, participants set off on a solo quest into the wilderness, listening, speaking and engaging with the natural world around them. 'Going out into nature, in order to journey more deeply inside ourselves, helps us to lay bare the bones of who we are and to strip away what's no longer useful. The extreme edge between longing and fear as they cross the threshold into this unknown ceremony is excruciating, beautiful and very emotional. We tell them to go slow, to notice, to speak, and listen to inner and outer voices. We tell them to question. A central pivot point for all of these quests is the question of fate or destiny. What's my life for? What should I be doing now? How do I live my life with the cards I've been dealt?' On the third day, they return to the group to relate and explore the gifts of their time alone on the land. The participants then work together to clarify insights they've gained into the ways they want to live in the future.

Mark's work is focused on men because he believes that ritual and ceremony are very much harder for men than for women. 'It's so rare for a man to mark the changes he's going through and explore them with intention. We might feel a shudder of joy or have a glimpse of meaning at a graduation, a marriage or a birth, but we rarely allow ourselves the space, the time and the creativity to mark the passage more deeply. It's so much more common for a

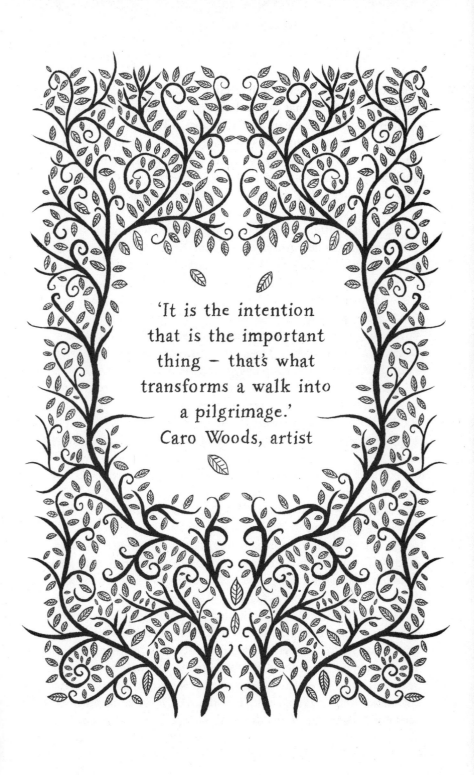

'It is the intention
that is the important
thing – that's what
transforms a walk into
a pilgrimage.'
Caro Woods, artist

woman to gather a community of other women around her to
mark her changes, to do some thoughtful artwork to express the
conscious and unconscious layers of her unfolding, or to speak
vividly and emotionally about her passages. But men don't, and
so it all goes underground. I tend to think it erupts to the surface
in things like spectator sports (with all the regalia of ritual and
emotional expression) or in drinking with the guys, where back-
slapping and (some) shared confidences become more acceptable
with every pint, each round of drinks opening another layer of
repressed longing for shared rites and rituals of depth and connection. But without a container, without intention, this kind
of thing can so easily slip into ego-building and ultimately soul-
crushing activities.

'On a vision quest, men often come to terms with their divided
lives – the ones which have them feeling one way about the world,
and yet speaking and doing things that contradict that feeling.
That's a big hurdle for a lot of the men I see, and there's a sense of
bafflement, and sometimes tears, but always an eagerness to overcome their divided lives and move toward wholeness and congruity.'

But it's not just about exploring your own personal needs, Mark
says: a quest is also a way to try to connect to community and the
wider world. 'At the heart of the archetypal quest is the idea that
we may be journeying for the sake of our soul, but our soul is
connected to the world, and so this also has to be about connecting to the world more deeply. It becomes about returning to our
home and community with the intention of sharing the gifts we've
received – there is always a gift – and perhaps sometimes sharing a
remedy for what ails us, and the community.

'So, after vision-questing in nature, you might see someone
devoting time, energy or money to supporting Earth health and
consciousness upon their return. The natural world gave them so
much on quest that they want to give something back to her. Or
someone who has been deeply healed from a particular trauma in
their life, comes back and is called to heal others with the same
or similar trauma in their community because of their gratitude.
The quester has gone out a wounded man, unable to tolerate the
prescribed or well-trodden path forward any more, and he's come
out of it a more gifted man, able to share his story of healing and
accomplishment. He seems to others now to be much more vivid

– in both his scars and his accomplishments – and this also helps them to see aspects of this in each other, so building a greater sense of tolerance and kinship.'

Pilgrimage can also perform this function, and in the UK and Ireland today there's a growing interest in it, as more and more organisations are focusing on renewing the ancient traditions. According to the British Pilgrimage Trust, pilgrimage 'offers initiation through making people reconnect with an ancient form of ritual, a journey on foot toward unknown outcomes. It takes away people's hard-won domestic insulation and convenience, and puts them simply on the ground – in a very real Britain that has always been there, just over the hills and beyond the woods.'[128] And it's the last phrase of that description which is beginning to resonate so deeply with people; pilgrimages these days are less likely to be taken for religious reasons than they are to achieve a sense of connection with something greater than ourselves – the Earth itself, and the community of life which inhabits it.

As with Mark's ritual journeys into the wilderness, people often make pilgrimages at turning points in their lives, in the hope that, somewhere along the journey, they'll find the answers they're looking for. In 2015, my friend Caro Woods set off from the Holy Island of Lindisfarne, in Northumberland on the north-east coast, on an epic thousand-mile journey across England, travelling along the ancient tracks, old drovers' roads and quiet country lanes to St Michael's Mount in Cornwall in the far south-west. This journey, she told me, was born out of adversity: the break-up of a relationship and its severe financial consequences. It was a search for transformation which took three-and-a-half months to complete – but what was unique about Caro's pilgrimage was that, rather than walking, she rode her Connemara pony, Tommy. 'I wanted the toughness and intelligence of a pony native to these islands who would be able to handle the rocky and rough terrain of our own native wild moorlands,' she said, 'and the repetitive rhythm of his hoof beats on the ground as we walked along became the beating heart of our journey.'[129]

As an artist, Caro is interested in pilgrimage as a creative journey, and so this was very much an inner exploration as well as an outer one. 'The adventures in my daily rides,' she told me, 'could be translated as mini-metaphors for the bigger journey of my life. Each new challenge along the road, whether mundane or profound, had to be met face to face, each problem solved with imagination and creative thinking, and dealt with, with little if no outside resources, while literally on the hoof. I often had to dig deep to find the resources to deal with situations as they arose. I hoped that by imposing this state of being in the wilderness, both physically and metaphysically, I might stumble upon a "bigger truth", something that could only be revealed beyond my everyday life.'

Caro's 'bigger truth' involved a renewed love for the landscape she was passing through – but she also found it in the heart of people's homes. 'I travelled without a pack horse,' she said, 'and so I had to rely on the goodness of others to help us find food and shelter along the way. I have, at times, been overwhelmed by the kindness and generosity of the strangers who not only embraced what we were doing but also took us into their homes, their own place of sanctuary, and shared a brief but intense moment of their lives with me and Tommy. And so I came back vowing to make more effort to help others along their own life's path in the future. The fact that we achieved what I had set out to do was hugely enriching and confidence-building. I learnt that with sheer bloody-mindedness, dogged determination and a touch of magic, you can achieve virtually anything.'

I asked Caro what advice she'd give to others who would love to embark on such a pilgrimage, but who find it hard to cut large swathes of time out of their everyday lives. 'Many people prefer to walk along traditional pilgrim routes,' she said, 'such as the route from London to Canterbury, or the Camino to Santiago de Compostela in Spain, following in the steps of countless other people. But I believe it is possible to turn any favourite walk into a pilgrimage – however big or little you want to make it. It could be a circular walk, a walk to a favoured destination or building, a singing walk or a silent meditation – alone or with others. A daily walk with the dog would do it! It is the *intention* that is the important thing – that's what transforms a walk into a pilgrimage. Whether it's a simple event or a more ambitious project, I believe that the potential for a deeper understanding of your own soul's purpose is a reward worth striving for.'

Creating rituals

A ritual requires the following ingredients:

- Having a reason or intention for the ritual.
- Finding a place in which to make it happen.
- Deciding on the action and/or words that the ritual will consist of.
- A closing: what will you take away from it, or what changes do you want to inspire?

Think about the kinds of ritual you might like to bring into your life:

- Ceremonies which celebrate seasonal cycles and festivals.
- Ceremonies and initiatory experiences which celebrate life passages: birth, death, the onset of menstruation, coming of age . . .
- Rituals and ceremonies carried out in times of need or illness.
- Rituals for transformation: pilgrimage or vision quests, for example.
- Public rituals to express solidarity or shared beliefs. One of my favourite examples is that of the 'Life Cairn' movement, which creates memorials for species that have been declared extinct. In their ceremonies, each participating individual lays a stone until a memorial cairn is formed.[130]

Ritual and ceremony in everyday life

- What can you do each morning to greet or mark the gift of a new day?
- What can you do each day to orient yourself to your surroundings and the world you live in? Here are some suggestions:

  - Open a door or window each morning and take the time to smell the air, say hello to the wind, nod your head to the sun.
  - Buy a moon calendar, so that even when you can't see it for clouds you always know the phase of the moon.
  - Wherever you are, be aware of the direction you're facing, and what lies beyond you in that direction.

- Choose a day that is important to you – your birthday, an anniversary, a seasonal festival. Get up at dawn and greet the sunrise, and take some time out to reflect upon the last year of your life.
- Take a midnight walk under the full moon. All places have a completely different atmosphere and reveal different things in the middle of the night.

The Enchanted Life

12. A manifesto for an enchanted life

Escape

When we get out of the glass bottles of our own ego,
and when we escape like squirrels turning in the
cages of our personality
and get into the forests again,
we shall shiver with cold and fright
but things will happen to us
so that we don't know ourselves.

Cool, unlying life will rush in,
and passion will make our bodies taut with power,
we shall stamp our feet with new power
and old things will fall down,
we shall laugh, and institutions will curl
up like burnt paper.

D.H. Lawrence

I<small>T'S A FUNNY</small> creature, the word 'hedge'; like all the best words, it's something of a shapeshifter. We use it mostly to convey a boundary – something which closes us in, keeps us neat and safe and well-behaved in the like-for-like boxes we live in. Think of the modern suburban hedge: regimented rows of neatly clipped, soulless leylandii; privet which has been so harshly pruned that it has forgotten how to bloom. These are the hedges we've created for ourselves; these are the hedges which define us. But we also use the word 'hedge' to indicate a quite different kind of boundary: the wild margins which surround the cultivated fields. Think now of the gnarly old hedgerows of Britain and Ireland: thick, richly flowering, berried hawthorn and elder, blackthorn and hazel. An abundance of food and shelter for wild things. Secret places, where treasure might be found, where birds might speak to you and foxes shelter while singing to the stars. The suburban hedge walls us in; the wild hedge marks the edge beyond which freedom lies – the place where village becomes forest. There's nothing safe about an ancient hedge: on the other side lies the dark wood and the road which goes ever on. An ancient hedge is an enchanted place; a place where anything might happen. A liminal place, where the wisdom of the wild margins is available to all. Hedge wisdom: the wisdom of the wild world, unfettered by rules and impossible to institutionalise.

Hedge wisdom is on the rise. As our social, political and religious institutions continue to fail us, and as we see them begin slowly to crumble; as we watch the consequences of our own actions deplete, pollute and choke the planet – more and more people are looking beyond the rigid and increasingly decadent Western 'establishment' for answers to the ever-more urgent question of how we should live now. People are looking to the wisdom which all the old stories tell us can be found on the fringes, in the forest, in the wild thickets of the ancient hedge.

This extended meaning of the word 'hedge' springs from a phenomenon which emerged in Ireland in the seventeenth century: the 'hedge school'. Hedge schools date back to the days when the old indigenous Bardic schools had finally been choked out. Persistent and repressive efforts were made by British invaders to force Irish children to attend schools which were designed to train them in the English language and customs, and the 'true religion' (Protestant Christianity). Rather than submit to such indoctrination, the Irish quite literally went back to the hedge and created their own schools. No institutions, just a healthy respect for the old ways. They might have been 'unofficial', but the hedge schools were run by teachers rich in learning: sometimes wandering poets or people who'd left their clerical training behind. These were teachers who understood the old ways of learning: not just useful things designed to get you a job, or pave the way to a 'profession' – but a love of language, story and poetry, and native land-based knowledge derived from the ancient bardic tradition.* These subjects were the stuff of life; they would not only enchant you, but they'd bind you into the community and the world around you. In 1655 Oliver Cromwell called the Irish hedge schools training places for 'superstition, idolatory and the evill customs of this Nacion.'[132] I'll go for that.

It's hedge wisdom that we need now, because hedge wisdom is the wisdom of enchantment. It's precisely the kind of wisdom we need, those of us who are seeking to re-enchant not only our own lives, but the world. It's a wild, loamy wisdom, unbound but deeply rooted. Are you feeling the rumblings of it, already? It's the gnawing feeling in our stomachs which tells us that the lives we've been instructed to want are empty things, devoid of fire or magic. It's the outrage we feel against those crumbling institutions which bind us and confine us and kill the planet while we look on,

---

* The hedge school curriculum offered an impressive array of subjects, including history, arithmetic, book-keeping, science, surveying and land measuring, astronomy, geography, Latin, Greek, Hebrew, English and Irish, chivalric romances – but it also included good agricultural practice, play, dancing, poetry, fairy tales and folklore and, in an age where it was considered largely to be dangerous fantasy, works of fiction. For more information, see Antonia McManus, *The Irish Hedge School and its Books, 1695–1831.*[131]

helpless. Above all, it's the deep longing of the searching, honest soul for Lawrence's 'cool, unlying life'.

How can we remythologise Western culture? How can we begin to change the cultural myths we live by, uprooting the outmoded and dying stories, and replacing them with something new, heartful and alive? What might a culture that was founded on enchantment look like? Above all, it would be focused on living in balance and harmony with the land and the non-human others which share it with us, rather than on 'mastering nature'. Its institutions would be small-scale and local; its political structures would be egalitarian and regional. Technology would be a tool, rather than the foundation of daily life. It would be founded on conservation and sufficiency, instead of mass production, growth and profit. What would we look like as individuals, if we adopted practices to enchant our everyday lives – focusing on quality of life rather than success or achievement, focusing on community instead of competition, on the needs of the living world around us, rather than our own selfish needs? How might we then re-enchant our children, and so re-enchant the future – with an educational system which valued craftsmanship and apprenticeship instead of the acquisition of paper qualifications, and which encouraged play, dance and storytelling, as well as traditional academic subjects?

It might sound utopian, but it's perfectly possible to achieve. It won't happen all at once, but there's nothing to stop us creating a better world, one step at a time, one person at a time. Sometimes, change begins simply, with a close reflection on the daily choices we make. Sometimes, it begins with some serious thinking about what exactly we choose to value in our lives. Our personal circumstances sometimes lead us to imagine that we can't possibly completely redesign our lives – but we can always start small. Examine your choices as you make them – everything from how you spend the next hour to what you buy and where you buy it from. For some of us, change will come like a whirlwind, sweeping us off our feet; for others, it needs to happen little by little, over a longer period of time. However it happens, at some stage during every journey to re-enchantment, we have to go back to the fundamentals: how do we actually *perceive* the world around us? And how do we imagine our place in that world?

But whatever changes we might make to the daily fabric of our lives – however much we might try to re-enchant our lives in this disenchanted culture – sooner or later, for real, lasting and meaningful change to occur in this world, we will need to turn our backs on that culture and plant the seeds for a new one. Social change is already beginning to happen through the actions of millions of people who've stepped aside, and refused to live by the rules of a civilisation which is killing not only the human spirit, but the planet. It's time to push through the wild hedge, and embrace the enchanted life which lies on the other side.

Manifesto for an enchanted life

1. Everything around you is alive: believe it. Tell stories to stones, sing to trees, start conversations with birds. Build relationships. You'll never be lonely again.

2. To be fully in your body is to be fully alive. Get out of your head and into the world.

3. Look for the wonder wherever you go. Be all your life, as American poet Mary Oliver suggested, 'a bride married to amazement'.

4. Embrace mystery – don't be afraid of what you don't know.

5. Cultivate your mythic imagination: the inner and outer landscape of myth.

6. Know your place. Learn to belong, because wherever you go, there you are. There's nowhere else real to be.

7. Cleave to the local and the ethical. Cultivate community spirit, and autonomy.

8. Slow down.

9. Create. Buy handmade. Live folklorically.

10. Don't have a career: have a life. Find your calling – but above all, find your meaning in the community of the world.

11. Foster meaningful ritual; make each day a ceremony, or make a ceremony in each day.

12. Cherish otherness, in all its forms; confront in yourself, and explore, the forms of otherness which make you uncomfortable or afraid.

13. Treasure change: it's the stuff from which lives are forged. Stop looking for the eternal and immutable, and enter into the daily dance with the transitory.

Acknowledgements

I'm immensely grateful to Hannah MacDonald, founder of September Publishing, for her enthusiasm, clarity of vision and insightful editing. And to Charlotte Cole, for her commitment throughout the publication process and her ever-thoughtful copy-editing. I've been fortunate indeed to work with these lovely and inspiring women on a second book.

It's been a pleasure too to work with editors Amelia Spedaliere and Maria Golikova at House of Anansi in Toronto. I'm grateful for their energy and their eagerness to take on the book, and for their sensitive assistance and support as the manuscript was completed.

Thanks also, as ever, to my agent Kirsty McLachlan for having faith in this new project.

In the middle of writing this book I helpfully decided that I needed to move back to Connemara, and into the bargain found a house which, although remarkable, was a bit of a wreck. My singular and most beloved husband David, as always, gritted his teeth and pulled out all the stops to help make it happen. And, landing in yet another Gaeltacht, managed to learn a second dialect of Irish while it was all going on. This book would never have been completed on time (and possibly not at all) without his support.

I've been blessed along this new writing path with much unexpected kindness and friendship. I'm especially grateful to the many women (and, sometimes, men) who took the time to write and tell me how much *If Women Rose Rooted* had meant to them. As well as stimulating this new book, those heartfelt messages-in-bottles kept me buoyant when the boat was taking on water and threatening to sink. I'm grateful to Moya for so many things – above all, and always, for Nell. And to the beautiful and soulful group of women I first, at a creative retreat on the wild western-most shore of Connemara, named the Mythical Misfits. Laura, Jenna, Gail, Katharine, Helen – and the two who so generously contributed to this book, Caro and Amy – you gave me more than you know.

References

Chapter 1: Enchantment matters

1 OECD, 'Better Life Index', 2016: http://stats.oecd.org/Index. aspx?DataSetCode-BLI
2 Office for National Statistics, 'Measuring national well-being: Life in the UK: 2016', 2016: https://www.ons.gov.uk/peoplepopulationand-community/wellbeing/articles/measuringnationalwellbeing/2016

Chapter 2: The unendurable everyday

3 Markham Heid, 'Why Men Have More Body Image Issues Than Ever', *Time* magazine, 5 January 2017: http://time.com/4622653/ men-body-image-muscle-steroids
4 Robert Berezin, 'Do Lower Life Forms and Inanimate Matter have Consciousness?', *Psychology Today*, 16 May 2014: https://www. psychologytoday.com/blog/the-theater-the-brain/201405/do-lower-life-forms-and-inanimate-matter-have-consciousness
5 René Descartes. *Discourse on Method and Meditations on First Philosophy*. Trans. Donald A. Cress. Indianapolis: Hackett (1998)
6 Francis Bacon. *Novum Organum*. (1620)
7 Pew Forum on Religion & Public Life, 'Many Americans Mix Multiple Faiths', 9 December 2009: http://www.pewforum.org/2009/12/09/ many-americans-mix-multiple-faiths/#ghosts-fortunetellers-and-communicating-with-the-dead
8 Pew Forum on Religion & Public Life, 'Religious Landscape Study', 2014: http://www.pewforum.org/religious-landscape-study/
9 The three novels in the trilogy are *Labyrinth* (London: Orion, 2006), *Sepulchre* (London: Orion, 2007) and *Citadel* (London: Orion, 2012)
10 Max Weber, 'Science as a Vocation' (1917) Trans. Rodney Livingstone in David Owen and Tracy Strong (eds), *The Vocation Lectures*. Illinois: Hackett Books (2004) This is the text of a lecture given at Munich University. Weber used the German word *Entzauberung*, which is usually translated into English as 'disenchantment', but which literally means 'de-magic-ation'.
11 Jordi Quoidbach, Daniel T. Gilbert and Timothy D. Wilson, 'The End of History Illusion', *Science*, 4 January 2013: http://science.sci-encemag.org/content/339/6115/96

12 John Tierney, 'Why You Won't Be the Person You Expect to Be', *New York Times*, 3 January 2013: http://www.nytimes.com/2013/01/04/science/study-in-science-shows-end-of-history-illusion.html?_r-0

13 Oxford Dictionaries, 'Definition of Enchantment in English', 2017: https://en.oxforddictionaries.com/definition/enchantment

Chapter 3: To inhabit the living world

14 Reproduced in Meredith Sabini (ed.), *The Earth Has a Soul: The Nature Writings of C.G. Jung.* Berkeley: North Atlantic Books (2002), 79–80

15 Kathleen Raine, *The Land Unknown.* London: Hamish Hamilton (1975)

16 Abraham Harold Maslow, *Religions, Values, and Peak Experiences.* Middlesex: Penguin (1964)

17 From Leslie Marmon Silko, *Ceremony.* New York: Penguin Classics (2006). Reprinted with the permission of Penguin Random House.

18 Erich Neumann, *The Place of Creation.* Princeton, New Jersey: Princeton University Press (1989)

19 Vine Deloria, *Spirit and Reason: The Vine Deloria Reader.* Golden, Colorado: Fulcrum Publishing (1999)

20 Val Plumwood, 'Surviving a Crocodile Attack', July–August 2000: http://www.utne.com/arts/being-prey

21 Graham Harvey, *Animism: Respecting the Living World.* London: Hurst & Co. (2005)

22 Val Plumwood, *Feminism and the Mastery of Nature.* Boca Raton, Florida: CRC Press (1993)

23 Freya Mathews. *For Love of Matter: a Contemporary Panpsychism.* Albany, New York: SUNY Press (2003)

24 Gregory L. Matloff, 'Can Panpsychism Become an Observational Science?', *Journal of Consciousness Exploration & Research*, 7:7 (2016), 524–43

25 Robyn Williams, Martin Redfern, Martin Rees, Paul Davies and Frank Tipler, radio interview: 'The anthropic universe', *The Science Show, 18 February 2006:* http://www.abc.net.au/radionational/programs/scienceshow/the-anthropic-universe/3302686

Chapter 4: The wonderment

26 Rachel Carson, *The Sense of Wonder,* New York: Harper & Row (1956)

27 A.H. Maslow, 'Cognition of Being in the Peak Experiences', *The Journal of Genetic Psychology*, 94:1 (1959), 43–66

28 Abraham Harold Maslow, 'Humanistic Education vs. Professional Education', *New Directions in Teaching*, 2 (1969), 3–10. Abraham Harold Maslow, *Farther Reaches of Human Nature.* New York: Viking Press (1974)

29 Amy Spittler Shaffer, 'The Wonderment: How it Works', *The Wonderment*, 2017: https://www.thewonderment.com/howitworks

30 Kyung Hee Kim, 'The Creativity Crisis: The Decrease in Creative Thinking Scores on the Torrance Tests of Creative Thinking', *Creativity Research Journal*, 23:4, 285–95

31 Carol Black, 'On the Wildness of Children', April 2016: http://carolblack.org/on-the-wildness-of-children/

32 George Duoblys, 'One, Two, Three, Eyes on Me!', *London Review of Books*, 5 October 2017: https://www.lrb.co.uk/v39/n19/george-duoblys/one-two-three-eyes-on-me

33 Ken Robinson, 'Do schools kill creativity?', February 2006: https://www.ted.com/talks/ken_robinson_says_schools_kill_creativity. See also Ken Robinson, *Creative Schools: The Grassroots Revolution That's Transforming Education*. New York: Viking (2015)

34 Abraham Harold Maslow, 'Self-actualizing and Beyond' in James F.T. Bugental, *Challenges of Humanistic Psychology*. New York: McGraw-Hill (1967)

Chapter 5: At home in our skin

35 'Ah, Not To Be Cut Off', translation copyright © 1995 by Stephen Mitchell; from *Selected Poetry of Rainer Maria Rilke* by Rainer Maria Rilke, translated by Stephen Mitchell. Used by permission of Random House, an imprint and division of Penguin Random House LLC. All rights reserved. Any third party use of this material, outside of this publication, is prohibited. Interested parties must apply directly to Penguin Random House LLC for permission.

36 Andrew Wilson, 'The Ecological Approach, Explained to an 8 Year Old', 5 April 2017: http://psychsciencenotes.blogspot.ie/2017/04/the-ecological-approach-explained-to-8.html

37 Reginald Ray, 'Touching Enlightenment', *Tricycle*, spring 2006: https://tricycle.org/magazine/touching-enlightenment

38 Suzanne O'Sullivan, *It's All in Your Head: True Stories of Imaginary Illness*. London: Chatto & Windus (2015)

39 Quoted in O'Sullivan (*ibid.*), p. 8

40 Charles E. Matthews, et al., 'Amount of time spent in sedentary behaviors and cause-specific mortality in US adults', *The American Journal of Clinical Nutrition*, 95:2, (2012), 437–45: https://www.ncbi.nlm.nih.gov/pmc/articles/PMC3260070/

41 Alice Park, 'Sitting Too Much Ages You By 8 Years', *Time*, 18 January 2017: http://time.com/4637898/sitting-aging-sedentary/

42 Erin Hoare, et al., 'The associations between sedentary behaviour and mental health among adolescents: a systematic review', *International Journal of Behavioral Nutrition and Physical Activity*, 13:108, (2016): https://ijbnpa.biomedcentral.com/articles/10.1186/s12966-016-0432-4

43 Michael Ondaatje, *The English Patient*. Toronto: McClelland & Stewart (1992)

44 Laura Sewall, *Sight and Sensibility: The Ecopsychology of Perception*. New York: J.P. Tarcher/Putnam (1999)

45 John Fowles, *The Aristos*. Boston: Little, Brown (1964)

46 Deborah Bird Rose, 'Dance of the Ephemeral: Australian Aboriginal Religion of Place' in: Makarand R. Paranjape (ed.), *Sacred Australia: Post-secular considerations*. Melbourne: Clouds of Magellan (1999)

47 Online Etymology Dictionary, 'enchantment', 2017: https://www.etymonline.com/word/enchantment

48 Laura Sewall, 'The Skill of Ecological Perception' in *Ecopsychology: Restoring the Earth, Healing the Mind*, Theodore Roszak, Mary E. Gomez and Allen D. Kanner (eds.). San Francisco: Counterpoint (1995)

Chapter 6: The mythic imagination

49 From Leslie Marmon Silko, *Ceremony*. New York: Penguin Classics (2006). Reprinted with the permission of Penguin Random House.

50 Walter Benjamin, 'The Storyteller', 1937. Reprinted in Walter Benjamin, *The Storyteller: Tales out of Loneliness*. New York: Verso Books (2016)

51 Thu-Huong Ha, 'What happens in the brain when we hear stories? Uri Hasson at TED2016', 18 February 2016: http://blog.ted.com/what-happens-in-the-brain-when-we-hear-stories-uri-hasson-at-ted2016

52 Marie-Louise von Franz, *The Feminine in Fairy Tales*. New York: Shambhala (2001)

53 Ursula K. Le Guin, 'Why Are Americans Afraid of Dragons?' in Ursula K. Le Guin and Susan Wood (ed.), *The Language of the Night: Essays on Fantasy and Science Fiction*. New York: Ultramarine Publishing (1989)

54 Marina Warner, *Once Upon a Time: A Short History of Fairy Tale*. Oxford: Oxford University Press (2014)

55 CentreParcs, 'Robin Who? British Folklore could be in danger of dying out within a generation', 22 June 2017: http://www.centerparcs.co.uk/press#/pressreleases/robin-who-british-folklore-could-be-in-danger-of-dying-out-within-a-generation-2031810

56 For more information about Rima, visit: http://intothehermitage.blogspot.com. See also www.hedgespoken.org.

57 René Guénon, *Symbols of Sacred Science*. Trans. Alvin D. Fohr. Hillsdale, New York: Sophia Perennis (2004)

58 Angela Voss, 'A methodology of the imagination', *Sacred Science Circle*, 2016: http://www.sacredsciencecircle.org/wp-content/uploads/2016/11/Voss-A_Methodology_of_the_Imagination.pdf

59 Toko-pa Turner, 'Tips for Dream Recall', 27 January 2012: https://toko-pa.com/2012/01/27/tips-for-dream-recall/

60 George Monbiot, 'The Gift of Death', 10 December 2012: http://www.monbiot.com/2012/12/10/the-gift-of-death/

61 Annie Leonard, 'Facts from The Story of Stuff', 2007: http://storyofstuff.org/movies/story-of-stuff/

62 For more information about Geoff, visit: https://geoffmead.blog/
63 Geoff Mead, 'Sustainability needs new narrative between catastrophe and utopia', *Guardian*, 30 April 2014: https://www.theguardian.com/sustainable-business/leadership-sustainability-new-narrative
64 Thomas Berry, 'The New Story: Comments on the Origin, Identification and Transmission of Values', *Teilhard Studies*, 1 (1978)
65 D. Stephenson Bond, *Living Myth*. Boston: Shambhala (1993)
66 Rollo May, *The Cry for Myth*. New York: Norton (1991)
67 A.S. Byatt, *Ragnarök: The End of the Gods*. Edinburgh: Canongate (2012)

Chapter 7: Coming home to ourselves

68 This poem is printed with permission from Many Rivers Press. 'Everything Is Waiting For You', by David Whyte, from *River Flow: New & Selected Poems*. © Many Rivers Press, Langley, WA, USA. www.davidwhyte.com
69 Gaston Bachelard, *The Poetics of Space*. Trans. Maria Jolas. New York: Penguin Classics (2014)
70 C.G. Jung, *Memories, Dreams, Reflections*. Trans. Richard Winston and Clara Winston. London: Fontana Press (1995)
71 See, for example: http://thetinylife.com/what-is-the-tiny-house-movement/
72 For more information about the Global Ecovillage Network, visit: https://ecovillage.org
73 For more information about Joanna, visit: www.fabularosa.co.uk
74 Mary Reynolds, *The Garden Awakening*. Cambridge: Green Books (2016)
75 An independent film, *Dare to be Wild*, based on her journey to compete in the Chelsea Flower Show, was released by Crow's Nest Productions in 2015.

Chapter 8: An ear to the ground

76 C.G. Jung, *Man and His Symbols: Approaching the Unconscious*. New York: Dell (1968)
77 Gregory Cajete, *Look to the Mountain: An Ecology of Indigenous Education*. Durango, Colorado: Kivaki Press (1993)
78 Pat Mora, 'Desert Women' in Pat Mora, *Borders*. Houston: Arte Publico Press (1986)
79 Yi-Fu Tuan, *Space and Place: The Perspective of Experience*. London: Edward Arnold (1977)
80 Frances Mayes, *Under the Tuscan Sun*. San Francisco: Chronicle Books (1996)
81 Wes Jackson, *Becoming Native To This Place (Annual E. F. Schumacher Lectures Book 13)*. Great Barrington, Massachusetts: Schumacher Center (1993)

82 'Building Dwelling Thinking' by Martin Heidegger, reprinted in *Poetry, Language, Thought*. Trans. Albert Hofstadter. New York: Harper & Row (1971)

83 C.G. Jung, *The Collected Works of C. G. Jung Volume 8: The Structure and Dynamics of the Psyche*. Eds. Herbert Read, Michael Fordham and Gerhard Adler. Trans. R.F.C. Hull. London: Routledge (2002), para 815

84 Edward S. Casey, *Getting Back into Place: Toward a Renewed Understanding of the Place-World*. Bloomington, Indiana: Indiana University Press (1993), xiii

85 Martin Heidegger, *The Question Concerning Technology* (1954). In *The Question Concerning Technology and Other Essays*. Trans. William Lovitt. New York: Garland Publishing (1977)

86 Susan Greenfield, *Mind Change: How Digital Technologies Are Leaving Their Mark On Our Brains*. London: Rider (2015)

87 Jonathan Bate, *The Song of the Earth*. London: Picador (2000)

88 Sean Kane, *Wisdom of the Mythtellers*. Peterborough, Ontario: Broadview Press (1998), 252

89 Sean Kane, *Wisdom of the Mythtellers*. Peterborough, Ontario: Broadview Press (1998), 33, 79

90 Keith Basso, *Wisdom Sits in Places*. Albuquerque: University of New Mexico Press (1996)

91 The word 'dinnseanchas' is made up of two elements: *dinn*, a landmark, eminent or notable place, and *seanchas*, which is usually translated as 'lore', but in fact refers to the entire body of work of the professional learned classes in early Irish society. The literary corpus which is known as the dinnseanchas consist of around 176 poems (sometimes called the 'metrical dinnseanchas') and a selection of prose tales and commentaries collected in manuscripts which date from the eleventh century – though analyses suggest that most of the stories have their origin in pre-Christian times, because many place-names appear which had fallen out of use by the fifth and sixth centuries, when Irish lore first began to be written down. Dinnseanchas stories are also scattered throughout the Irish sagas, so deeply and thoroughly woven into the fabric of them that it sometimes seems that the main action is secondary.

92 Australian Government, 'The Dreaming', 2015: http://www.australia.gov.au/about-australia/australian-story/dreaming

93 Big Bill Neidjie, Stephen David and Allan Fox, *Australia's Kakadu Man: Bill Neidjie*. Darwin: Resource Managers Pty Ltd (1986)

94 Deborah Bird Rose, 'Journey to Sacred ground: Ethics and Aesthetics of Country' in Makarand Paranjape (ed.), *Sacred Australia: Post-Secular Considerations*. Melbourne: Clouds of Magellan (2009)

95 Gary Snyder, 'The Place, the Region, and the Commons' in Gary Snyder, *The Practice of the Wild*. Berkeley: Counterpoint (2010)

96 John Moriarty, *Dreamtime*. Dublin: Lilliput Press (1999)

Chapter 9: Kinship and otherness

97 Nickole Brown, 'A Prayer to Talk to Animals', *The Academy of American Poets*, 2017: https://www.poets.org/poetsorg/poem/prayer-talk-animals. Reprinted with the permission of the author. www.nickolebrown.com

98 Aldo Leopold, 'Thinking Like a Mountain', in Aldo Leopold, *A Sand County Almanac*. Oxford: Oxford University Press (1968)

99 Aisling Irwin, 'There are five times more urban foxes in England than we thought', *New Scientist*, 4 January 2017: https://www.newscientist.com/article/2116583-there-are-five-times-more-urban-foxes-in-england-than-we-thought/

100 John Lane, *Coyote Settles the South*. Athens, Georgia: University of Georgia Press (2016)

101 Katherine D. Kinzler and Elizabeth S. Spelke, 'Do infants show social preferences for people differing in race?', *US National Library of Medicine: National Institutes of Health*, April 2011: https://www.ncbi.nlm.nih.gov/pmc/articles/PMC3081609

102 Henry Beston, *The Outermost House*. New York: Owl Books (2003)

103 You can find out about Moya's work with animals here: http://www.tranquilpaths.com/

104 Terri Windling, 'Married To Magic: Animal Brides And Bridegrooms In Folklore And Fantasy, 2004: http://www.endicott-studio.com/articleslist/married-to-magic-animal-brides-and-bridegrooms-in-folklore-and-fantasy-by-terri-windling.html

105 For a review of some of the evidence on plant communication, see this article: Dan Cossins, 'Plant Talk', *The Scientist*, 1 January 2014: http://www.the-scientist.com/?articles.view/articleNo/38727/title/Plant-Talk/

106 More details about Asia's work can be found here: https://onewillowapothecaries.com/

107 Linda Hogan, *Dwellings: A Spiritual History of the Living World*. New York: Norton (2007)

108 WWF, 'Deforestation', accessed 2017: https://www.worldwildlife.org/threats/deforestation

109 S.L. Pimm, G.J. Russell, J.L. Gittleman and T.M. Brooks, 'The Future of Biodiversity', *Science* 269 (1995): 347–50

Chapter 10: Hands on the clay of life

110 Max Paradiso, 'Chiara Vigo: The last woman who makes sea silk', 2 September 2015: http://www.bbc.com/travel/story/20170906-the-last-surviving-sea-silk-seamstress; Helen Scales, *Spirals in Time: The Secret Life and Curious Afterlife of Seashells*. London: Bloomsbury (2016). Sumitra, 'Chiara Vigo – The World's Last "Sea Silk" Seamstress', 11 September 2015: http://www.odditycentral.com/news/chiara-vigo-the-worlds-last-sea-silk-seamstress.html

111 All figures retrieved from: https://www.etsy.com

112 https://www.etsy.com/ie/shop/HannahWillow?ref-profile_shopname
113 D.W. Winnicott 'Transitional Objects and Transitional Phenomena', in *Through Paediatrics to Psycho-Analysis*. New York: Brunner/Mazel (1992)
114 Cas Holmes, *The Found Object in Textile Art*. Loveland, Colorado: Interweave (2010)
115 Carl Honoré, *In Praise of Slow: How a Worldwide Movement is Challenging the Cult of Speed*. San Francisco: HarperSanFrancisco (2004)
116 Matt Kaplan, 'Why great ideas come when you aren't trying', *Nature*, 21 May 2012: https://www.nature.com/news/why-great-ideas-come-when-you-aren-t-trying-1.10678

Chapter 11: Life as if it mattered

117 William Stafford, 'The Way It Is' from *Ask Me: 100 Essential Poems*. Copyright © 1998, 2014 by William Stafford and the Estate of William Stafford. Used with the permission of The Permissions Company, Inc., on behalf of Graywolf Press, www.graywolfpress.org
118 James Hillman, *The Soul's Code: In Search of Character and Calling*. New York: Random House (1996)
119 Investors in People, '60 per cent of UK workers not happy in their jobs', 19 January 2015: https://www.investorsinpeople.com/press/60-cent-uk-workers-not-happy-their-jobs
120 Louis Studs Terkel, *Working: People Talk About What They Do All Day and How They Feel About What They Do*. New York: Pantheon Books (1974)
121 Max Weber, *The Protestant Ethic and the Spirit of Capitalism*. (1930) Oxford: Oxford University Press (2010)
122 Carl Benedikt Frey and Michael A. Osborne, 'The Future of Employment', 17 September 2013: www.oxfordmartin.ox.ac.uk/downloads/academic/The_Future_of_Employment.pdf This work elaborates on conclusions reached by two MIT economists, Erik Brynjolfsson and Andrew McAfee, in the book *Race Against the Machine: How the Digital Revolution is Accelerating Innovation, Driving Productivity, and Irreversibly Transforming Employment and the Economy*. Lexington, Massachusetts: Digital Frontier Press (2012)
123 Oxford Dictionaries, 'Definition of ritual in English', 2017: https://en.oxforddictionaries.com/definition/ritual
124 Caroline Newman, 'The Evolution of Modern Rituals: 4 Hallmarks of Today's Rituals', 28 March 2017: https://news.virginia.edu/content/evolution-modern-rituals-4-hallmarks-todays-rituals
125 Arnold van Gennep, *Rites de Passage*. Paris: Émile Nourry (1909)
126 Andrew Forsthoefel, *Walking to Listen*. New York: Bloomsbury (2017)
127 For more information about Soul and Stream, visit: http://www.soulandstream.com/

128 The British Pilgrimage Trust, 'An Unbroken Journey on Foot to Holy Places', *The British Pilgrimage Trust*, 2017: http://britishpilgrimage. org/what/

129 You can read the archive of Caro and Tommy's travels at her blog, here: https://pilgrimonehorseback.com/

130 The Life Cairn memorial programme was started by BBC TV presenter Reverend Peter Owen Jones, and Andreas Kornevall, the Director for the Earth Restoration Service, an environmental charity. www.facebook.com/Thelifecairn

Chapter 12: A manifesto for an enchanted life

131 Antonia McManus, *The Irish Hedge School and its Books: 1695– 1831*. Dublin: Four Courts Press (2004)

132 Commonwealth Records, P.R.O. Ireland, A 5.99, Dublin, March 19, 1655. In Timothy Joseph Corcoran, *Education Systems in Ireland from the Close of the Middle Ages*. Dublin: University College Dublin (1928), p. 27